THE PLEASURES OF REASON IN PLATO, ARISTOTLE, AND THE HELLENISTIC HEDONISTS

Human lives are full of pleasures and pains. And humans are creatures that are able to think: to learn, understand, remember and recall, plan and anticipate. Ancient philosophers were interested in both of these facts and, what is more, were interested in how these two facts are related to one another. There appear to be, after all, pleasures and pains associated with learning and inquiring, recollecting and anticipating. We enjoy finding something out. We are pained to discover that a belief we hold is false. We can think back and enjoy or be upset by recalling past events. And we can plan for and enjoy imagining pleasures yet to come. This book is about what Plato, Aristotle, the Epicureans, and the Cyrenaics had to say about these relationships between pleasure and reason.

JAMES WARREN is a Reader in Ancient Philosophy at the University of Cambridge and a Fellow of Corpus Christi College. He is the author of *Epicurus and Democritean Ethics* (2002), *Facing Death: Epicurus and his Critics* (2004), and *Presocratics* (2007), and the editor of *The Cambridge Companion to Epicureanism* (2009) and, with Frisbee Sheffield, *The Routledge Companion to Ancient Philosophy* (2014). He has published articles on a wide range of topics in ancient philosophy.

THE PLEASURES OF REASON IN PLATO, ARISTOTLE, AND THE HELLENISTIC HEDONISTS

JAMES WARREN

CAMBRIDGE
UNIVERSITY PRESS

CAMBRIDGE
UNIVERSITY PRESS

University Printing House, Cambridge CB2 8BS, United Kingdom

Cambridge University Press is part of the University of Cambridge.

It furthers the University's mission by disseminating knowledge in the pursuit of education, learning and research at the highest international levels of excellence.

www.cambridge.org
Information on this title: www.cambridge.org/9781107025448

© James Warren 2014

First published 2014

A catalogue record for this publication is available from the British Library

Library of Congress Cataloguing in Publication data
Warren, James, 1974–
The pleasures of reason in Plato, Aristotle, and the Hellenistic hedonists / James Warren.
pages cm
Includes bibliographical references and index.
ISBN 978-1-107-02544-8
1. Plato. 2. Aristotle. 3. Epicureans (Greek philosophy) 4. Pleasure. 5. Reason. 6. Learning. I. Title.
B398.P56W37 2014
180–dc23
2014018779

ISBN 978-1-107-02544-8 Hardback

For Dad, in memory of Mum

ἡδὺ πανταχόθεν ἡ φίλου μνήμη τεθνηκότος.
Epicurus in Plutarch, *Non Posse* 1105E

Contents

Acknowledgements

I would like to thank the following people for comments on earlier versions of these chapters: Jenny Bryan, Victor Caston, Sylvain Delcomminette, Nicholas Denyer, Mehmet Erginel, Benjamin Harriman, Dhananjay Jagannathan, Georgia Moroutsou, Olivier Renaut, Malcolm Schofield, David Sedley, Oliver Thomas, Voula Tsouna, Junyi Zhao, and the anonymous readers for Cambridge University Press. I would also like to thank Michael Sharp at Cambridge University Press and Jan Chapman for her keen-eyed copy-editing.

Parts of this work have been presented to audiences in Cambridge, London, Oxford, and Paris. The reactions of the audiences on these occasions have been invaluable.

Parts of this book are based on work published elsewhere as parts of Warren 2001a, 2010, 2011a, and forthcoming b. I thank the respective publishers and editors for their permission to reuse this material. Translations of ancient texts are my own except where a translator is named.

I would like to thank my colleagues in the Faculty of Classics at the University of Cambridge and Corpus Christi College for their encouragement and advice and for covering my teaching and administrative duties during my sabbatical leave for the academic year 2012–13, particularly the members of the B Caucus in the Faculty and Marina Frasca-Spada, Thomas Land, and Emma Wilson at Corpus Christi.

I also thank my family and, most of all, Sara Owen.

Abbreviations

Arist.	Aristotle
APo.	*Posterior Analytics*
De An.	*De Anima* (*On the Soul*)
De Insom.	*De Insomniis* (*On Dreams*)
De Mem.	*On Memory*
EE	*Eudemian Ethics*
GA	*On the Generation of Animals*
HA	*Historia Animalium*
MA	*On the Motion of Animals*
Metaph.	*Metaphysics*
NE	*Nicomachean Ethics*
PA	*De Partibus Animalium* (*On the Parts of Animals*)
Phys.	*Physics*
Poet.	*Poetics*
Rhet.	*Rhetoric*
Sens.	*De Sensu* (*On Perception*)
Top.	*Topics*
Aul. Gell.	Aulus Gellius
Noct. Att.	*Attic Nights*
Cic.	Cicero (Marcus Tullius Cicero)
Fin.	*De Finibus*
Tusc.	*Tusculan Disputations*
Clement of Alexandria	
Strom.	*Miscellanies*
Damascius	
In Phileb.	*Lectures on Plato's Philebus*
DK	H. Diels and W. Kranz, *Die Fragmente der Vorsokratiker*, 6th edition (Berlin, 1952)
DL	Diogenes Laertius, *Lives of Eminent Philosophers*

Epic.	Epicurus
Ep. Hdt.	*Letter to Herodotus*
Ep. Men.	*Letter to Menoeceus*
Ep. Pyth.	*Letter to Pythocles*
KD	*Kyriai Doxai*
Nat.	*On Nature*
SV	*Sententiae Vaticanae* (*Vatican Sayings*)
Eur.	Euripides
Or.	*Orestes*
Euseb.	Eusebius
PE	*Praeparatio Evangelica*
Hom.	Homer
Il.	*Iliad*
Od.	*Odyssey*
Iambl.	Iamblichus
Prot.	*Protrepticus*
Lucr.	Lucretius
DRN	*De Rerum Natura* (*On the Nature of Things*)
PHerc.	*Herculaneum papyrus*
Plat.	Plato
Gorg.	*Gorgias*
Phaed.	*Phaedo*
Phdr.	*Phaedrus*
Phileb.	*Philebus*
Prot.	*Protagoras*
Rep.	*Republic*
Symp.	*Symposium*
Theaet.	*Theaetetus*
Tim.	*Timaeus*
Plut.	Plutarch
Adv. Col.	*Against Colotes*
An Seni	*On Whether an Old Man Should Be a Ruler*
De Adul.	*On Flattery*
De An. Procr. in Tim.	*On the Generation of the Soul in the Timaeus*
De Aud. Poet.	*On How to Listen to Poets*
De Soll. An.	*On the Cleverness of Animals*
De Stoic. Repug.	*On Stoic Self-contradictions*
Lat. Viv.	*On the Maxim 'Live Unknown'*

Non Posse	*On the Fact That It Is Impossible to Live Pleasantly Following Epicurus*
Quaest. Conv.	*Dinner-party Questions*
Quaest. Plat.	*Platonic Questions*
Virt. Mor.	*On Moral Virtue*
Polyst.	Polystratus
De irrat. cont.	*On Irrational Contempt for Common Opinions* (*PHerc.* 336/1150)
Procl.	Proclus
In Plat. Rem Pub.	*Commentary on Plato's Republic*
Sen.	Seneca (the Younger)
Ep. Mor.	*Moral Letters*
Sext. Emp.	Sextus Empiricus
PH	*Pyrrōneioi Hypotupōseis (Outlines of Pyrrhonism)*
SSR	G. Giannantoni, *Socratis et Socraticorum Reliquiae* (Naples, 1990)
Suda	Greek Lexicon formerly known as *Suidas*
Thuc.	Thucydides, *History of the Peloponnesian War*
Usener	H. Usener, *Epicurea* (Leipzig, 1887)
Xen.	Xenophon
Mem.	*Memorabilia*

CHAPTER I

Introduction: the pleasures of reason

Human lives are full of pleasures and pains. And humans are creatures that are able to think: to learn, understand, remember and recall, plan and anticipate. Ancient philosophers were interested in both of these facts and, what is more, were interested in how these two facts are related to one another. There appear to be, after all, pleasures and pains associated with learning and inquiring, recollecting and anticipating. We enjoy finding something out. We are pained to discover that a belief we hold is false. We can think back and enjoy or be upset by recalling past events. And we can plan for and enjoy imagining pleasures yet to come. This book is about what Plato, Aristotle, the Epicureans, and the Cyrenaics had to say about these relationships between pleasure and reason. It focusses on Plato, Aristotle, and these two Hellenistic schools because, as I hope will emerge from the chapters to follow, we find there some of the richest material on the topic. There are also thematic and dialectical links between these philosophers, so when we consider them together an ancient philosophical conversation arises about the pleasures of reason.

Pleasure and *logismos*

Early in Plato's *Philebus*, Socrates and his interlocutor, Protarchus, come to agree that a human life must involve not only experiences of pleasure and pain but also various activities that they classify as falling under the umbrella term 'reasoning' (*logismos*). At the very opening of the dialogue Socrates gives a list of the activities he has in mind when he first introduces to Protarchus the dispute between himself and Philebus:

> Φίληβος μὲν τοίνυν ἀγαθὸν εἶναί φησι τὸ χαίρειν πᾶσι ζῴοις καὶ τὴν ἡδονὴν καὶ τέρψιν, καὶ ὅσα τοῦ γένους ἐστὶ τούτου σύμφωνα· τὸ δὲ παρ' ἡμῶν ἀμφισβήτημά ἐστι μὴ ταῦτα, ἀλλὰ τὸ φρονεῖν καὶ τὸ νοεῖν καὶ μεμνῆσθαι καὶ τὰ τούτων αὖ συγγενῆ, δόξαν τε ὀρθὴν καὶ ἀληθεῖς λογισμούς, τῆς γε ἡδονῆς ἀμείνω καὶ λῴω γίγνεσθαι σύμπασιν ὅσαπερ αὐτῶν δυνατὰ

μεταλαβεῖν· δυνατοῖς δὲ μετασχεῖν ὠφελιμώτατον ἁπάντων εἶναι πᾶσι τοῖς οὖσί τε καὶ ἐσομένοις. (*Phileb.* 11b4–c2)

So Philebus here says that for all animals what is good is enjoyment, pleasure, delight, and everything consonant with this. My position, in disagreement with his, is that these are not good but that being wise, understanding, remembering and things like that, and correct belief and true reasoning, are better than pleasure and more desirable for all things that can have a share in them. Sharing in them is the most advantageous thing of all for all those who can do so, both now and in the future.

A little later, when Socrates and Protarchus consider in turn a life of just those things that Philebus thinks are good and a life of just those things that Socrates prefers, we find a similar list of cognitive capacities (21a14–d1). Socrates sets aside being wise (*to phronein*), understanding (*to noein*), reasoning (*to logizesthai*), memory (*mnēmē*), knowledge (*epistēmē*), and opinion (*doxa*). Socrates sums up a life without any of these capacities as a life deprived of *logismos* (21c5).

Socrates and Protarchus soon agree that a choice-worthy human life cannot be deprived either of thinking or of pleasure. A good human life will be a mixture that combines these activities of reason with pleasures, perhaps ideally only pleasures of a certain kind, to produce a harmonious and ordered result. That claim leaves a lot still to be worked out and many of the details of Socrates' eventual and considered proposals are unclear. What is clear, however, is that these activities of *logismos* have a series of complex relationships with pleasures and pains; certainly, Socrates does not think of a good human life as simply a collection of a set of experiences of pleasure and pain on the one hand and then, on the other hand, a set of activities of reasoning. Rather, human reasoning gives rise to pleasures and pains of its own: there are pleasures of thinking, believing, learning, remembering, and so on. And this gives rise to another of Socrates' concerns since he also insists that there are some such pleasures that should and others that should not be part of the eventual mixture of a good human life. Pleasures can be false, he notoriously maintains, and such false pleasures should not be part of a good human life. The falsehood of these false pleasures is itself not a simple thing to understand, but it is certainly connected with these pleasures being intimately involved with, or stemming from, or arising out of, certain human capacities for reasoning. To put it very crudely, the same capacity for forming true beliefs will also allow us to form false beliefs. And, in so far as pleasures may similarly arise from our taking the world to be a certain way, Socrates thinks that those pleasures themselves may also be thought of as true or false. The precise understanding of the claim that there are false and true pleasures will return later in my discussion. For now, it is mentioned just to signal the simple point that, for Socrates in the *Philebus*, and indeed for many of the ancient philosophers, pleasures and pains can have a subtle but important relationship with our reasoning capacities: we can enjoy or be distressed by things we believe or know or calculate or remember or anticipate. And just as we can be correct or mistaken in our beliefs and calculations and expectations, there might be something similar to be said about the relevant pleasures too.

In some ways 'the pleasures of reason' might appear to refer to a narrower subject matter than in fact I go on to discuss. The choice of the title is determined to some extent by an attempt to respect a widespread ancient psychological presumption that humans differ from all other animals by possessing a certain rational capacity. But that might make it reasonable to question why 'the pleasures of reason' in this sense can include pleasures of remembering and anticipating. After all, memory and anticipation of a sort are agreed by Plato and Aristotle to be psychological capacities present not only in humans and therefore they are not capacities whose presence is dependent on the presence of a rational part of the soul. On the other hand, 'the pleasures of cognition' threatens to make the field too broad: it would include the pleasures of all forms of perception in so far as our ancient philosophers tend to think of the activity of our senses as a form of cognition. 'The pleasures of thinking' might have been a compromise between these two. I emphasise 'reason' rather than 'thinking', however, since these philosophers agreed that there is a distinctively human faculty of reason and my topic is their account of the pleasures and pains that occur in human lives because we are animals with that capacity of reason.[1] If some of what is said turns out also to be applicable to other animals because they too are in fact capable of some of the relevant psychological functions then that will not diminish the relevance of those same accounts for us humans. Besides, even granted that some of these are capacities we share with other animals, it seems to me that, for those of the ancient thinkers whose views on the matter we can reconstruct, this distinctively human rational capacity is what is ultimately responsible in humans for our being able to learn about and understand the world in the way that we do. It is also, furthermore, responsible for the way in which we humans can remember and anticipate, and plan ahead. Even if other animals have memories and can

---

[1] Aristotle makes the possession of understanding (*nous*), thought (*dianoia*), or *logismos* the criterion for differentiating humans from non-human animals (at least non-divine ones): *De An.* 2.3 414b16–18, 415a7–12. See Johansen 2012, 221–6.

perhaps in some sense think ahead, they do not do either of these in quite the same way that humans do.

In any case, it is a plausible idea that the pleasures and pains we humans experience through sense perception are also affected by our being rational creatures. Plato and Aristotle, for example, would happily say that we humans can enjoy seeing things that are well proportioned or listening to music that is harmonious and ordered.[2] Our capacity for reason makes a significant difference to how we perceive things and therefore to the pleasures and pains we experience from those perceptions. Such pleasures and pains will play only a minor role in what follows since my interest is in the main focussed on the range of activities that Socrates in the *Philebus* assigned to *logismos*. But they are perhaps worth bearing in mind as showing what the next step would be in tracing the effect that our reasoning capacities have on our experience of pleasure and pain generally.

This is merely an initial sketch of the subject matter. We can now turn to set out in some more detail the three broad categories of pleasures and pains to be discussed and outline some of the ways in which they are related to one another. Those categories are: (1) pleasures and pains of learning, knowing, and understanding; (2) pleasures and pains involved in planning and prudential reasoning; (3) pleasures and pains from anticipating and remembering.

Knowing and learning

The clearest examples of the pleasures that might be associated with this human capacity for reasoning are the pleasures that arise from our learning, discovering, and knowing something. In Plato's *Protagoras*, Prodicus notes that there are pleasures of learning as well as those concerned with bodily experiences and explains that, in his opinion, we ought to mark this distinction linguistically.

> ἡμεῖς τ' αὖ οἱ ἀκούοντες μάλιστ' ἂν οὕτως εὐφραινοίμεθα, οὐχ ἡδοίμεθα – εὐφραίνεσθαι μὲν γὰρ ἔστιν μανθάνοντά τι καὶ φρονήσεως μεταλαμβάνοντα αὐτῇ τῇ διανοίᾳ, ἥδεσθαι δὲ ἐσθίοντά τι ἢ ἄλλο ἡδὺ πάσχοντα αὐτῷ τῷ σώματι. (*Prot.* 337c1–4)[3]

---

[2] See e.g. Arist. *EE* 3.2 1230b38–1231a5.

[3] Denyer 2008, 141–2, notes that this distinction is in tension with the argument at the end of the dialogue, which appears to treat all pleasures as homogeneous or, at least, commensurable. (At 358a7–b2 Socrates explicitly comments that he will ignore Prodicus' distinctions.) On Prodicus' distinctions see also Arist. *Top.* 2.6 112b21–6 and compare the vocabulary for pleasure used in the report of

Let those of us who are listening be cheered, not pleased. For 'being cheered' is what happens when one learns something or shares in understanding through thinking itself, while 'being pleased' is what happens when one eats something or experiences some other pleasure with the body itself.

It is sometimes pleasant to discover a new truth; it is sometimes pleasant to acquire a belief. It can also be painful to learn things or to come to believe things. All these pleasures and pains are such that they seem to be available to us humans and not to other animals in virtue of our possession of a certain kind of intellectual or rational capacity. This will be the first kind of 'affective thinking': pleasures and pains brought about by learning, discovering, and knowing. Examples of this kind of affective thinking are the pain Oedipus experiences when he discovers his true ancestry and the pleasure the philosopher-ruler of Plato's *Republic* is supposed to experience when he or she comes to know the Good.

These capacities for learning and knowing involve the use of memory and recollection in various ways. Learning has an obvious connection with memory, both in the sense of learning skills and learning facts. Plato, at least in some of his dialogues, offers the most radical connection between learning and remembering by simply identifying the two. At *Meno* 81d4–5 Socrates asserts that 'inquiry and learning, as a whole, are recollection (*anamnēsis*)'. And he means by recollection here the retrieval of what a person's immortal soul has learned prior to entering into a body (81c5–d5). Of course, this need not mean that everything a living person can be said to know in any reasonable sense of the word 'know' is somehow recalled from a prior non-corporeal existence, but Socrates is sure that some forms of learning and knowledge are to be explained in that way. Others follow his lead in exploring the role of memory in learning and inquiry in more mundane ways. Aristotle is interested in the relation of memory to experience, skill, and the acquisition of knowledge, most obviously in *APo.* 2.19 and *Metaph.* A.1. And the Epicureans are interested in the role that memorising the central tenets of their philosophy can play in assuring a good and pleasant life. Having available a stock of important lessons and arguments is important for equipping the Epicurean with ready material to counter any novel anxieties or challenging situations. It is perhaps best to treat memory of this kind as part of the general mechanism of learning and retrieving

Prodicus' story of the choice of Heracles: Xen. *Mem.* 2.1.23–4. Wolfsdorf 2011 discusses all the evidence and argues that this passage from the *Protagoras* does not faithfully report Prodicus' view. Timaeus distinguishes between *hēdonē* and *euphrosynē* at *Tim.* 80b5–8, noting that harmonious music produces the former in fools and the latter in the wise because only the wise appreciate how these mortal movements imitate divine harmony.

learned information. This is distinct from 'autobiographical memory', which I shall introduce below.

Planning ahead

Humans also possess the ability to think about, evaluate, plan, and deliberate about different possible future courses of action. This capacity is relevant to the present study in two ways. First, there are discussions of the use of reason to plan ahead and maximise pleasures and minimise pains. In this way our rational capacity is considered prominently in Plato's *Protagoras* in connection with a specifically hedonist axiology and Socrates there famously develops an account of a hedonic calculus, recommending ways in which we might better plan and evaluate future outcomes in terms of the pleasures and pains involved and thereby maximise our pleasures and minimise our pains over the course of a life. The afterlife of this account of hedonist prudential reasoning and its use in more recent accounts of consequentialist reasoning might itself warrant our considering the *Protagoras* in this study. Epicurus, for example, takes up something like this model of hedonist calculation and recommends it as part of a good and pleasant life. But there is another connection that is rather more important, in part because it is relevant for considerations of practical reasoning that are not themselves committed to a hedonist account of value.

The account in the *Protagoras* does not consider the use of our reasoning capacities in the evaluative procedure it recommends to be potentially pleasant or painful itself. But in the *Philebus* Plato notes that planning of this kind can produce pleasures and pains because it involves some kind of anticipatory consideration of the various goods and bads (including pleasures and pains) on offer and such anticipation can be pleasant or painful. He also notes that such pleasures and pains can be termed 'false' if they are produced by inaccurate estimations of the future experience. Aristotle does not pursue the idea of false pleasures, but he does recognise in rational creatures the faculty of deliberative imagination (*phantasia bouleutikē*), which involves some kind of measuring by a single standard (*De An.* 3.11 434a5–10; he does not there discuss whether in the process of such imagination there might also be experienced pleasures and pains but it is reasonable to think that he would agree that there might). Epicurus notes that ideally such a procedure will not only ensure pleasure in the future but will also generate a pleasant confidence in the present. These accounts of the affective aspect of thinking ahead to future experiences are best considered in tandem with a similar discussion of the affective aspects of remembering past experiences.

Remembering and anticipating

In addition to the general capacity for memory that is part of the mechanism of learning and the general capacity for anticipating the future, we humans are also able deliberatively and reflectively to look backwards to recall our own past experiences and to look forwards to anticipate possible future experiences. This ability allows us to stitch our lives together across time and also to have some kind of access in the present to temporally remote parts of our lives. Memory and anticipation in the sense I mean here are to be distinguished from a more general ability to think about the past and the future. Rather, in this particular sense, they are involved in a person's thinking about his or her own past and own future.[4] By 'memory' therefore I mean what is variously called 'personal memory', 'autobiographical memory', 'recollective memory', 'episodic memory', 'experiential memory', or 'introversive memory'.[5] By 'anticipation' here I mean just the counterpart of this sense of memory: not the ability to look forward into the future generally and wonder what might or might not happen, but an agent's ability to consider, bring to mind, or think over what he or she might do and experience in the future. We can call it 'introversive anticipation'.

This might be thought to be a limited activity of a more general ability since memory in this sense is restricted to a person's thinking of past events in his or her own life. However, memory and anticipation in this sense are also richer than the bare ability to think about the past and future. They allow us to do things such as remember pains and pleasures or anticipate joy and sadness. Our ability to think about our own past and future affective experiences also allows us to plan and consider how best to maximise our pleasures by thinking in a useful way about different possible future experiences. It allows us to draw on our past experiences to learn and benefit from them. And perhaps most intriguing of all, the ability to look forward and backward to our future and past experiences allows us to generate further affective responses in the present. We can remember and anticipate with pleasure or with pain. We can remember our pleasures with pleasure and be pained when we anticipate pains.

I will not offer my own account of what precisely is involved when we remember an experience with pleasure or look forward to an experience

---

[4] This is what makes memory interesting to people who are trying to offer an account of the criteria for the persistence of a person over time. It also makes it unclear whether memory can serve as such a criterion or, rather, is itself dependent on there being some persistent subject to prior parts of whose life memory then may give access.

[5] Cf. Annas 1992, 299–300; Bernecker 2010, 11–45.

with trepidation.[6] Nevertheless, that we do engage in both of these kinds of introspective thinking and are affected as we do so is itself not a trivial observation and it attracted the attention of thoughtful ancient writers too. In Chapters 6, 7, and 8 I explore some of what they had to say about it. There are two important themes that deserve to be briefly noted here. First, there is in these thinkers' discussions a strong emphasis on the connection between memory, anticipation, and the agent's character over time. Autobiographical memory and the affective aspects of autobiographical memory, for example, are related to how the agent's character changes or remains constant over time. In brief, they tend to think that a person of good and stable character ought to take pleasure in and be pained by the same things now as in the past. This is also supposed to hold, *mutatis mutandis*, for an agent's affective responses to considerations of future experiences. Second, I suggest that we might distinguish in these thinkers two broad ways of thinking about the fact that we can take pleasure and pain in our memories and in our anticipations.

On the first model, anticipating and recalling are thought to be means of, so to speak, reaching out to the past or future and hauling some temporally remote experience from there into our present. Within this model, we can distinguish two further ideas. The first idea is that this ability to set together a present with a non-present affective state allows an agent to arrange some kind of comparison between the present affective state (pleased, pained, neither pleased nor pained) and the anticipated or recollected state (pleased, pained, neither pleased nor pained). The comparison between the two is then noted and used to draw various further conclusions, for example about the nature of pleasure and pain themselves, or this particular person's consistency of character and the like. The second idea is that the recollected or anticipated pleasure can be used to help to improve one's state in the present by allowing us to 'relive' or 'pre-live' a pleasure. For example, the Epicureans claim that recollecting and thereby reliving a past pleasant experience is useful in producing a balance against a present pain.

The second model is a less common approach and is perhaps best illustrated by contrast with the dominant form. In brief, unlike its counterpart, this model does not assume that an experience that was painful to us in the past will always be painful when we remember it. Sometimes a past painful experience can be recalled with pleasure. What is more, the pleasure we may feel in recalling that past painful experience is not simply because,

---

[6] Such an account would need to build a story about affective content into a general account of introversive memory or anticipation. The analysis in Bernecker 2010, ch. 8, offers some helpful steps in this direction.

when placed in comparison with our present situation, that past experience is merely revealed not to have been as bad as we once thought. Rather, we can recall even with pleasure something that was genuinely painful at the time. While this picture is less common in the ancient texts, we can detect signs of it in Aristotle's discussion of pleasure and memory in *Rhet.* 1.11.

Reason and emotion

In some cases it is less clear whether, in the view of these ancient philosophers, the cognitive capacities involved in the relevant affective experience belong exclusively to humans – and are therefore candidates for being 'pleasures of reason' – or may also belong to non-human animals. I have already mentioned the pleasures and pains of perception. Another class of pleasures and pains that might be approached in a similar fashion are those associated with emotions or, as the ancient Greeks would describe them 'affections': *pathē*. These will not form a major part of my discussion, but it is worth dwelling on them just briefly. In humans emotions such as anger or fear are certainly accompanied by pleasures and pains. And in humans emotions might be thought to involve some kind of cognitive component since they seem to involve 'taking things to be' in a certain fashion. Fear, for example, might involve an agent in taking there to be some impending danger or harm and therefore involve some cognitive input besides what is plausibly given by sensory perception alone. Anger, for example, often seems to involve the angry person in having a belief such as that some undeserved slight has been suffered. On the other hand, it is also common both nowadays and in our ancient sources to ascribe emotions such as fear and anger to non-human animals that are incapable of reasoning or of forming beliefs.

The moral psychology of the *pathē* is a large and difficult topic which would demand a different treatment for each of the various ancient philosophers and schools.[7] For the Stoics, for example, the answer is relatively clear because they take an extreme view of the nature of emotions. For the Stoics, non-human animals are not able to experience emotions and their relevant pleasures and pains since emotions – *pathē* – are attendant upon if not identical to a belief of some kind (e.g. the belief that someone has illegitimately wronged you). For a Stoic, a dog cannot, properly speaking, experience the emotion of anger since it cannot form such a judgement.[8] For Plato,

---

[7] For a good introduction see Price 2009.

[8] It also follows that all emotions are based on false judgement since they take things to be good or bad that are neither good nor bad; virtue is the only good and vice the only bad.

things are more complicated. We should probably say that different dialogues offer different accounts of the emotions since they offer different general accounts of the soul. Some seem to envisage the human soul as exclusively a reasoning soul; others famously divide the embodied human soul into distinct parts only one of which is identified as the rational soul and between which there can be conflict as well as harmony. The analysis of the emotions will depend upon these more general accounts which determine which activities are psychic activities and which psychic activities are activities of the rational or non-rational parts of the soul.

The case of Aristotle is perhaps more complicated still. Some commentators argue that Aristotle's account of the emotions does not see a necessary role for rational capacities in every experience of a *pathos*.[9] Aristotle sometimes talks about emotions arising when we come to believe something, for example that something terrifying is present (e.g. *De An.* 3.3 427b21–4). But he also sometimes talks about emotions being triggered just because things 'appear' to us a certain way, despite a belief to the contrary or in the absence of a relevant belief.[10] We can feel fear, for example, even in the absence of the belief that things are as they currently appear to us (e.g. *De Insom.* 2 459b32–460a27). We may not act always on the basis of such an appearance when there is a belief to the contrary but in the absence of such a belief we will instead act and be moved, as non-human animals act and are moved, simply on the basis of how things appear to us. We might therefore also be subject to various emotions just on the basis of how things appear to us.[11] The pleasures and pains that are associated with emotions are not necessarily, in that case, to be connected with our human rational capacities. Any animal capable of perceiving or equipped with *phantasia* has the requisite psychological equipment for experiencing emotions and the pleasures and pains they involve.[12] The alternative, and now perhaps the less common, interpretation of Aristotle's view of the emotions holds that the references to the human agent 'being appeared to' in a certain way in cases of emotion is

---

[9] For a clear introduction to the debate see Moss 2012a, 69–71, and see the remainder of the chapter for her own view.

[10] Cf. *NE* 7.6 1149a32–b1: either *logos* or *phantasia* can 'make clear' to a person that he has been slighted, after which spirit (*thumos*) 'as if having reasoned it out' (ὥσπερ συλλογισάμενος) becomes enraged. Aristotle argues that *phantasia* and opinion must be distinct capacities because the sun 'appears' to be about a foot in diameter even to people who believe that it is vastly larger than Earth (*De An.* 3.3 428b2–4; cf. *De Insom.* 2 460b18–20).

[11] For interpretations of Aristotle's account of the emotions on these lines see Cooper 1996 and Striker 1996a. See also Moss 2009 and 2012a, 100–33, who builds on such a view to interpret Aristotle's account of *akrasia*.

[12] The discussion in Sihvola 1996 makes good use of references to animal emotions in the biological works.

sufficient for us to infer that in those cases too there must be some involvement of our rational capacities.[13]

It is worth noting that there is a case for seeing Aristotle's account of the pleasures and pains of the *pathē* in human lives as related to our reasoning capacities even if he is sometimes inclined to account for them as caused by perception or *phantasia*, capacities which he does not restrict only to human animals. Lions see things; they have a capacity for memory, some ability to foresee consequences, form desires, and so on. Nevertheless, given that humans are rational creatures, Aristotle will hold that our cognitive grasp of the world around us is different from that of non-rational creatures. This difference lies not only in the sense that we are able to form beliefs and non-rational creatures are not. We also perceive the world differently in virtue of the possession of reason. We can perceive something as a tree, or a threat, or an insult. Hence, we remember or envisage things in ways that non-human animals cannot. We humans are not, in other words, just non-human animals with a reasoning capacity bolted on. The presence of that reasoning capacity transforms the cognitive capacities that we possess and that are also possessed by other animals and will therefore affect any pleasures and pains arising from the *pathē* that these shared capacities produce.[14]

What the lion anticipates

Considering Aristotle's view a little further will illustrate how even when we do find examples in his writings of relevant pleasures that are experienced by both human and non-human animals – for example, the pleasure involved in anticipating some future experience – there is nevertheless often a distinction to be drawn between the experiences of human and non-human animals that is explained by the presence in humans alone of certain rational capacities. There are similar points that might be made about the other philosophers' attitude to non-human animal psychology but Aristotle is perhaps the most interesting case because we have quite a lot of evidence for his view and also because his view has been subjected to more recent interpretative scrutiny.[15]

---

[13] A recent defence of the view that emotions must involve some kind of opinion can be found in Dow 2009 (cf. Dow 2011). This involves reading references to 'being appeared to' in accounts of the emotions – especially in the *Rhetoric* – as references to how the agent believes things to be and not to the activities of *phantasia* as attributed to some non-human animals.

[14] See Heath 2009, 53–7; cf. Moss 2012a, 22–47, esp. 40, 64–6, 88–9.

[15] For the Epicureans, for example, it seems that other animals do not experience emotions as humans do even though they do experience the *pathē* of pleasure and pain and may as a result be said to experience something like an instinctive fear of imminent danger. See Konstan 2008, 18–22. There is

The details of Aristotle's account of human and animal psychology are often controversial. Some things, however, are clear. He says that humans have a certain capacity for reason while non-human animals do not (*De An.* 3.3 428a23–4).[16] Some non-human animals are nevertheless able to exercise a capacity for memory and, like humans, also to possess the capacity for 'imagination' (*phantasia*) (*De An.* 3.3 428a19–24). There are differences between kinds of non-human animals. Some of them are only just capable of perception and are incapable of self-motion. Not all of them have the capacity of memory (*Metaph.* A.1 980a27–9; cf. *APo.* 2.19 99b34–100a3). Not all of them have the capacity of *phantasia*.[17] The psychological landscape is varied; levels of psychological abilities vary between different species of animal and not only between humans and all other animals.[18]

So there are some things that humans can do that might be captured by the broad category of 'thinking' that non-human animals cannot do and there are other things that we might capture in the broad category of 'thinking' that both human and some non-human animals share.[19] From Aristotle's perspective, the capacities that Socrates used to gloss the notion of *logismos* at *Phileb.* 21c1–d1 do not map neatly and exclusively on to the psychological capacities that belong only to human animals. There are, in fact, signs also in the *Philebus* that Socrates recognises important continuities between the types of cognition available to human and some non-human animals. A simple mollusc will be an extreme contrasting case with a rational human but other animals might share some important capacities with us.[20] Nevertheless, Socrates and Protarchus are guided in their discussion by the principal concern of outlining the nature of a good human life. Something similar is also the case for Aristotle. His inquiry into human *eudaimonia* in the ethical works requires him to think principally about human psychology. His inquiry into the nature of the soul in his physical works has a different focus and will include also accounts of the psychology

---

certainly evidence for the Epicureans thinking that other animals cannot anticipate or recollect their own past experiences. See Polyst. *De Irrat. Cont.* (*PHerc.* 336/1150) I–IV Indelli 1978 and Warren 2002a, 137–8.

[16] Some texts bracket these lines for deletion.

[17] See *De An.* 3.3 428a10–11: ants, bees, and grubs do not have *phantasia*. (The text here is debated but certainly *some* animals are denied this capacity. This is one of the premises in Aristotle's argument for the conclusion that perception and *phantasia* are distinct.) Compare *De An.* 3.10 433a12–13: Aristotle refers to 'the other animals' that have the capacity *phantasia* but not understanding (*noēsis*) or calculation (*logismos*). Cf. *De An.* 3.10 433b27–30.

[18] Osborne 2007, 87–94, stresses the continuities of psychological capacities between humans and non-human animals. See also Coles 1997. Cf. Sorabji 1993, 12–20; Heath 2009, 52–8.

[19] The class of 'non-human animals' I have in mind here excludes divine living things, which both Plato and Aristotle are inclined to think of as possessing rational capacities.

[20] See e.g. *Phileb.* 35c9–10 and 36b8–9; this is emphasised by Lorenz 2006a, 102.

of non-human living things. His inquiries into animals in the biological works will also have a different focus and, sometimes, explanations of non-human animal behaviour will involve attributing to them some means of foresight or understanding.

Even once we recognise that there are psychological continuities between human and non-human animals, we might qualify the sense in which humans and animals have some of the same capacities. For Aristotle, even those capacities that are shared by other animals – for example, memory – are not the same in a lion as in a human. It is clear that dogs have an ability to retain in some way a memory of past experiences. At least, their behaviour suggests that they are able to remember their owners, know that the post arrives in the morning, and so on.[21] In the wild, some animals' hunting behaviour also suggests that they have an ability to anticipate events in some way. However, it is much less plausible to imagine that a dog sitting by the fire in the evening is able deliberately to reminisce about the fun he had playing in the park that afternoon or to think ahead to what fun he might have the next day. (That dogs might dream of such things – indeed enjoy dreaming of such things – is a different matter since dreams too are not voluntary.) Humans can deliberately reminisce and anticipate and we can experience pleasures and pains as we do so.[22]

There is a well-known passage, however, which suggests that Aristotle holds not only that non-human animals anticipate pleasures and pains but also that they can take pleasure in the anticipation of a future pleasure.

οὐκ ἔστι δὲ οὐδ' ἐν τοῖς ἄλλοις ζῴοις κατὰ ταύτας τὰς αἰσθήσεις ἡδονὴ πλὴν κατὰ συμβεβηκός. οὐδὲ γὰρ ταῖς ὀσμαῖς τῶν λαγωῶν αἱ κύνες χαίρουσιν ἀλλὰ τῇ βρώσει, τὴν δ' αἴσθησιν ἡ ὀσμὴ ἐποίησεν· οὐδ' ὁ λέων τῇ φωνῇ τοῦ βοὸς ἀλλὰ τῇ ἐδωδῇ· ὅτι δ' ἐγγύς ἐστι, διὰ τῆς φωνῆς ᾔσθετο, καὶ χαίρειν δὴ ταύτῃ φαίνεται· ὁμοίως δ' οὐδ' ἰδὼν "ἢ [εὑρὼν] ἔλαφον ἢ ἄγριον αἶγα," ἀλλ' ὅτι βορὰν ἕξει. περὶ τὰς τοιαύτας δ' ἡδονὰς ἡ σωφροσύνη καὶ ἡ ἀκολασία ἐστὶν ὧν καὶ τὰ λοιπὰ ζῷα κοινωνεῖ, ὅθεν ἀνδραποδώδεις καὶ θηριώδεις φαίνονται· αὗται δ' εἰσὶν ἁφὴ καὶ γεῦσις. (*NE* 3.10 1118a16–26)

Nor is it the case in other animals that there is even any pleasure from these senses [*sc.* sight, smell, and hearing] except incidentally. For it is not the case

---

[21] Consider the case of Argus, Odysseus' dog, who waits for years for his master's return and then recognises him just by his scent (since Odysseus is in disguise): Hom. *Od.* 17.290–327, esp. 301.

[22] *De An.* 3.3 427b14–26; *phantasia* is 'up to us whenever we wish'. Aristotle also distinguishes between animals that also use *phantasia* for deliberation and those that do not. The former are those that are also able to reason. *De An.* 3.11 434a5–10: *aisthētikē phantasia* is present in other animals too but *bouleutikē phantasia* is only in those with *logismos*. Cf. Nussbaum 1978, 263–4: not every *phantasia* of a rational creature will be a rational *phantasia*.

that hunting dogs take pleasure in the scents of hares; rather, they take pleasure only in eating them (though the smell made the dogs notice the hares). Nor does the lion take pleasure in the sound of the ox; rather, it enjoys devouring it. The lion perceived that the ox was close through its lowing and merely appears to take pleasure in the sound. Similarly, the lion is not pleased by the sight of 'a dear or a fierce goat', but because it will have food. Those are the sorts of pleasures with which self-control and wantonness are concerned and which the other animals share, as a result of which they are revealed as slavish and bestial: the ones to do with touch and taste.

The immediate aim of this passage is to bolster Aristotle's assertion that self-control and wantonness (*sōphrosynē* and *akolasia*) concern only the pleasures of touch and taste and not those of the other senses. These pleasures are shared by non-human animals and are therefore rightly sometimes termed 'bestial'.[23] In passing, Aristotle offers some brief comments on non-human animals that might suggest that they too are capable of taking pleasure in imagining some future pleasant experience. For example, it might be claimed that this passage suggests that the lion takes pleasure in the prospect of eating in the sense that it enjoys 'envisaging the prospect' of the meal. The quotation at 1118a22–3 is from Homer, *Il.* 3.21–9 and is part of a description of Menelaus, who has seen Paris in the Trojan ranks and, like a lion spotting prey in the distance, feels great joy (ἐχάρη, 3.23, 27). Menelaus is pleased not simply by the sight of Paris but also by the anticipation of killing the man who stole away his wife. Similarly, the lion does not take pleasure in the mere sound of the stag nor does a dog take pleasure in the mere scent of a rabbit. But nevertheless the sound or smell of nearby prey might occasion the predator to be pleased that it will get a meal.

It is certainly true that a predator is provoked into action when it perceives the sound or scent or even the visual image of a prey animal. And its actions do appear to be goal-directed in the sense that the lion, for example, will take certain steps to hide until it is ready to pounce, will move downwind of the

---

[23] See Pearson 2012, 92–100, who also notes that 3.10 1118a27–32 shows that in so far as taste is primarily a discriminatory sense then it too, strictly speaking, is not something that can provoke self-indulgence. The parallel discussion at *EE* 3.2 1231a6–12 does not use the example of the hungry lion although it does affirm again that non-human animals do not take pleasure in odours *per se*. This is also true of us humans. When we take pleasure in the smell of dinner cooking on the stove, we are not taking pleasure in the smell *per se* but in our expectation or memory of food or drink. We can however take pleasure *per se* in the scent of a flower (ἀλλὰ καὶ τῶν ὀσμῶν ταύταις χαίρουσιν ὅσαι κατὰ συμβεβηκὸς εὐφραίνουσιν, ἀλλὰ μὴ καθ' αὑτάς. λέγω δὲ <μὴ> καθ' αὑτάς, αἷς ἢ ἐλπίζοντες χαίρομεν ἢ μεμνημένοι, οἷον ὄψων καὶ ποτῶν (δι' ἑτέραν γὰρ ἡδονὴν ταύταις χαίρομεν, τὴν τοῦ φαγεῖν ἢ πιεῖν), καθ' αὑτὰς δὲ οἷον αἱ τῶν ἀνθῶν εἰσίν). We can call wanton someone who really enjoys fancy perfumes and condiments, but only because they are ways of triggering recollections of objects of *epithumia* (3.10 1118a9–13).

prey so as not to be detected, and so on. The motivation for these actions is surely the goal of eating the prey and it is reasonable to think that eating its natural prey is a pleasant experience for the lion. Aristotle specifies that the lion is pleased 'because it will get food' (ὅτι βορὰν ἕξει, 1118a23). There is therefore a pleasant affective aspect to the lion's reaction to the sound of the stag which is related to the lion's goal of eating the stag.[24] The lion is, in some sense, pleased at anticipating the meal.

Although Aristotle does not mention the psychological capacity of imagination (*phantasia*) here in *NE* 3.10, given what he says elsewhere about desire in general and non-human animal psychology in cases of purposive action, *phantasia* must be the psychological capacity that is involved when the lion is pleased that it will get a meal: an 'image' (*phantasma*) is provoked by the sound of the stag and generated from the lion's memories. This *phantasma* is pleasant because it is generated from memories of past pleasant perceptions. This *phantasma* is involved in the lion's desire to eat the stag and in its actions to achieve the object of that desire. Aristotle says that an object of desire moves the animal by being thought of or imagined and, since the lion cannot think, it must be imagining the object of its desire. Consider a dog that is provoked by a feeling of thirst into desiring a drink in the absence of a direct external perceptual stimulus. It cannot see or smell a bowl of water but its capacity of *phantasia* allows it to bring to its mind the bowl of water in the next room. (It has perceived the bowl there before.) It says to itself (as it were): '*This* is something to drink' and off it goes; there is an obvious role for *phantasia* to supply the otherwise imperceptible object of desire. The complication in the case of the lion is that the lion does after all perceive the stag; it can hear it. However, we are told that the lion does not take pleasure in the sound but only in what the sound leads it to expect. Aristotle here presumably thinks that imagination is required in order for the lion to recognise the sounds as coming from something pleasant to eat. If so, some combination of the perception of the sound and the imagination anticipating the pleasant meal is needed.[25]

However, the precise specification of the content of what the lion envisages is not a simple matter. It is not clear whether *phantasia* in

---

[24] On desire as involving envisaging prospects see Pearson 2012, 41–7. Cf. Lorenz 2006a, 128–37.

[25] See Schofield 2011, 124–5 on *MA* 7 701a32–3 and esp. 124 n. 14. There has been a lot of recent discussion of the roles of perception and *phantasia* in animal desire and animal locomotion. The general view is that *phantasia* is always involved in animals that move as a whole (unlike animals such as anemones, which are stationary but which can move parts of their bodies in reaction to pleasant and painful perceptions) and that pursue something not immediately available to perception. See for the most recent contributions to the debate: Moss 2012a, 61–3; Corcilius 2011, 137; Pearson 2012, 51–60; Johansen 2012, 210–18.

non-human animals is able to do anything as complex as 'envisage prospects' or, perhaps better, it is unclear what sense of 'prospect' it would be right to think that these animals can envisage. It must be something provided by the lion's *phantasia* drawing on its past leonine perceptions and memories. But then we will need to wonder about the range and richness of things that a lion's *phantasia* might be able to provide and this, in turn, will depend upon the way in which a lion perceives the world and remembers past perceptions. On a generous view, *phantasia* allows the lion to envisage the prospect 'that it will get food': when a hungry lion perceives the stag it forms a desire to eat the stag, which involves envisaging 'the prospect of stag-eating'.[26] The generous view will make the content of the *phantasma* cognitively rich: the lion envisages 'a meal' or 'stag-eating'. This would seem to require that the lion perceive things as 'stag' or at least 'prey'. A more parsimonious view is that what the lion enjoys is the *phantasma* of the pleasant experience of tasting something it needs to satisfy its hunger. *Phantasia* reproduces the content of past perceptions and, furthermore, past perceptions of taste will suffice to explain the lion's motivation just as present perceptions are at other times motivationally sufficient.[27] The generous view would make the lion's behaviour closer to what humans can do when they form desires for things or take pleasure in anticipating some future state of affairs since the content of what *phantasia* can conjure for humans is cognitively rich. The parsimonious view holds that simple perceptions and the reproduction of just those simple perceptions are sufficient to explain non-human behaviour.[28]

This passage does confirm Aristotle's idea that we should explain some non-human animals' behaviour in terms of their being able, on the basis of some present stimulus, to look ahead to achieving some object of desire. Some human actions, no doubt, should also be explained in this same way.

---

[26] Lorenz 2006a, 131–7, argues that the lion enjoys envisaging the prospect of 'stag-eating'.

[27] See e.g. Moss 2012a, 38: 'Creatures who cannot recognise predators as such can experience fear (a species of pain) at the sight of a proper perceptible, and thus will flee. Thus animals can discriminate the beneficial from the harmful without recourse to sophisticated forms of cognition: simple perception even of proper perceptibles will suffice, by being pleasurable or painful.' Moss 2012a, 55–7 and esp. 56 n. 23 takes issue with Lorenz's interpretation of the example of the lion in *NE* 3.10.

[28] The Homeric quotation does not help us very much. In the Homeric simile the lion is said to take pleasure in devouring the carcass of a deer or goat that it has simply chanced upon (*Il.* 3.23–5); the hungry animal is not envisaging the prospect of a meal but is taking pleasure right now in the present satisfaction of its desire. This contrasts with Menelaus, who takes similar pleasure at the mere sight of his enemy and, we presume, at the thought of killing Paris that this perception provokes. And this is precisely the distinction between humans and other animals that Aristotle wishes to draw. For Aristotle is here insisting that the lion will not take pleasure in the mere sound of the ox as Menelaus takes pleasure at the mere sight of Paris. Contrast: Lorenz 2006a, 132 n. 23.

But although Aristotle does think that a lion might experience some pleasure as it goes about trying to bring down its prey, there is nevertheless room to find important distinctions between even that rich account of non-human anticipation and what we humans are capable of doing. Even granted the richest interpretation of the cognitive resources of the lion in this example, there are two differences between it and humans. First, the lion experiences the anticipatory pleasure as a result of a direct and present perceptual stimulus. It is implausible to imagine that it would be able to take pleasure in the thought of its next meal as it lies under a tree with no prey in the vicinity. It cannot deliberately and voluntarily turn its thoughts to its next meal and simply enjoy the prospect without such an immediate perceptual stimulus. Humans can. Second, humans can anticipate pleasures and have desires for things as pleasant in a way that requires reason to conceive of the specific end in question. The dog desires the pleasure of drinking the water but it cannot form a desire for the drink on the grounds that it believes that the water is healthy; humans can. Nor can the dog desire a particular brand of mineral water. Humans can.[29] In short, dogs and lions do not deliberately think back and take pleasure just in recalling a particularly tasty meal or a particularly pleasant drink, let alone a thoroughly enjoyable weekend in the mountains or a joyful reunion with a friend. Nor do they take pleasure simply in looking forward to such things. But humans do.

To be sure, at *NE* 6.7 Aristotle notes that just as a person can be said to be practically wise (*phronimos*) because of the way in which he deals with his own particular affairs, so too, 'they say', some non-human animals are also wise (*phronima*) in this way because they appear to have a capacity for foresight over their lives.[30] But he has perhaps instructively chosen to present this merely as an opinion held by some unnamed others and does not explicitly endorse this view. But elsewhere he is less guarded. Often in the zoological works Aristotle appears to attribute relatively high-grade cognitive powers to non-human animals. He describes their characters as courageous or timid and notes that some behave intelligently or are *phronimoi*. This is perhaps just a loose, traditional, or anthropomorphising way of talking: animals behave 'as if' they are intelligent and able to plan; for example, he describes how the

---

[29] See Pearson 2012, 190–5. Aristotle also comments that non-human animals cannot be subject to *akrasia* since they act only on the basis of *phantasia* or memory of particulars and therefore there can be no conflict between acting on the basis of an evaluative cognition from *phantasia* and an alternative action that knowledge or belief would recommend: *NE* 7.3 1147a35–b5; cf. *De An.* 3.3 429a4–8. Cf. Moss 2012a, 127.

[30] *NE* 6.7 1146a26–8: διὸ καὶ τῶν θηρίων ἔνια φρόνιμά φασιν εἶναι, ὅσα περὶ τὸν αὑτῶν βίον ἔχοντα φαίνεται δύναμιν προνοητικήν.

panther has 'realised' that other animals like its scent and therefore conceals the scent while it is hunting.[31] But even in the zoological works in which he is most relaxed about describing non-human animals in such a fashion, Aristotle also denies that they are properly capable of deliberation or of deliberate recollection (*anamnēsis*).

> βουλευτικὸν δὲ μόνον ἄνθρωπός ἐστι τῶν ζῴων. καὶ μνήμης μὲν καὶ διδαχῆς πολλὰ κοινωνεῖ, ἀναμιμνήσκεσθαι δ' οὐδὲν ἄλλο δύναται πλὴν ἄνθρωπος. (*HA* 1.1 488b24–6)

> Of all the animals, only humans are capable of deliberation. And while many of them share in memory and learning, only humans are able to recollect.

Therefore, although when he is being a keen empirical zoologist Aristotle is prepared to describe non-human animal behaviour in terms that often use the vocabulary of intelligent rational behaviour, he never goes so far as to deny that there is a significant psychological distinction between humans and all other animals. True, animals that perceive share in an intelligence of a sort (*gnōsis tis*), since perception is knowledge of a sort (*GA* 1.23 731a31–b4). But when he is being more scrupulous Aristotle insists that what we find in the other animals are just resemblances of understanding or thought and behaviour analogous to human craft and wisdom (*HA* 8.1 588a18–31).[32]

Aristotle is clear that deliberate recollection is an activity of reasoning and therefore a capacity restricted to humans. The point we have already seen made in *HA* 1.1 is restated at *De Mem.* 2 453a6–11: Aristotle explains that is the case because deliberate recollection is a kind of inference or reasoning (*syllogismos tis*) and inquiry (*zētēsis*). It is therefore legitimate to talk of a specifically human capacity for the deliberate recollection and anticipation of past and future experiences such as is involved, for example, in Eumaeus' reminiscences discussed in *Rhet.* 1.11.[33] Aristotle does occasionally talk of non-rational animals as having forward-looking capacities and, as we saw, is prepared to say, for example, that a lion takes pleasure in the appearance that he will eat the nearby stag (*NE* 3.10 1118a20–3). But he also says at *PA* 3.6 669a19–21 that only humans have hope (*elpis*) or expectation for the future

---

[31] *HA* 9.6 612a12–15: the verb is κατανοέω. This example is preceded, perhaps instructively, by the comment that 'people say' (λέγουσι) that the panther does this.

[32] On this general topic see Cole 1992, 45–51. Coles 1997 also provides an excellent catalogue of the ascriptions of intelligent behaviour and *phronēsis* to non-human animals in Aristotle's works and some strong arguments in favour of interpreting them as sincere attributions. Compare Lloyd 1983, 18–26.

[33] This passage is discussed in more detail in Chapter 7 below.

(*prosdokia*); this is why only humans experience their heart 'jumping'.[34] We can characterise the sense of 'hoping' or anticipating here as the counterpart of recollection (see e.g. *Rhet.* 1.11 1370a27–30). Anticipation in this sense will also involve some kind of deliberate inference or reasoning and is therefore also restricted to humans.

It is legitimate in that case to investigate the pleasures and pains of such 'autobiographical' anticipation or recollection as revealing an aspect of the affective lives we humans live. They will be the focus of my Chapters 6, 7, and 8.

Damascius and the donkey

Let us finally take a brief look at a much later ancient text that appears to be still grappling with the question of how to distinguish human affective expectation from what non-human animals experience. Damascius, in his lectures on Plato's *Philebus*, contrasts the sort of expectation that it is appropriate to attribute to a non-human animal with those appropriate only for a human animal capable of reasoning.[35]

ὅτι τριττὴ ἡ ἐλπίς, ἡ μὲν μόνου τοῦ λόγου, ἡ δὲ μόνου τοῦ ἀλόγου· τούτου μὲν γὰρ παράδειγμα ὁ πρὸ τῆς πόλεως θᾶττον ἐπιτρέχων ὄνος ἐλπίδι τοῦ μεταλήψεσθαι τροφῆς, ἐκείνου δὲ φανερὸν τὸ παράδειγμα· ἡ δέ ἐστιν ἐλπὶς τοῦ συναμφοτέρου, ὅταν δοκιμάζοντος τοῦ λόγου τροφὴν προσενεχθῆναι ἅμα καὶ τὸ ζῷον ἐνδεὲς ᾖ καὶ ἐλπίζωσιν ἅμα παρέσεσθαί τι τῶν πρὸς τὴν χρείαν. (*In Phileb.* §178)

Expectation comes in three kinds. One belongs to reason alone; another to the non-rational alone. Of the latter, an example is the ass that quickens its pace as it nears the city in expectation that it will be fed. Of the former there is an obvious example. There is also expectation that belongs to both together, whenever reason thinks that food should be acquired at the same time as the animal is in need. And simultaneously they expect that something will be present to satisfy this need.

Damascius goes on to claim that it is expectation of this third kind that Socrates has in mind at *Phileb.* 40a and distinguishes between such expectations in pious and good and in impious and wicked people. This is a little puzzling since the example he gives here seems to be of a simple case of

---

[34] Aristotle also discusses hope (*elpis*) as the future-directed counterpart of memory at *De Mem.* 1 449b25–8. He then discusses the role of *phantasia* in memory in such a way that we can assume it plays a role in hope too.

[35] For more on Damascius' interpretation of the psychology of the *Philebus* see Van Riel 2000, 142–54, and 2012.

desire in which a bodily need is combined with reason looking forward to a relevant object whose acquisition will satisfy that need, while the example Socrates gives at 40a seems not to involve any bodily need. But, for now, we should notice that Damascius too, no doubt quite rightly, identifies a sense in which even a donkey can be said to have a pleasant expectation.[36] It is unfortunate that he thinks examples of the other unmixed kind of expectation – that of reason alone – are so obvious that it is not worth mentioning any. He cannot have in mind any expectation that would fit into the third category and involve both rational expectation and some kind of bodily need. Later (§§206–7), Damascius gives as examples of pure pleasures seeing the evening star or a fine pasture and, as an example of a pure pleasure belonging just to the soul, contemplation of and grasping something intelligible (compare the 'pleasure in *gnōsis*' mentioned at §13). We can therefore imagine two animals walking home to the city: the ass which takes pleasure in expecting a meal when it reaches the city and the philosopher quickening his pace as he heads home in the pleasant expectation of an evening thinking about intelligible reality. The most basic point, however, is that here too in one of the latest ancient authors there is the recognition of both a continuity and a distinction between the ways in which rational and non-rational animals are capable of expectation and, therefore, of taking pleasure in expectation. The ass can manage with only the expectation that belongs to what is without reason (*to alogon*). We humans might sometimes act on just this basis but we also have two other kinds of expectation. There is the expectation that belongs to reason all by itself and there is also a third kind of expectation: the mixed expectation that belongs to reason and the irrational working together. These are, I suppose, human embodied desires and hopes and they too are important parts of our human lives that are not shared by animals that do not possess reason.

---

[36] Westerink 1959 ad loc. notes that the donkey might represent *epithumia*: see Plat. *Phaed.* 81e6–82a2.

CHAPTER 2

Plato on the pleasures and pains of knowing

Plato often assures us that it is pleasant to acquire knowledge. In the *Republic* a philosopher is said to live the most pleasant life because only a philosopher experiences the true and pure pleasures to be had from acquiring knowledge of the special intelligible objects that are the Forms. In the *Phaedo* Socrates' attention is focussed particularly on the damaging effects on the soul of the pleasures and pains of the body. But even here he mentions other pleasures – the 'pleasures of learning' (114e3–4) – that are the concern of the philosopher. Similarly, Socrates claims in the *Philebus* that the pleasure of learning is a good example of a pure pleasure: a pleasure that is neither preceded nor followed by pain. Nevertheless, Plato is also well aware of the fact that neither the process of coming-to-know something nor the final acquisition of knowledge will always be entirely pleasant. Indeed, in matters that would seem to be for Plato of the utmost importance, he is quite clear that our progress towards knowledge can be accompanied by a variety of affective experiences and it can often be difficult and painful.

For example, in the *Laches* Nicias explains how participating in a discussion with Socrates can be challenging but, with luck, can also result in important benefits. It can even be pleasant. But many people find it difficult.

οὔ μοι δοκεῖς εἰδέναι ὅτι ὃς ἂν ἐγγύτατα Σωκράτους ἦ καὶ πλησιάζῃ διαλεγόμενος, ἀνάγκη αὐτῷ, ἐὰν ἄρα καὶ περὶ ἄλλου του πρότερον ἄρξηται διαλέγεσθαι, μὴ παύεσθαι ὑπὸ τούτου περιαγόμενον τῷ λόγῳ, πρὶν <ἂν> ἐμπέσῃ εἰς τὸ διδόναι περὶ αὑτοῦ λόγον, ὅντινα τρόπον νῦν τε ζῇ καὶ ὅντινα τὸν παρεληλυθότα βίον βεβίωκεν· ἐπειδὰν δ' ἐμπέσῃ, ὅτι οὐ πρότερον αὐτὸν ἀφήσει Σωκράτης, πρὶν ἂν βασανίσῃ ταῦτα εὖ τε καὶ καλῶς ἅπαντα. ἐγὼ δὲ συνήθης τέ εἰμι τῷδε καὶ οἶδ' ὅτι ἀνάγκη ὑπὸ τούτου πάσχειν ταῦτα, καὶ ἔτι γε αὐτὸς ὅτι πείσομαι ταῦτα εὖ οἶδα· χαίρω γάρ, ὦ Λυσίμαχε, τῷ ἀνδρὶ πλησιάζων, καὶ οὐδὲν οἶμαι κακὸν εἶναι τὸ ὑπομιμνήσκεσθαι ὅτι μὴ καλῶς ἢ πεποιήκαμεν ἢ ποιοῦμεν. (*Laches* 187e6–188b1)

21

I don't think you understand that whoever is closest to Socrates and encounters him in discussion is forced, whatever the original topic of the conversation, not to be released from being spun round in argument until he manages to give an account of himself, of his manner of life and the life he has led previously. Then, if he manages this, Socrates will not let him go before testing whether all these things are fine and good. I'm used to him and I know that you have to undergo these things and I know full well that I will undergo them as well. For, Lysimachus, I take pleasure from this man's company and I think it no bad thing to be reminded that we have acted and do act poorly.

Nicias goes on to explain that he considers the potential benefits of submitting to Socrates' question to be worth the effort and that as far as he is concerned there is nothing unusual or unpleasant about the procedure (οὐδὲν ἄηθες οὐδ' αὖ ἀηδές, 188b5). However, it is clear that some people might find such self-examination difficult and troubling, even painful, no matter what potentially life-changing benefits it could bring. Nicias does after all compare Socrates' questioning with being subject to a kind of testing (*basanizesthai*) which has connotations even of torture and admits that he has prior experience in talking with Socrates on which he can base his confidence. The implication is that for others – for novices or perhaps people less open to Socrates' methods – this can be a painful experience.[1] And there are examples in the dialogues of people who complain that Socrates is not doing them any good at all.

In the light of such reasonable concerns about the difficulties of submitting to Socrates' brand of philosophy, the claim in book 9 of the *Republic* that the philosopher's life is the most pleasant possible has often been thought to be problematic, not least because of the various passages in that dialogue which appear to depict the philosophical life and philosophical education as painful.[2] But Socrates' proposal can be illuminated first by considering a stretch of argument at *Phileb.* 51e–52b, in which he tries to give an account of the nature of the pleasures of learning and which includes a specification of the conditions under which certain kinds of learning might be painful or a mixture of pleasure and pain. Teasing out the precise implications of what is said there will allow us to reconsider the pleasures

---

[1] Roberts and Wood 2007, 100–1, discuss this passage and insist that Nicias recognises that the procedure will be beneficial but painful. In fact, Nicias denies that the procedure is painful, at least for him. But the description of the procedure gestures towards the fact that other people might think it painful and perhaps that it was indeed painful for Nicias before he became fully acquainted with Socrates and his methods.

[2] Note also *Rep.* 539e6–540a1: before being finally allowed to rule, the student philosophers must be tested in difficult circumstances (βασανιστέοι).

and pains of the philosopher's life outlined in the *Republic*, since Protarchus' suggestion of the conditions under which learning might not be a pure pleasure but will instead be a relief from pain turns out to be directly applicable to the experience of the prisoner released from the cave in the allegory in the seventh book of the *Republic*. However, there remain some important obstacles in the way of producing a fully satisfying account of the hedonic life of the philosopher. One of these problems stems from an objection sometimes raised against the portrayal in book 9. This objection holds that the understanding of the nature of pleasure presumed in that argument should force Socrates to claim that only the acquisition of new philosophical knowledge and not the continued possession and exercise of philosophical knowledge is wonderfully pleasant. I canvass some possible answers to this problem and conclude that the analysis of various pleasures of learning in the *Philebus* can usefully be brought to bear on this question.

Pleasures and pains of learning in the *Philebus*

In the *Philebus* Socrates and Protarchus discuss the pleasures associated with learning and try to give an account of their nature.

ΣΩ. ἔτι δὴ τοίνυν τούτοις προσθῶμεν τὰς περὶ τὰ μαθήματα ἡδονάς, εἰ ἄρα δοκοῦσιν ἡμῖν αὗται πείνας μὲν μὴ ἔχειν τοῦ μανθάνειν μηδὲ διὰ μαθημάτων πείνην ἀλγηδόνας ἐξ ἀρχῆς γιγνομένας.
ΠΡΩ. ἀλλ' οὕτω συνδοκεῖ.
ΣΩ. τί δέ; μαθημάτων πληρωθεῖσιν ἐὰν ὕστερον ἀποβολαὶ διὰ τῆς λήθης γίγνωνται, καθορᾷς τινας ἐν αὐταῖς ἀλγηδόνας;
ΠΡΩ. οὔ τι φύσει γε, ἀλλ' ἔν τισι λογισμοῖς τοῦ παθήματος, ὅταν τις στερηθεὶς λυπηθῇ διὰ τὴν χρείαν.
ΣΩ. καὶ μήν, ὦ μακάριε, νῦν γε ἡμεῖς αὐτὰ τὰ τῆς φύσεως μόνον παθήματα χωρὶς τοῦ λογισμοῦ διαπεραίνομεν.
ΠΡΩ. ἀληθῆ τοίνυν λέγεις ὅτι χωρὶς λύπης ἡμῖν λήθη γίγνεται ἑκάστοτε ἐν τοῖς μαθήμασιν.
ΣΩ. ταύτας τοίνυν τὰς τῶν μαθημάτων ἡδονὰς ἀμείκτους τε εἶναι λύπαις ῥητέον καὶ οὐδαμῶς τῶν πολλῶν ἀνθρώπων ἀλλὰ τῶν σφόδρα ὀλίγων.
ΠΡΩ. πῶς γὰρ οὐ ῥητέον; (*Phileb.* 51e7–52b9)

SOC.: So let us therefore add in the pleasures to do with learning, if in fact we do think that these have no associated hunger for learning and that there are no pains that come about from and have as their origin a hunger for learning.
PROT.: That seems right to me too.
SOC.: What, then? If at a later time there should come about for those who have been filled with knowledge the loss of it through forgetting, do you discern any pains from that loss?

PROT.: None by nature, at any rate. But perhaps there are in our thinking about what we have undergone, whenever someone who has been so deprived is pained because of the usefulness of what has been lost.

SOC.: But, my friend, for now we are dealing with only the nature of those experiences themselves, distinct from our thinking about them.

PROT.: Then you are correct that each time we forget something we have learned this occurs without pain.

SOC.: So we should say that the pleasures of learning are unmixed with pains and never belong to the majority of people but only to the very few.

PROT.: How could we not say that?

Socrates is looking for another example of a pure pleasure: a pleasure which is neither necessarily preceded nor necessarily followed by a pain. His first example was the pleasure of smell. The pleasure of learning is the second example. It too, Socrates thinks, is a process and the filling of a lack but since simply not-knowing-X is not painful and having-forgotten-X is not painful then the pleasure of learning X is a pure pleasure.

A brief comment a few lines later specifies that these pleasures of learning that are unmixed with pains belong to 'the few and not the many' (52b7–8), and this suggests that Socrates has in mind here cases of learning that are not mundane examples of simply coming-to-know something. Most probably, the sort of learning Socrates has in mind is to be connected with the dialogue's later discussions of the various special *epistēmai*.[3] There are, of course, important differences between how the *Philebus* and the *Republic* conceive of *epistēmē* and its objects. Nevertheless, in both dialogues there is an evident commitment to the idea that certain kinds of special cognitive achievements are to be associated with a particular and superior form of pleasure. Furthermore, in both cases the dominant model for understanding the pleasure of this form of achievement is the filling of some kind of lack which may or may not be recognised or painful.

However, it seems quite implausible to think that a philosopher's cognitive progress is unaccompanied by pains, frustrations, and the like which are essentially connected with the fact that there is a conscious desire to know or understand something as yet un-grasped.[4] Plato himself is acutely aware that philosophical understanding is often hard-won. In fact, the *Philebus* passage is very careful to clarify the precise sense in which the pleasures of learning are unmixed with pain. Protarchus voices an important qualification at 52a5–7 when he notes that, although the simple fact of forgetting is not itself painful, the fact of *having forgotten* can perhaps be said

---

[3] Cf. Delcomminette 2006, 470.   [4] Cf. Frede 1997, 301, and Delcomminette 2006, 471 and 476–7.

to be painful just in cases when a person comes to reflect upon his lack of previous knowledge and on occasions when that knowledge is needed. Socrates swiftly brushes aside Protarchus' concern as irrelevant to the precise point he wishes to make. As he reminds Protarchus, what they want to grasp is precisely the nature of these experiences themselves, shorn of any further complicating factors. Socrates is right. There are lots of things I do not know and am entirely indifferent about not knowing; the fact of my not knowing them causes me no distress. There are also lots of things I did know and no longer know and am entirely indifferent about no longer knowing. To be sure, if I think that something I do not know (or used to know) is something that I ought to know or ought still to know then that secondary thought might be something that causes me distress. But the first order fact of simply not knowing is not painful. So learning something need not be a relief from something painful.

And yet, Protarchus has pointed to something important. He has given an important set of conditions under which a lack of knowledge (whether the result of forgetting something previously known or, we might add, the simple lack of a piece of knowledge never previously possessed) might rightly be thought to be painful. The conditions are twofold: (i) the lack of knowledge must be noticed or reflected upon and (ii) the knowledge that is lacking must be recognised as needed or necessary in some way. Each of the two is necessary but insufficient for the state to be painful: I might recognise I do not know something but feel no pain at that realisation so long as I think I have no need to know what I realise I do not know. Similarly, I might believe I need to know some important truths for my life to be good and worthwhile. But, so long as I do not recognise that in fact I do not currently possess such knowledge, then I will not feel any pain at its absence. When combined, however, the two conditions will be sufficient to generate pain attendant upon a desire to know. While the first of these conditions is often noted, the second is often missed.[5] Yet both are obviously necessary since it is the second which is required to generate in the person concerned a desire to know whatever it is that he does not know and it is crucial for the presence of some kind of negative affective response.[6]

---

[5] E.g. Delcomminette 2006, 471: 'En effet, pour qu'il ait désir, il faut qu'il y ait non seulement manque, mais encore manque *conscient*, si du moins le désir doit avoir une direction, un object.'

[6] Vogt 2012, 25–50, offers a detailed account of some of Plato's discussions of forms of ignorance, including *Phileb.* 48c2–49e8, and emphasises the sense in which unnoticed ignorance may be morally reprehensible even if it is not painful to the ignorant person himself. These cases of ignorance often

The full psychological commitments of Protarchus' comment at 52a8–b1 are worth further thought. Clearly, he is distinguishing between an 'affection' (*pathēma*), which we can presume is what is later glossed as a kind of deprivation (*tis sterētheis*) – the state of lacking some piece of knowledge – and something else which we have already identified as a necessary condition for this affection to be painful. Protarchus refers to this additional factor as our thinking about the affection (our '*logismoi*').[7] The *Philebus* provides a satisfying account of what *logismos* amounts to in this context in its initial stipulation that the best human life must consist in some kind of combination of both pleasure and reason (20e–22e). Socrates and Protarchus consider two extreme cases: on the one hand, a life which contains pleasure but is devoid of any cognitive capacities such as memory, knowledge, opinion, and wisdom – a life, Socrates explains, of a mollusc or some other such sea creature – and, on the other hand, a life which retains all those capacities but is without even the least experience of pleasure. Neither alternative seems to them to be choiceworthy and the remainder of the dialogue proceeds with this conclusion taken as its basis.

From Socrates' account of the 'mollusc life' at 21c4–8 and, in particular, his account of what it will lack as a result of the absence of reasoning (*logismos*), it seems that *logismos* is, first of all, something that is an essential prerequisite for living a recognisable human life and, more specifically, is related to what we might call a capacity for self-awareness and for considering one's wellbeing or hedonic state at non-present times. Such a capacity might not exhaust the range of what *logismos* may do, but it is the important characteristic for present purposes.[8]

In Protarchus' proposal at 52a–b too an important condition of feeling the pain of an absence of understanding is the human capacity to reflect upon or notice that condition and perhaps also compare it with some previous or hoped-for future state. It is possible, in that case, to give an account of the conditions under which an absence of knowledge is painful by making use of a distinction between first- and second-order knowledge, according to which the presence or absence of the first-order knowledge can be the object of a second-order form of knowledge and in which this second-order knowledge will be the exercise of the human capacity here referred to as *logismos*. Take a case in which I come to know that I do not

---

involve falsely inflated beliefs about one's own self, one's abilities and ethical worth. Many of Socrates' interlocutors are ignorant in this sense: they have a falsely inflated conception of their own grasp of a topic of ethical importance.

7   The plural form is clearly not significant since Socrates' immediate reply replaces it with the singular *logismos* (b3) with no apology, and the replacement does not seem to bother Protarchus.

8   Compare 11b4–c2. I return to discuss 21c in Chapter 6.

know X. Imagine also that coming-to-know that I do not know X is painful to me. It remains true that I do not know X, of course, so what I have acquired in coming-to-know that I do not know is a different truth. I know more than I did when I simply did not know X and did not know that I did not know X. We noted, remember, that for such a second-order knowledge of an absence of first-order knowledge to be registered as painful there would need in addition to be some awareness that the first-order knowledge that is lacking is something worth having. There must, in other words, be a recognised need for that first-order knowledge. The *Philebus'* analysis of human psychological capacities can also supply that additional requirement, once again by referring to the capacity of *logismos*.

The prospective and retrospective faculties associated with *logismos* at 21c are not only stressed as essential characteristics of human psychology; they are both also involved in desire. Later in the dialogue Socrates states clearly that he thinks all desires and impulses which initiate a drive for the removal or replenishment involve some sort of memory (35c–d). Specifically, the memory involved in desire is a memory of the opposite state to that in which the agent currently finds himself. This memory then provides a representation of the object of the forward-looking desire and the agent anticipates that desired state. Socrates then distinguishes two cases involving a person who is in pain but can remember the pleasant things he lacks. In the first, the person has a 'clear hope or expectation' of attaining what he lacks and the memory provides pleasure while he is also experiencing pain (36a–b). In the second, he is both in pain and also aware that there is no hope of replenishment. In that case he suffers both from the recognised lack and also from the despair of fulfilling that lack in the future (36b–c). We shall return to this account in a later chapter when we come to consider the *Philebus'* account of memory and anticipation in more detail.[9] But for now we should note that hopes and desires all involve some activity of memory, since it is memory which provides the store of experiences which can be drawn upon to generate the appropriate objects of pursuit in any given situation and which allows the animal to bring to mind some state (which it has experienced in the past) which is the opposite of its present condition.[10]

---

[9] Below, Chapter 6.
[10] See Frede 1985, 164–5; Russell 2005, 175–6. Delcomminette 2006, 470–6, has a good account of the sense in which philosophy itself in the *Philebus* is imagined as a kind of desire (see 58d4–5, 67b4–7); this is an image familiar from other dialogues such as the *Symposium* or *Phaedrus* but present also in the *Republic*.

We can now offer a full account of the painful cases of coming-to-know which Protarchus mentions at 52a–b: these are cases in which an example of first-order ignorance is recognised as a result of second-order reflection on a person's own cognitive state. This ignorance might be simply something that the person has never known or it might be the result of a loss of memory. In the latter case, the agent may recall the prior state of knowing without recalling the content of what was known; this might generate a desire to remember. The same capacity for second-order reflection that can recognise present ignorance is also responsible for the person's being able either to reflect upon a prior state of knowledge or to imagine a future state of comprehension and, in cases where the possession of the relevant piece of knowledge would serve some recognised end, this will generate a desire to know. That desire can be painful. Indeed, if it is to motivate the person sufficiently then its painful nature might itself be something instrumentally useful. In such a way we can imagine that knowledge can cause pain. This is a possibility which might be initially surprising but on reflection it is something that is only to be expected, particularly when the knowledge concerned is of a certain sort, namely the knowledge of an important personal failing.

Before we turn to the *Republic* we might compare, briefly, perhaps the best-known case in the dialogues of someone being brought to recognise an important lack of knowledge. Meno begins his discussion with Socrates certain that he knows what virtue is (71e1–72a5). Only a few pages later, when Socrates asks again what virtue is, Meno confesses that he now has no idea and compares his state to that of someone paralysed by a stingray (79a7–80b7). It is not clear whether this is a painful state to be in; the paralysis need not be a state of numbness or lack of feeling but is rather an inability to speak or act (80a8–b2). But Meno is certainly not pleased to be in this position.[11] Later, Socrates brings a slave to the very same state when he is puzzling over a geometrical problem. At the outset the slave did not know the answer but thought that he did. Then, at 84a3–b1, Socrates notes that the slave still does not know the answer but at least now knows that he does not know. Rather than inducing a form of paralysis, however, it engenders a new desire to discover the answer, 'for now he would be pleased to inquire (ζητήσειεν ἂν ἡδέως), though he does not know' (84b10–11). It is perhaps not surprising, given the generally protreptic aim of Socrates' demonstration, that there is no reference to this newly recognised ignorance

---

[11] See Scott 2006, 69–74.

being painful. Instead, Socrates stresses how the slave has a new longing to find the answer he realises he lacks (84c6), in contrast to Meno's disgruntled complaints of paralysis, and that the inquiry is something the slave will enjoy, perhaps because in the slave's case there is a confident expectation of success. But we find here too an interest in second-order knowledge and, in the implied analysis of the nature of the slave's desire to find the answer, an interest in the affective aspects of discovering one's own ignorance.

The pleasures and pains of the cave

Book 9 of the *Republic* contains the longest sustained account of the pleasure associated with a life of philosophy and also presents the most difficult problems for anyone trying to claim that the life of a fully-fledged philosopher is pleasant while holding firm to the analysis of pleasure – including intellectual pleasure – as the process of filling some kind of lack. Before we apply to this problem the analysis in the *Philebus* of the pleasures of learning and the pain of some kinds of ignorance, we should first consider the most famous Platonic account of the experience of radical and transformative cognitive progress, namely the story of the prisoner's release from bondage and ascent from the cave into the sunlight at the beginning of book 7.[12] The description of the ascent from the cave emphasises not the pleasures of discovery and the satisfaction of intellectual lack but quite the opposite: the dizzying and startling effect produced by the taxing and disorienting acquisition of a new perspective on reality and value. Indeed, Socrates repeatedly notes the pain and discomfort felt by the student on his way up out of the cave as the bright light and the journey take their toll (*algoi*, 515c8; *algein*, 515e1; *odunasthai*, 515e7).[13]

We might also relate his experience to the analysis offered by Protarchus. The release of the prisoner from his bonds and his ignorance (*aphrosynē*, 515c5) is painful perhaps because it makes that ignorance obvious to him. The first stage of his education reveals to him the fact that although he previously thought that he was viewing real objects, in fact he was viewing only shadows cast by the light behind the puppeteers. Such a realisation is hard to endure and the prisoner may well prefer his previous comfortable acceptance of mere shadows. Indeed, the prisoner will be confused if he is told that, despite his struggles to cope with the glaring light, his eyesight is in

---

[12] See Frede 1997, 300–2.
[13] There is a helpful account of the experience of the freed prisoner in Schofield 2007, 225–8, which does not, however, ask specifically why it is painful.

fact now working better (515d2–7). Socrates notes that when presented with new and more real objects for consideration the prisoner will become confused or at a loss and will perhaps even initially refuse to consider them, preferring instead to turn back towards the objects with which he is more familiar. A degree of compulsion is needed to force him to persist through the uncomfortable – indeed, painful – initial transition. The freed prisoner feels pain not only when he emerges into the light outside but also when he first turns round and looks away from the shadows to the fire within the cave. In that case, if the first stage of the conversion might plausibly be likened to the unsettling effects of a Socratic elenchus and the undermining of the passive acceptance of mere cultural norms, then this too – as well as the eventual first encounter with the dazzling realities of genuinely intelligible objects – is said to be a painful process. The prisoner is confronted with his own ignorance about things which he previously thought that he knew and also acquires a need or desire to know something of which he now realises he is ignorant: just the two conditions noted by Protarchus as sufficient to make a case of acquiring knowledge only a mixed pleasure.[14]

The overall portrayal of the prisoner's experience might therefore pose a problem for what Socrates will eventually claim for the great intellectual pleasures of philosophical enlightenment. The budding philosopher-ruler will certainly turn his gaze towards new and more knowable objects and he too might have to come to realise his prior ignorance. In some passages any pleasures that the philosopher will eventually experience from finally acquiring the truth does indeed seem to be connected to a kind of pain, presumably closely linked to the philosopher's tremendous desire to acquire the truth.[15] Socrates refers to the philosopher's 'birth pangs' as he struggles to grasp each thing's nature (490a–b) and, once the philosopher has achieved the goal of his intellectual desire, Socrates says that he then:

γνοίη τε καὶ ἀληθῶς ζώη καὶ τρέφοιτο καὶ οὕτω λήγοι ὠδῖνος. (*Rep.* 490b6–7)

would understand and truly live and be nourished and, in this way, be relieved of his pain.

---

[14] A similar phenomenon is illustrated by the case of what Socrates calls 'summoners' of thought (παρακαλοῦντα, 523b9; cf. παρακλητικά, 524d2). Faced with conflicting appearances, the soul is forced into an *aporia* and is compelled to find a resolution to its lack of understanding (524e2–525a3).

[15] Gibbs 2001, 20, comments: 'In Bk 9 Socrates appears to have forgotten his own warnings about the toils and pains and hardships involved in becoming a philosopher and living the philosophical life.' I see no reason to think there is an inconsistency.

Such comments invite us to think that the pleasure involved is mixed rather than pure. Perhaps the student's intense desire to know that is often associated with the life of a philosopher, coupled with the realisation that there are some terribly important things that he does not know, will always make philosophical progress a rather mixed affair in hedonic terms; the final hoped-for understanding will be experienced as a great pleasure, but also as a kind of relief. In that case there might appear to be a tension between these passages and the optimism of book 9.

Such concerns can be set aside, fortunately, once we understand properly the reasons for the prisoner's pain. The prisoner is pained at being forced suddenly to view objects of increasing brightness. We can distinguish three aspects here: (i) the glare of the new objects of his sight, (ii) the fact of his being forced to view them, and (iii) the fact of this being a sudden turn from familiar to unfamiliar objects. The first aspect is presumably part of Socrates' demonstration that the prisoner is being asked to turn his cognitive apparatus to objects that are more and more real – that is, have a greater share of 'being', are more purely 'just', 'beautiful', and so on – and are therefore more and more knowable (cf. 477a2–4). The cognitive apparatus, the 'eye of the soul', that had previously been dealing only with the dimmest objects is now being presented with objects that activate its powers of cognition more and more. But such things take some getting used to, particularly when they occur by compulsion: it is difficult to adjust when moving from a dark room out into the light even though it is true to say that out in the daylight is where a person's powers of sight work best.[16] It is not therefore simply the fact of being faced with these more knowable objects that generates the pain; rather, the prisoner is pained at being compelled all of a sudden to turn from his previous and familiar objects of attention – the shadows – and being forced to keep his gaze on these new and surprising things.

A life of philosophical progress and understanding is not *per se* painful, but it is so in the case of the prisoner in the cave because of the necessary compulsion and the shocking revelation involved in effecting a rapid transition from the prisoner's dreadful initial state. When Socrates goes on to describe the education of the budding philosophers, on the other hand, he makes clear that they have to undergo a lengthy process of careful preparation that begins very early in life (see e.g. 519a–b). We can therefore

---

[16] For more discussion of Plato's use of imagery and metaphor in describing the philosophical life see Nightingale 2004, 94–138.

be more optimistic about the experience of philosophical students in the ideal city, since there is a significant difference between the tremendous involuntary cognitive upheavals experienced by someone plucked out of the cave and dragged into the light and the altogether less horrific experience of a young person educated in the ideally organised city and led willingly and carefully through a programme of philosophical education which has an assured, if far from universal, level of success. As the *Philebus* notes, there is also a great difference between cases in which a desire is coupled with the realisation that its satisfaction is extremely unlikely and a desire accompanied by the assurance that it will be fulfilled (36a–c). Philosophical progress may never be entirely straightforward but we should be able to grant to Socrates the concession that under ideal circumstances the pain involved will be significantly lessened. And, in any case, elsewhere in the dialogue Socrates is often upbeat about the pleasures of intellectual discovery. Consider, for example, his description of the 'philosophical natures' beginning at 485a, especially 485d10–e1.[17] These fortunate people, fitted with all the traits of character necessary to allow them to be potential philosopher-rulers desire 'the pleasure of the soul itself by itself' (τὴν τῆς ψυχῆς ἡδονὴν αὐτῆς καθ' αὑτήν), a description very reminiscent of book 9's characterisation of the pure and true pleasures at 585b–e. There is no mention here that the 'pleasure of the soul by itself' is always accompanied by pain.

Coming-to-know and continuing to know

There are also, no doubt, distinctions to be drawn between the experiences of someone progressing towards philosophical understanding and a fully qualified philosopher-ruler, and those distinctions will be important in what follows. Still, Socrates is clearly interested in explaining the affective aspects of the philosophical life as a whole and is also interested in explaining them in part by reference to the specific kinds of knowledge and ignorance – including knowing that one is ignorant and knowing that one knows – that are involved in acquiring and possessing philosophical understanding. We can now approach directly the most significant difficulty which has been raised both for the characterisation of the pleasures of learning in the *Philebus* and also for the account of the philosophers' pleasures in the *Republic*. In both works, the emphasis is squarely on the pleasures of the process of coming-to-know something previously unknown

[17] On this passage see Lane 2007, esp. 50–9.

or previously known but now forgotten. In that case it might remain mysterious how the philosopher might be said to continue to live a pleasant life once the necessary and previously lacking knowledge has been acquired. The case of the *Republic* is perhaps the most pressing since there Socrates is most intent on insisting that the philosophical life, a life dedicated to the pursuit and then retention of knowledge, is the most pleasant life a human can live.

The difficulty begins with the closest Socrates comes in the dialogue to an explicit statement of what he thinks pleasure and pain are. In the course of an argument intended to secure the conclusion that pleasure and pain are both to be distinguished from an intermediate state of calm or rest (*hēsukhia*), he clearly states that pleasure and pain are both changes or motions (*kinēseis*: 583e9–10). That comment is left without further expansion until he comes some two pages later to give a more elaborate account of the different pleasures of the body and the soul. At *Rep.* 585a Socrates begins a new argument for the superiority of the philosopher's life by offering two premises. They deal with first the body and then the soul and assert an analogous relationship between their respective states of need.

(i) Hunger, thirst, and the like are 'emptyings' (κενώσεις) of the state (ἕξις) of the body (585a8–b1).

(ii) Ignorance (ἄγνοια) and foolishness (ἀφρονύνη) are 'emptyings' of the state of the soul (585b3–4).

He then infers:

(iii) Someone taking in nutrition (ὁ τῆς τροφῆς μεταλαβάνων) and someone having understanding (ὁ νοῦν ἴσχων) would be filled (585b6–7).

By this, he presumably means that the ingestion of food and drink would remove the 'emptying' identified in (i) and the acquisition of understanding would remove that in (ii).[18] One of the fundamental problems in interpreting this argument is the question whether Socrates exploits an ambiguity in the terms 'emptying' (κένωσις) and the associated 'fulfilment' (πλήρωσις) since they can both refer both to a state (of being empty, of being fulfilled) and to a process (of emptying, of fulfilling). From what we have seen of the argument so far, it is difficult to think that anything other than the state of

---

[18] Pappas 1995, 168–9, mistakenly detects an inconsistency here: '[W]hereas the first half of the argument shrank from praising any pleasure that follows from the *relief* of pain, the second half endorses the *relief* from ignorance as though it could raise a person higher than the middle state of calm (586a). Nothing in the argument prepares for this claim, which feels like a gratuitous insistence on the pleasure of philosophy.' The inconsistency disappears when we note that Socrates nowhere claims that ignorance is itself painful. Rather, it is a painless lack and so the pleasure of learning is not necessarily preceded by pain. It is therefore analogous to the 'pure' pleasures of smell described earlier.

'being empty' is intended in (i) and (ii). Certainly, it is not easy to imagine that the ignorance in (ii) is meant to be only a process of becoming less knowledgeable. On the other hand, the present participle μεταλαμβάνων in (iii) might suggest a process of ingestion rather than a state of being free from hunger, for example, whereas ἴσχων might rightly be thought to suggest a continued possession of understanding. The most satisfying overall interpretation remains one in which the states of ignorance or hunger are painful but the processes of eating or learning are pleasant.

The question whether pleasures are always *kinēseis* becomes acute, of course, when we glance forward to the intended conclusion of the argument, which holds that the philosopher is the one most truly fulfilled since he grasps objects which are themselves most pure and true and 'are' without qualification. If this refers merely to the process of acquiring understanding then we might agree that the process of becoming a philosopher is exquisitely pleasant but think that the resulting state of understanding is not (much as we might think that the process of eating when hungry is present while the state of feeling no hunger is not). Socrates does offer some more information about how he understands the pleasures of the philosophical life, but regarding the specific question whether these pleasures are associated entirely with the process of acquiring knowledge or may also include pleasures associated with the possession of knowledge, there is unfortunately only limited help to be found in the immediate context of this argument.

A survey of the various references in the surrounding discussion to the sorts of pleasures said to characterise the philosophical life proves to be frustrating. In the description of the discussion between three spokesmen for the three kinds of life, each dedicated to the cultivation of one of the three parts of the soul, Socrates has various ways of describing the pleasures characteristic of the life of the lover of wisdom. Sometimes these expressions point in the direction suggested by the argument thus far: intellectual pleasures are associated with the process of acquiring knowledge, that is to say, with learning. For example, when Socrates imagines the attitude of the other two sorts of people – the profit-lover and the victory-lover – to the philosopher's life he often puts it emphatically in terms of their attitude to the pleasures of learning (e.g. 581d2: *manthanein*; d6: *manthanein*; e1: *manthanonta*). This lends support to the conception of the philosophical pleasures as primarily – and perhaps exclusively – the pleasures of coming-to-know special objects. But this manner of expression is not applied consistently. Elsewhere, Socrates is prepared to talk about the pleasures of knowing (582a10: τῆς ἀπὸ τοῦ εἰδέναι ἡδονῆς) or about the pleasures of contemplating what is (582c7–8: τῆς δὲ τοῦ ὄντος θέας, οἵαν ἡδονὴν ἔχει). There are also occasions on which Socrates refers in the same sentence both to the pleasures of learning and to the pleasure of knowing. For example, at 581d9–e1, he wonders how the philosopher will think of other pleasures in relation to his own preferred intellectual pleasures. He compares the other pleasures with the pleasure 'of knowing how the truth stands' (τὴν τοῦ εἰδέναι τἀληθὲς ὅπη ἔχει) and 'always being in such a state [*sc.* of pleasure] when learning' (καὶ ἐν τοιούτῳ τινὶ ἀεὶ εἶναι μανθάνοντα).[19] It is hard to be sure whether Socrates means in this case to refer to two different kinds of pleasure that the philosopher may experience and to contrast both with the pleasures of the spirit or the appetites and it is unclear whether the adverb 'always' is supposed to show that the philosopher is always learning or that he is always experiencing pleasure when he learns. But it certainly suggests that there is pleasure associated with knowing the truth, of having acquired knowledge, whatever it may or may not then claim about that state.

In short, the problem is that much of the argument so far is plausible only on the understanding that pleasure is the replenishing of a desire or lack. On the other hand, Socrates is apparently happy to talk as if there are also pleasures to be had from knowing, rather than learning, the special objects of the philosophers' expertise. To be sure, we might understand ignorance as a state of cognitive lack much as hunger is a state of bodily lack, but if pleasure is associated with the process of replenishing that lack, there seems no other conclusion possible than that the pleasures of replenishing the soul – exquisite and intense though they might be since they are trained on pure and true objects – will be experienced only while the philosopher is acquiring knowledge. What pleasures can be left for the philosopher once he has the understanding he requires?[20] It is essential for the overall political project of the *Republic* that the ruling philosophers take up their role in the possession of a kind of knowledge that makes them experts in the areas relevant for political decision making. Readers of the *Republic* are familiar with the concern that as soon as the philosophers have acquired the required expertise they may be made to live a worse life by being forced to give up

---

[19] The phrasing echoes an earlier description of the special characteristic of the rational part of the soul, being that 'with which we learn and which quite evidently is entirely focussed upon knowing how the truth lies (πρὸς τὸ εἰδέναι τὴν ἀλήθειαν ὅπη ἔχει πᾶν ἀεὶ τέταται) and is least of all of them concerned with money and reputation' (581b5–7).

[20] If pleasure ceases when the process of replenishing ends, then 'the more successful a philosopher is, the sooner his life will cease to be pleasant': Gosling and Taylor 1982, 122–3.

their intellectual pursuits and descend back into the cave and rule. The present worry is that the fully fledged philosophers may also be made to live a less pleasant life simply because the ascent out of the cave comes to an end.[21]

We have already seen that the *Republic* contains a complex and varied story of the affective aspects of intellectual advancement, beyond the arguments concerning pleasure in book 9. And we have seen indications that Socrates wants to say that even the accomplished philosopher's intellectual life will display a similarly complex affective aspect. Such considerations might alleviate some of the worries about the hedonic life of the philosopher-rulers or, less charitably, they might be taken merely to demonstrate a contradiction between what Socrates evidently wishes to claim about their pleasant lives and the inadequacy of the model of pleasure in *Republic* book 9 to support that view. It would be preferable if we could construct an account that will allow this expanded sense in which the philosopher, even once he or she has attained the knowledge required for being a ruler, will continue to live a life characterised by great intellectual pleasures and which also remains consistent with Socrates' explicitly professed account of the nature of those intellectual pleasures in terms of a process of satisfying some kind of cognitive lack. But we are hampered in the construction of such an account by the fact that although Socrates spends rather a lot of time on describing the various epistemological and psychological, not to mention ethical, aspects of someone's progress towards philosophical understanding and the comprehension of the Good itself, what that person's life might be like after that point is left relatively underexplored.[22] Perhaps this is excusable in the sense that Socrates' major task is to persuade us that such an understanding is possible for a human to acquire and that, once properly installed as the rulers of a city, such rulers would set things up so as to be the best they could possibly be. Quite what it would be like to be such a ruler is not such a pressing concern. We are told, of course, that they will desire and endeavour to enact whatever is good and just and we can extrapolate something about their having no desire for certain things the rest of us might hanker after – money, fame, familiar familial relationships, and the like – but that is about it.

---

[21] See also Taylor 1998, 69, who objects to Socrates' argument on the grounds that 'no doubt a truth once discovered does not have to be rediscovered, but a meal once eaten does not have to be eaten again, and an intellectual *life* will require repeated acts of thought (whether new discoveries or the recapitulation of truths already known) no less than a life of bodily satisfactions will require repeated episodes of bodily pleasure'. See also Gibbs 2001, 28–30; Russell 2005, 128 n. 45.

[22] For a good discussion of the various psychological, epistemological, and ethical aspects of dialectic, see McCabe 2006.

Resolving the difficulty

A recent attempt by Sylvain Delcomminette to resolve the problem seems to me to be ultimately unsatisfactory. Nevertheless, it deserves serious consideration since it helpfully points the way to what I think is a more promising solution. Delcomminette's overall interpretation aims to show that for Plato knowing ('connaissance') and learning ('apprentisage') are regularly held to be one and the same or, perhaps better, that for Plato human knowledge always consists in the regular re-learning of previously known things.[23] Delcomminette's principal piece of textual evidence comes from the immediate context of *Republic* book 9. He notes the following questions from earlier in Socrates' defence of the superior pleasures of the philosopher's life which we have already considered briefly above:

τὸν δὲ φιλόσοφον, ἦν δ' ἐγώ, τί οἰώμεθα τὰς ἄλλας ἡδονὰς νομίζειν πρὸς τὴν τοῦ εἰδέναι τἀληθὲς ὅπῃ ἔχει καὶ ἐν τοιούτῳ τινὶ ἀεὶ εἶναι μανθάνοντα; οὐ πάνυ πόρρω; (*Rep.* 581d9–e1)

'What', I said, 'are we to think that the philosopher will think of the other pleasures in relation to the pleasure of knowing how the truth is and always being in such a state when learning? Won't he think they fall far short?'

Delcomminette argues that Socrates here refers to the pleasure of 'knowing the truth and being always in such a state of learning'.[24] If that is indeed how the second half of the sentence must be understood then it would appear to lend explicit support to his proposal that the philosopher's life is best understood as a kind of 'apprentisage permanent'. He further supports this interpretation by appealing to the *Symposium*'s famous account of human psychological flux, in which Diotima claims that not only in respect of our various character traits and emotional states but also in respect of our knowledge we are constantly in a state of change. Knowledge comes and goes and we are never the same with respect to what we know from one moment to another.

ὃ γὰρ καλεῖται μελετᾶν, ὡς ἐξιούσης ἐστὶ τῆς ἐπιστήμης· λήθη γὰρ ἐπιστήμης ἔξοδος, μελέτη δὲ πάλιν καινὴν ἐμποιοῦσα ἀντὶ τῆς ἀπιούσης μνήμην σῴζει τὴν ἐπιστήμην, ὥστε τὴν αὐτὴν δοκεῖν εἶναι. (*Symp.* 208a3–7)

---

[23] Delcomminette 2006, 477: 'En réalité, tant dans la *République* que dans le *Philèbe*, le plaisir pur résulte bien du processus d'apprentissage, main *en tant précisément qu'il est identique à la connaissance*' (original emphasis).

[24] Delcomminette 2006, 477: '[Le] plaisir de connaître le vrai tel qu'il est et d'être toujours dans un tel état en apprenant.'

> What is called studying happens because knowledge is departing. For forgetting is the departure of knowledge and studying puts back new memory in place of what has left and preserves knowledge in such a way as to make it seem the same.

I have already noted that the passage at *Rep.* 518d9–e1 is not entirely clear in its commitments. The text itself is debated and it is therefore understandable that different translators render the sentence differently.[25] In that case, it is prudent not to rely heavily on a particular interpretation of a controversial passage. In addition, the reference to the *Symposium*'s notion of psychological flux is not consistent with the most plausible interpretation of the contrast between the pleasures of the body and those of the soul as outlined in the *Republic*. To make clear that inconsistency it is necessary to return to the argument we left at 585b with Socrates having set out an initial analogy between fillings and emptyings of the body and the soul. With a full account of Socrates' conception of the nature of the philosophers' pleasures, we might then be able to give an informed answer to the question of the pleasures of a philosopher's life after he has come to know the Forms. Socrates continues:

(iv) A filling with what 'is' to a greater degree is truer / more truly a filling than a filling with what 'is' to a lesser degree (πλήρωσις δὲ ἀληθεστέρα τοῦ ἧττον ἢ τοῦ μᾶλλον ὄντος; δῆλον ὅτι τοῦ μᾶλλον, 585b9–10).

The central difficulty here is in making good sense of the notion of degrees of being and then applying it to the intended analogue of degrees of filling.[26] Socrates himself helps only a little with the first of these problems, since he merely reminds Glaucon in a brisk fashion of a previously agreed distinction between things which share in 'pure being' and those which do not. Even so, there is enough spelled out in these lines for us to be fairly confident about Socrates' view. The general contrast he invokes is between bodily nutrition and the means of caring for the soul (585d1–3); the former

---

[25] J. Adam 1902 devotes Appendix III of his commentary on book 9 to the discussion of how to construe these lines and, in particular, whether they contain one or two questions. I have cited them, following Slings' Oxford text, with two questions. Burnet punctuates similarly, bracketing τῆς ἡδονῆς, which appears in some manuscripts after μανθάνοντα. Adam retains τῆς ἡδονῆς to read: '. . .καὶ ἐν τοιούτῳ τινὶ ἀεὶ εἶναι μανθάνοντα τῆς ἡδονῆς; οὐ πάνυ πόρρω καὶ καλεῖν. . .', translating: '. . . compared with that [pleasure] of knowing how the truth stands and always enjoying a kindred sort of pleasure while he learns? Will he not think them very far away and . . .?'

[26] Cf. Rosen 2005, 344–6. Annas 1981, 312–13, is also unhappy with this section. She wonders (312) 'how what is changeless can *come about in* what is changeless' and also is concerned because (313) 'it is not clear how this passage should be related to claims elsewhere about the Forms. For the contrast drawn here is not one between Forms and other things, since it has as much application to soul and body as to other things (585d), and the soul is not a Form.' There is a helpful discussion in Wolfsdorf 2013a, 70–4; cf. Erginel 2011.

obviously includes food, drink, and the like, while the latter includes true opinion, knowledge, understanding, and every virtue (585c1–2). The question of degrees or categories of 'what is' is then explained by a contrast between two kinds of filling – their objects, and their proper location – which is spelled out in the next few exchanges between Socrates and Glaucon. The contrast is complex but worth exploring carefully because it holds the key to the remaining argument. There is both a kind of filling related to what is always the same, what is immortal, and the truth, which is itself of such a kind and comes to be in such a thing and, in contrast, another kind of filling which is related to what is never the same and mortal, is itself of such a kind and comes to be in such a thing. It emerges, therefore, that there are three variables in play in the complex set of associations which Socrates wishes to use. They are what we might call: (a) the thing to be filled, (b) the method of filling, and (c) the object of filling.

Learning, for example, is a method of filling which is taken to be a means of seeing to the care of the soul, and knowledge is necessarily related to objects which are changeless and true. Eating, on the other hand, is a means of seeing to the care of the body but it is related to objects which are changeable and inconsistent. Socrates insists that the character of the kind of filling is determined by the character of its object, so learning itself is of a kind with its objects. He also insists that the kind of filling comes to be in something which is also of such a kind as it and its objects, so knowledge – which is stable and unchanging – comes to be in a soul which is also immortal and, in important ways, unchanging. The fulfilment of the body's needs, in contrast, has as its objects perceptible items, bits of food, and so on, is itself only temporary – because it has to be constantly repeated using always new items – and comes to be in something equally temporary and changeable, namely the body.

A chain of explanation is set in place. The important determining factor is the nature of the ultimate object in each case. The nature of the object then determines the nature of the filling, which must in turn be related to an appropriate subject. It remains only for Socrates to spell out the distinctions between the two sets of relations and to rank them. Unfortunately, the text of 585c8 has been transmitted in a corrupt state, so it is not easy to see how the argument begins.[27] The conclusion, however, at 585d1–3 is what we might have expected, namely that the forms of care for the body have a lesser

---

[27] Slings comments in the Oxford Classical Text ad loc.: 'locus desperatus'. See Adam 1902 ad loc. and his Appendix VI to book 9 for further discussion and for his own preferred solution. Cf. Ferrari 2002; Erginel 2011, 518–20.

share in being and truth than do the forms of care of the soul. And at 585d5 it is added that the body differs from the soul in the same way, because the body shares less in being and truth than does the soul. Something that is always the same shares more in being and truth than something which is not always the same. And if that is the case for the objects of the fillings, then it must also be the case for the fillings themselves.

It should be clear why the thrust of this argument sits poorly with the idea that Socrates here holds the view that the philosopher's soul is in a state of permanent learning of the kind suggested by Diotima at *Symp.* 207e–208a. The argument as a whole rests on the assumption that the filling appropriate for the soul is the filling of something that is always alike, immortal, and true with something that shares those characteristics. The central contrast is between the stability and permanence of the filling appropriate to the soul and the impermanence and changeability of the body and the objects in which it takes pleasure. The upshot of this argument in book 9 is that filling a bodily need is less truly a filling than filling a psychic need.[28] The subject being filled (the body), the means of filling (eating), and the items used for the filling (food), are all changeable and inconstant. Hunger is sated only temporarily. The body and the food used to feed it are such that the filling cannot be permanent and is at best only ever partial. As Socrates later comments, those who are trying to satisfy their bodily desires fail to do so because they are filling something 'which neither is, nor is watertight, with things which are not' (586b3–4). He tellingly compares their state to that of the Danaids, who were condemned to toil fruitlessly trying to fill a leaky vessel by carrying water in a sieve, reusing an image he exploits to good effect in his conversation with Callicles at *Gorg.* 493a1–c7.[29] It would be very surprising – not to say unhelpful to his argument – if Socrates were to hold simultaneously that the intellectual pleasures he is praising for the stability of their objects and the stability and permanence of the soul which they fulfil in fact also display a similar kind of impermanence. And Socrates stipulated back at 485c–d that a philosophical nature would have to display an excellent memory. It is therefore very unlikely that the kind of psychological fluidity emphasised in the *Symposium* is something we are invited to bring to bear on the understanding of intellectual pleasures in the *Republic*.

---

[28] Annas 1988, 312, complains of an illegitimate slide from 'being filled with what really/truly is' to 'being really/truly filled'; cf. Erginel 2011; Wolfsdorf 2013b, 119–29.

[29] Cf. Gosling and Taylor 1982, 128: 'the thought seems to be that a firm lasting container filled with firm lasting contents can truly be said to be filled, whereas when one has a non-stable container and volatile contents it is only in a dubious sense to be called a filling at all: can one fill a hair-sieve with liquid?'; see also Bobonich 2002, 55–6.

As the discussion progresses there are more reasons offered in support of the view that the intellectual pleasures are thought of as being provoked by a change that is permanent and, moreover, that they are associated with that part of us that is also permanent and unchanging. At 585d11 Socrates finally brings all of the complicated discussion about different kinds of filling of different kinds of vessel with different kinds of object to bear on the question of pleasure.

(v)   Fulfilment by what is appropriate to our nature is pleasant (585d11).

(vi) That which is to a greater degree filled really and with things that are generates to a greater degree the enjoyment of true pleasure really and more truly. That which receives things that are to a lesser degree would be filled less truly and securely and would receive more untrustworthy and less true pleasure (585e1–5).

Critical attention has focussed on (vi), but premise (v) is undoubtedly just as important. When Socrates considers the pleasures enjoyed by those who are focussed on bodily delights, it is not coincidental that he casts such people and their pleasures in decidedly bestial terms. They are 'like cattle, always looking down and bent over towards the ground, feeding at the table, growing fat and mounting one another' (586a6–7). The metaphor of rutting herd animals continues as these people are described as butting one another with 'iron horns and weapons' (586b2). Clearly, Socrates is encouraging us to disown such behaviour as not appropriate to our proper, human and rational, nature. It is a mere bestial nature which such pleasures fulfil, to the extent to which they can fulfil anything at all.[30] The strong implication is that this vignette sketches the state of people who are focussed on enjoying the pleasures produced when they try to satisfy the desires of the appetitive part of the soul. They have become misled by these impure and false pleasures and have created for themselves a misinformed conception of the good life. Tragically, the subsequent constant pandering to the desires of the appetitive part of the soul merely compounds their misfortune and further distorts their conceptions of value.[31] Socrates goes on to refer explicitly to the elements familiar from the tripartition of the soul when he turns at 586c7 to consider the pleasures of the spirited, money- and victory-loving part of the soul. The discussion of pleasure is, after all, part of a much more extensive discussion of the relative happiness of different

---

[30] Gibbs 2001, 31, cannot be correct in reading this passage as merely rhetorical.

[31] See 439b3–6, 588b10–e1 and Lorenz 2006a, esp. 31. There are important continuities between this view and the claims about false and impure pleasures made in the *Philebus*. See e.g. Cooper 1999a, 157–8.

character types, an inquiry which has taken up much of this and the previous book and in which Socrates has made extensive use of the three parts of the soul to explain the origin and nature of various ways of living.[32]

The question of the precise account of our human nature offered by Socrates in the *Republic* is complicated and controversial. But, in general terms, Socrates appears to be committed to an account of our nature which encourages us to identify ourselves, first and foremost, with the rational part of our soul, which should take care of and guide the other two parts.[33] That is the overall message of the concluding sections of book 9 and their depiction of a person as composed of a human, a lion, and a many-headed beast (see 589a–92b). The fulfilment of the needs of the rational soul is what best fulfils the best part of our nature and produces the most and finest pleasure. (It is impossible, at least while the soul is incarnated, to rid ourselves entirely of the desires and influence of the appetites and of spirit, but they ought at least to be controlled and reined in as far as possible: 571b–572b.) Such an identification with the rational part of the soul is necessary for the proper harmony of the soul's parts and also, apparently, for the proper functioning of each individual part of the soul. Certainly, in the coda to this argument, which once again surveys the various character types distinguished by the prominence of each one of the three parts of the soul, Socrates notes that in the absence of proper guidance by reason even the pleasures of the spirited or appetitive parts are not maximised. Only the philosophical and just soul, ruled by reason, properly enjoys the pleasures of the appetitive and spirited parts since only with the guidance of reason will each enjoy 'the best and truest of its own pleasures, in so far as it is possible' (586e4–587a2). A glutton, for example, will not enjoy the pleasures of the appetite as much as the philosopher will, since the glutton's desires are not controlled by reason. Socrates spells out this view in the case of the money- and victory-loving character: constant irascibility and the overwhelming desire for victory in fact prevent the successful satisfaction of such a person's predominant desires (586c7–d2).[34]

Premise (vi) adds very little that has not been explained or, at the very least, discussed already; it adds only the association of pleasure with the degree of fulfilment attained and the kind of object being used for the fulfilment. If we have by now accepted the notion outlined and explained at

---

[32] For discussion see Annas 1981, 294–305; Scott 2000; Ferrari 2003; Lorenz 2006b.

[33] See Long 2005 for a discussion of Platonic personhood.

[34] Cf. Russell 2005, 131–5. Compare also Socrates' diagnosis of the constant futile toils of the tyrannical man, trying desperately to satisfy his uncontrolled and changing appetites: 573b–581c.

585b11–c6 that bodily fulfilment is less a fulfilment than proper intellectual fulfilment, then this new point follows without much trouble. We might still imagine a staunch supporter of the pleasures of eating and drinking objecting that he sees no particular reason to think that his preferred pleasures are less truly *pleasures* than those of his more intellectually inclined counterpart. Certainly, he might object, there is no reason to think that they are any less intense. And, indeed, perhaps Socrates would agree with him; the problem with bodily pleasures, after all, is that they are based in such violent fluctuations and contrasts between satiety and emptiness that they can mislead people into concentrating on them to the detriment of the health of their souls (586b7–c5). He also explains the problem in terms familiar from the epistemology and metaphysics of the central books: the pleasures in question here are not only mixed with pain but are also 'copies and shadow-pictures of true pleasure' (εἰδώλοις τῆς ἀληθοῦς ἡδονῆς καὶ ἐσκιαγραφημέναις, 586b7–8).

The exact connotations of that description and the precise relationship between the account of those pleasures and the general epistemological and metaphysical commitments of the dialogue can be left aside for now.[35] Whatever we finally decide about these 'shadow-pictures' of true pleasure, we are still faced with the problem of what to say about the hedonic life of the fully fledged philosopher. The argument so far, after all, strongly implies that the true pleasure to be had is associated with the *kinēsis* that is learning – filling up the cognitive lack that is ignorance – and that this filling is something which takes place in a stable and everlasting container, uses stable and everlasting objects, and therefore does not have to be repeated. Indeed, the fact that, unlike the bodily pleasures with which it is contrasted, such true pleasure is not in constant need of repetition is one of the reasons why Socrates thinks it is a superior form of pleasure.

There are a number of ways in which Socrates can respond to the concern that the philosophical life will contain great and exquisite pleasures while the philosopher is in the process of acquiring knowledge but, after that point, will seem to have many fewer opportunities for continued enjoyment of those same pleasures. A first general point to bear in mind is that Socrates nowhere promised to show that the philosopher is at every moment of his life experiencing the greatest pleasures; we are not to imagine him in a constant state of intellectual ecstasy. Rather, the *demonstrandum* is that the philosopher's life, taken as a whole, is most pleasant. This lessens the need

---

[35] For discussion of this see, for example, Wolfsdorf 2013b, esp. 119–29 and 133–6.

for us to show that the philosopher is at all times experiencing the greatest pleasures since we might well agree that the philosopher's life will contain at some point in it the greatest, most true, and purest pleasures.

Second, the hedonic life of a fully-fledged philosopher will nevertheless contain a great variety of pleasures and, moreover, will contain pleasures which are still superior to those found in any other possible life. Socrates asserts at 586e4–587a2 that only in the light of the rule of reason in the soul is a person able to experience appetitive and spirited pleasures of the best and truest variety available. Of course, these pleasures are never going to be pure and true in the sense that the intellectual pleasures are, but nevertheless this passage serves as an important reminder that the philosopher will also continue to enjoy the pleasures of eating and so on and, more to the point, we are assured that because of the harmonious arrangement of his soul, free from internal conflict (586e5), and the fact that therefore his desires are all correctly marshalled and arranged by reason, he will be able to do so to the greatest extent possible for any person.[36] In contrast, when one of the other parts of the soul is dominant, it forces its fellow soul-parts to pursue pleasures which are alien to them (587a4–6).

This observation remains unsatisfying to the extent that it concerns pleasures that are not related directly to the philosopher's special emphasis on living a life identified with the best activities of reason. A philosopher might well take great pleasure in eating his healthy diet, perhaps even more pleasure than the gluttons or gourmands take in eating theirs, because he eats in a way that is ultimately guided by a conception of the good. But that still falls short of the account we want of why a philosophical life remains most pleasant and Socrates himself seems most interested in locating the superiority of the philosopher's hedonic life in its being related closely to the experience of pleasures that are both true and also – as we have seen – appropriate to our best nature.

Third, perhaps Socrates imagines that a philosopher will be qualified to rule once he has grasped various essential moral truths – knowing what is good and just, for example – but there will remain a number of other Forms that the philosopher might come to know even once he has taken up his role

---

[36] This is important additional support for the earlier contention (580d–583a) that the philosopher's life is the most pleasant because only he has experienced true and pure intellectual pleasures and, as an expert in all pleasures, he would judge his life to be the most pleasant. On that argument see Taylor 2008, who rejects Socrates' claim that the philosopher excels other types of men in his experience of pleasure. Erginel 2004, ch. 3, has a wide-ranging discussion of this argument and compares it fruitfully with similar arguments in Mill's *Utilitarianism* §10.

as a ruler in the city.[37] This proposal will postpone the difficulty: the philosopher's life can contain the marvellous pleasures of learning for longer than his required period of training. But it does little more than that. There is no guarantee, I think, that there is an indefinitely large number of Forms to learn such that a philosopher will never run out of potential new sources of the pleasures of intellectual discovery. (The *Republic* is unfortunately unclear about the precise range of the Forms.) And this proposal nevertheless still faces the problem that there is no sense in which the possession of knowledge already acquired is itself a source of pleasure for the philosopher.

Another possibility is that Socrates has in mind a wider conception of intellectual pleasures than just those concerned with Forms.[38] Perhaps the fully qualified philosopher will continue his intellectual development by acquiring various true beliefs, finding out various facts about the world, reading literature or history, even doing some mathematics or revisiting his old harmonic theory text-books and trying out some new problems. There is some textual support for such a view since at 585b11–c2 Socrates groups not only the pleasures of knowledge and understanding but also true beliefs and generally all virtue against those concerned with food, drink, and nutrition as a whole. All of the former types, it seems, will produce pleasures that are superior to those of the latter type. Now, the precise ramifications of this proposal for the classification of this wider group of pleasures will depend to a large extent on what view is taken of the ontological stance of the *Republic* as a whole and also of the capacities for the acquisition of true beliefs of not only the other classes of citizen but also the non-rational soul parts themselves. But it is an important reminder that the philosopher-ruler will not be a disembodied soul; he will continue to live and take enjoyment in various pursuits and activities beyond the special case of acquiring knowledge of perfect, intelligible, and everlasting Forms. But yet again, the proposed pleasures that are said to characterise the philosopher's life are not obviously of a kind that cannot also be enjoyed by those less fortunate people who cannot be said to live a philosophical life. A rather wide group of

---

[37] This proposal was suggested by one of the anonymous readers for Cambridge University Press.

[38] An interpretation of this kind is offered by Erginel 2011 (cf. Erginel 2004, ch. 4), which he further supports by relying on a scalar interpretation of the being and truth of various objects of pleasure: there are, in other words, objects that stand between those that are 'always the same, immortal, and the truth' and those that are 'never alike and mortal' (585c2–6) such as the objects of true beliefs. There are signs that some ancient readers were tempted by a version of this approach. For example, Plutarch's criticism of the Epicureans in his *Non Posse* seems to accuse them of neglecting a wide range of apparently intellectual pleasures. See Chapter 4 below.

people, we might imagine, can come to acquire and perhaps enjoy acquiring true beliefs or a grasp of empirical facts, even if we grant the possibility that such learning would be transformed significantly by a proper grasp of the nature of the Good.

A proposal

A better answer can be given if we allow ourselves to work with a richer conception of the workings of the reasoning part of the soul. We have already seen signs in the discussion of the pleasures and pains involved in the philosopher's ascent from the cave that the *Republic* must be using something like the conception of first- and second-order knowledge that Protarchus expresses in more explicit terms and that in both cases there is an evident interest in the pleasure and pain to be associated with a kind of reflexive knowledge. My further claim is that the analysis taken from the *Philebus* can be used to alleviate the problem of the philosopher's intellectual pleasures in the *Republic* by pointing to a set of pleasures that the philosopher will be able to experience after the point of coming-to-know the Forms and that are not accessible in any way or to any degree by someone who has not similarly come to know the Forms. It is certainly wrong to say that the philosopher, once he has acquired knowledge of the Forms, will continue to experience the pleasures of that initial and extremely satisfying discovery because he will 'forget' what he has learned. It is hard to square such a proposal with the evident emphasis in the *Republic* on the stability and permanence of not only the object of philosophical knowledge but also the rational soul with which that knowledge is acquired, not to mention the insistence that philosophers will have excellent powers of memory (487a). However, Delcomminette's proposal is on the right lines because it is true that the philosopher's life will continue to be characterised by various changes in the soul that might reasonably be said to be examples of coming-to-know of the sort that would qualify as potential pleasures. We do not need, on the other hand, to posit some kind of constant state of learning and forgetting of any first-order knowledge since any psychological changes necessary can be restricted to the second-order kinds of knowing.

Protarchus drew our attention to the possibility of there being a second order of reflection on what a person knows and the connections this might have to experiences of pleasure or pain in coming to know something, since it allows a distinction between coming-to-know in some cases in which one does and in others in which one does not also know that one does not know that something. There are cases in which this second-order knowledge that one does not know something is coupled with the fact that one previously did know that something, in which case we are right to talk in terms of 'forgetting' or 'remembering'.[39] But this is not true of all cases. There is surely, we might insist, an important distinction between having forgotten something and merely not having to mind something that we still know. That distinction is brought out most forcefully by the fact that in the case of something forgotten but now recognised as necessary to know, the previously held piece of knowledge is not easily remembered. Indeed, the difficulty of remembering that previously held piece of knowledge coupled with the recognised need for it is precisely the combination of factors that would make it plausible to say that the experience is a painful one.

Once again we can turn to the *Philebus* for a more explicit expression of an idea that I want to suggest is relevant to Socrates' claims in the *Republic*. In his discussion with Protarchus, Socrates articulates a distinction between 'remembering' something that has been forgotten and 'calling to mind' something that has not been forgotten but has simply not been the focus of attention. At 34b–c he distinguishes between two forms of 'recollection', *anamnēsis*: one in which the soul 'takes up' (*analambanēi*, 34b8) a memory, which is something originally experienced together with the body, and another in which the soul 'unearths' or recovers (*anapolēsēi*, 34b11) a memory which it previously had lost (*apolesasa*, 34b10) of a perception or a piece of learning. Both, he says, can rightly be called examples of *anamnēsis*, although it is evident that we are not meant to think on this occasion of the special kind of recollection considered in the *Meno* and *Phaedo*: both forms of *anamnēsis* in the *Philebus* deal with perceptions or things learned during a person's life.[40] This distinction between the two forms is embedded in a longer section that tries to clarify what memory is (33c–34c) since Socrates wishes to use the pleasures belonging to memory as an example of pleasures which belong only to the soul and not to the soul and body together. His principal concern, therefore, is to show that even in cases where what is being recalled is something that originally involved the body (a perception or some other kind of experience) the recollection of it involves only the soul. But whatever the other subtleties of the passage, it is reasonable to identify here some recognition on Socrates' part that there is

---

[39] And there is also the further aspect of whether the person concerned knows *that* he has forgotten, which is a complicated combination of (i) not knowing X, (ii) knowing that he does not know X, and (iii) knowing that he previously did know X.

[40] There is a helpful discussion of this passage in Delcomminette 2006, 324–30.

an important difference between the soul's remembering something that has been forgotten – that is, a memory that has been lost (33e2–4) – and the soul's recovering something stored in the memory. Calling a piece of latent knowledge to mind can hardly be called 'learning', of course, nor can it really be called 'remembering'. But the Socrates of the *Philebus* apparently thinks it might still be called a case of *anamnēsis*, and what matters for our purposes is that he does identify a psychological capacity involving the taking up of things stored in the memory.

At this point we might be put in mind of not only Aristotle's discussion of *anamnēsis* in *De Mem.* 2, but also his useful distinction between the first and second actualities of knowing in *De An.* 2.5. Of course, Aristotle has his own account of how it can be both pleasant to learn and also pleasant to possess and use already-learnt knowledge. And that account is in turn related to a more general disagreement between him and Plato on the necessity of thinking of pleasure as a kind of *kinēsis*. That disagreement will be further explored when we consider Aristotle's own account of the pleasures of learning and knowing.[41] Still, it seems that Plato needs something that will do the same job as Aristotle's useful distinction. He needs some distinction between the *kinēsis* that is the remembering of something previously known that has been forgotten and a *kinēsis* that is the bringing to mind of something known that has become somehow latent but can be activated at will and without effort when it is found to be necessary. The first of the two species of *anamnēsis* at *Phileb.* 34b seems to satisfy this need. My hope is that we now have sufficient evidence that Plato does consider there to be a complexity of psychological activity concerning learning, knowing, and remembering such that we can move beyond a simple and exhaustive dichotomy between the philosopher-ruler's 'knowing' the Form and his being engaged in the process of learning the Form.[42]

Philosopher-rulers will not spend all of their time in ruling. Indeed, we are told explicitly that for the most part they will be able to spend their time in philosophy (540a–b). Socrates does not say much about what kind of philosophy a philosopher-ruler will do, nor does he give a detailed account of what a philosopher-ruler will do as he rules, but some of what he does say will allow me to illustrate some of the pleasures which will characterise the

---

[41] See Chapter 3.
[42] A similar idea appears at *Theaet.* 198d–e, where Socrates and Theaetetus are investigating the 'aviary' analogy. Socrates distinguishes between 'possessing' a piece of knowing and 'holding' it. And this distinction corresponds to two senses of learning: the initial acquisition of some piece of knowledge and the retrieval of a piece of knowledge already learned.

fully fledged philosopher-ruler's life. When the philosopher is not ruling but instead doing philosophy, we can assume that either he is acquiring more philosophical knowledge – which is pleasant in an uncontroversial way – or he is reviewing and revisiting philosophical knowledge he already has. The latter activity is neatly characterised as the first kind of *anamnēsis* canvassed in the *Philebus*: the soul takes up something stored in the memory. The philosopher will turn his attention back to this or that Form or consider how the Forms are related to one another. Whatever he does, precisely, it is reasonable to think that it involves a change of a kind in his soul, the bringing to mind of latent knowledge, and is therefore something we can readily classify as an intellectual pleasure. These pleasures are both plausibly imagined as *kinēseis* and, furthermore, are related directly to his being a philosopher-ruler.

When the philosopher ruler is actively engaged in ruling, although it is evidently not his preferred activity, it too presents opportunities for intellectual pleasures. At 501b Socrates likens the activity of the philosophers in constructing the ideal city to that of a painter. Just as the painter will work by looking back and forth between his picture and the original that he is attempting to depict, so too the philosophers will turn their attention first to the Forms they are attempting to instantiate as best they can, then to their city, then back to the Form, and so on. Throughout this process they of course know, for example, what Justice is but the constant movement back and forth between the model and the original might rightly be said to correspond to a psychological shift of attention from the perceptible construction to the ideal model and back again. They call to mind the original and then, in the light of that original, they turn their attention back to the city. And the process goes on, stopping not when the city is complete but also being called into action whenever the philosophers are called to make a judgement about a specific question of the city's affairs.

To borrow the apparatus of Protarchus' observation, we might say that the philosopher-ruler will continue to use his faculty of *logismos* and in doing so call to mind and reconsider various things that he knows both when he is doing philosophy and when he is ruling. He needs to do this not because he has forgotten the nature of the Just or the Fine but because, although he does know these things, his attention is moving between these intelligible objects and various perceptible objects and particular instances of justice and fineness in the city. It is not at all implausible to imagine that on each occasion when he turns once again to consider, for example, the Just, this will involve a coming-to-know that, while not of the significance of the first time he came to know its nature, will share enough of the characteristics of that first occasion to be thought of as a *kinēsis* that fills a kind of lack in the soul. And, as such, it can be thought of as a true and pure pleasure. Finally, it is a kind of pleasure that is entirely unavailable to anyone who is not a philosopher-ruler.

Philebus 55a: pleasure, thought, and the divine life

There is a final twist in the story. In the *Philebus* Socrates and Protarchus are happy to identify various pleasures associated with learning and they also make some headway in outlining a number of processes involved in learning, remembering, and then retrieving items of knowledge. But they do not claim that there is a pleasure to be had in the state of the continued possession or the continual active contemplation of knowledge. In fact, the account of the pleasures of learning and remembering at 51e7–52b9 turns out to be relevant only for human knowers and learners since it is contrasted with a different kind of life at 55a5–8: a 'third kind of life' which is characterised by neither destruction nor coming-to-be. This life is characterised, however, by being a life of neither pleasure nor pain but of 'thinking in the purest way possible' (φρονεῖν δ' ἦν ὡς οἷόν τε καθαρώτατα). Protarchus agrees that this life would not be one a human should choose since he and Socrates have agreed that a human life ought to contain some pleasure (21d9–e4). This conclusion that the life of continued and pure thinking is not a human life had, in fact, been advertised as a possibility earlier in the dialogue. They had reminded themselves that, according to the original comparison of lives (21d9–e2), the life of understanding (*noein*) and thinking (*phronein*) would not contain any pleasure or pain at all (33b2–4). And they had even recognised the possibility that this would be the most divine (*theiotatos*) life (33b2–7) since it is not likely (*eikos*) that the gods will experience either pleasure or its opposite (33b8–9).[43] What is surprising about this claim is not that gods will not feel pain but that they will not feel pleasure either.[44]

Now, at 55a Socrates and Protarchus have a metaphysical argument for this same conclusion. If pleasure is a coming-to-be, then a life that contains

---

[43] The divine life is also described at 30d1–3: οὐκοῦν ἐν μὲν τῇ τοῦ Διὸς ἐρεῖς φύσει βασιλικὴν μὲν ψυχήν, βασιλικὸν δὲ νοῦν ἐγγίγνεσθαι διὰ τὴν τῆς αἰτίας δύναμιν... For an illuminating account of the gods in the *Philebus* see Carpenter 2003.

[44] It is common to deny that the gods feel pain but divine lives are usually thought to be pleasant. For example, the demiurge seems to be pleased at *Tim.* 37c6–d1. The claim that god lives a life free from pain or toil can be traced back in the philosophical tradition at least as far as Xenophanes (DK 21 B 25).

no coming-to-be will contain no pleasure. A life of continual thinking of the purest kind and no destruction or coming-to-be at all will therefore include no pleasures. Socrates embraces just this difficulty sometimes identified with the account in the *Republic*. And perhaps it should remind us that the philosopher-rulers of the *Republic* are indeed still humans and still subject to the processes of destruction and restoration that characterise human lives. Nevertheless, the *Philebus* denies that a life of continual pure thought will be a pleasant life. There are some important consequences of this result. It implies that in so far as the divine life of the gods is a life of thought and subject to no destruction or coming-to-be then it too will be without pleasure. Furthermore, if the goal of a human life is to become as much like god as possible, the presence of pleasure and pain in a human life is a marker of the limits of such assimilation and therefore the best human life may well always fall short of the divine life.[45]

The conclusion that a divine life is without pleasure is doubtless supposed to be striking and perhaps even shocking. It may also be a consequence that Plato himself would find uncomfortable but which he is prepared to air in the *Philebus* because it is dictated by the account of the nature of pleasure he finds most plausible. As we shall see in the next chapter, Aristotle argues that a significant virtue of his own alternative account of the nature of pleasure is that it allows there to be pleasure associated not merely with the coming-to-be of knowledge but also – indeed primarily – with the possession and active contemplation of knowledge: 'thinking in the purest way possible'.

---

[45] Perhaps Socrates and Protarchus deny that the life of thinking which is free from pleasure and pain is preferable to a life which includes pleasure and pain because a choiceworthy human life must include both reason and pleasure. (This is a plausible interpretation of 21a8–22a6.) Alternatively, they may hold that the divine life is indeed preferable for humans to a life including pleasure and pain but think that the divine life is an ideal which humans can only approximate at best. For further discussion see Carone 2000; Russell 2005, 198–9; Delcomminette 2006, 188–90, 310–13; Evans 2007c, esp. 352–6, and 2007b, 134–45.

CHAPTER 3

Aristotle on the pleasures of learning and knowing

It is well known that Aristotle disagrees with what he takes to be the analysis of the nature of pleasure dominant among his predecessors and contemporaries, namely that pleasure is some kind of change (*kinēsis*) or coming-to-be (*genesis*). He often connects this view of the nature of pleasure with the related claim that pleasure is a kind of fulfilment or replenishment (*anaplērōsis*). This view of the nature of pleasure is indeed not hard to find in Plato's works. We have already seen that the idea of pleasure as a process of replenishment allows Socrates in the *Republic* to make a case for the pleasantness of cases of coming-to-know something. But we also noted that it is not obvious how such a framework for understanding pleasure will allow Socrates to claim that the continued possession or use of knowledge already acquired might also be pleasant. It was difficult, in short, to see how a philosopher-ruler's life might continue to be pleasant once he or she has come to possess the knowledge of the pure intelligible forms required for ruling, even if we granted that the initial acquisition of such knowledge is pleasant in the way Socrates insists. Aristotle shares Plato's view that the life of the best kind of intellectual activity is the best kind of life for a human to live. And he agrees also that it will be the most pleasant life for a human to live. Aristotle's solution to the difficulty of reconciling these two views depends on his general revision of the metaphysics of pleasure, denying the Platonic view that it is a kind of change or coming-to-be and instead insisting that pleasure is to be associated with his metaphysical notion of 'activity' (*energeia*).[1] In this way he stands in stark opposition to Plato.

---

[1] This is not an unproblematic revision. While Plato may struggle to account for the pleasures of knowing and contemplating a geometrical proof, Aristotle may find it difficult to make good sense of obvious pleasures such as those involved in the process of satisfying a hunger or of satisfying a desire for revenge. Frede 1996b, 278: '[B]oth the Platonic and the later Aristotelian accounts of pleasure suffer the same defect: neither is sufficient to cover the whole range of phenomena that it supposedly explains. In principle, Aristotle at least could have known better.' For a recent interpretation that tries to attribute to Aristotle a more plausible account of the pleasures of restorative processes, see Aufderheide 2013.

But this opposition ought not to obscure the ways in which he and Plato think very much alike, particularly when it comes to the value and importance of the pleasures that come from rational activities and the close connection between the possession or active use of knowledge and the fulfilment of the best parts of our human nature.

A natural desire to know

Aristotle thinks that humans all have a natural desire for knowledge. And the presence of this desire for knowledge is indicated by a certain kind of pleasure:

> πάντες ἄνθρωποι τοῦ εἰδέναι ὀρέγονται φύσει. σημεῖον δ᾽ ἡ τῶν αἰσθήσεων ἀγάπησις. (*Metaph.* A.1 980a21–2)

> All humans desire to know. An indication of this is the joy they take in perceiving.

Of course, the specific pleasure being referred to here is one that we experience through the use of our senses and not through reasoning as such. But Aristotle thinks that this is a good piece of evidence for there being a general desire for and, we presume, enjoyment of knowledge. As we shall see, both perception and thought are for Aristotle prime examples of activities that produce pleasure; he often uses them in tandem to make points about the metaphysics of pleasure and he will then often contrast the two or note some kind of cognitive progression from perception to thought. Sight in particular is for Aristotle the sense we value above all others and it produces the best pleasures, even though we would choose to see even if it provided no pleasure at all.[2] The same goes for thinking (cf. *NE* 1.6 1096b16–19). The general thrust of the famous passage at the beginning of the *Metaphysics* is that, beginning from the most basic form of cognition that we all share (and which other animals also share), Aristotle shows how this is the basis of other kinds of cognition and understanding: memory, experience, skill, and understanding. The details of how these are to be distinguished from and related to one another need not concern us here, but we should remember that cognition of a more elevated sort than perception is not far from Aristotle's mind.

The claim about perception is twofold: first we take a certain kind of delight in it whether or not it serves some particular end and, second, the

---

[2] Johansen 2012, 206–7, notes that in *Sens.* 1 437a1–17 Aristotle claims that, in a way, hearing is more important for thinking in so far as its accidental objects are *logoi*.

reason why we do take delight in it is because it makes us knowers (ποιεῖ γνωρίζειν ἡμᾶς) in the sense of revealing differences (980a24–7).[3] The vocabulary used in these lines will not withstand any particularly fine-grained scrutiny that might distinguish between different kinds of knowledge or objects of knowledge. Aristotle is pointing to a very general and universal human impulse for knowledge understood very broadly.[4] Rather, the delight in knowing and the associated claim that we would choose to engage in such activities just for their own sake is supposed to show that this is something we all desire by nature. This is of course compatible with Aristotle's also holding, as he does, that there is a specific form of understanding that is the best kind of knowledge for humans, is involved in the kind of activity that ought to be recognised as the goal of a human life and is, in that sense, something that all humans desire just as all humans desire to live well. In other words, there is a special kind of knowing that is to be identified as the fulfilment of our human nature: this is the best thing we can do and is the activity of the very best part of us. But there is no reason to think that the message of these opening lines of the *Metaphysics* should be confined to the assertion of a specific kind of desire for a specific kind of understanding.[5]

Aristotle also offers an elaborate analysis of what it is first to learn and then to know something. This analysis allows him to deal with the problems that we identified for Plato's connection between pleasure and knowing since they allow Aristotle to make clear the distinction between the possession of already-acquired knowledge and the active contemplation and use of such knowledge. He can also account for the movement between these states. Finally, he will be able to identify a way in which it can be pleasant both to acquire knowledge and actively to contemplate already-acquired knowledge.

In *De An.* 2.5 he is explaining the kinds of change that are involved in perception. Part of his explanation involves him in offering an analysis of

---

[3] Cambiano 2012, 3–4, notes that *agapēsis* is a hapax: 'Aristotle presumably aimed at emphasizing that what we are faced with is a peculiar kind of pleasure, more exactly a kind of delight, as Ross rightly translates it. Nor should it be confused with any sort of pleasure by whatever sense and for every thing.'

[4] Cf. Burnyeat 2011.

[5] The verb *oregesthai* is perhaps chosen for its similarly broad scope, on which see Pearson 2012, 17–87. At *NE* 3.1 1111a30–4 Aristotle refers to an appetite (*epithumia*) for learning (*mathēsis*) since he is emphasising the pleasures that are supposed to come from satisfying this appetite. For this expanded notion of *epithumia* see Pearson 2012, 100–4. Cf. Lear 1988, 1–10, who takes the opening of the *Metaphysics* to be emblematic of a general account of Aristotelian philosophy and Aristotle's account of human nature.

different cognitive states and the changes from one to another. Starting at 417a21, he draws distinctions between different kinds of 'knowers':

(1) Someone who is a knower in the sense that he is a human and humans are animals who are knowers and have knowledge;

(2) Someone who is a knower in the sense that he has knowledge of, for example, grammar;

(3) Someone who is a knower in the sense that he is now contemplating some particular piece of knowledge.

The person in (3) is a knower because he is 'in fulfilment and knows in the proper sense this particular thing' (ἐντελεχείᾳ ὢν καὶ κυρίως ἐπιστάμενος τόδε τὸ Α). He stands as the end-point or goal of intellectual achievement to which the other two should be compared and related.[6]

Then, at 2.5 417b5–28 Aristotle contrasts the following:

(i) Someone who has knowledge and who comes to contemplate (θεωροῦν γὰρ γίνεται τὸ ἔχον τὴν ἐπιστήμην 417b5–6);

(ii) Someone who has the capacity to know and who, through the agency of someone who has fulfilled that capacity and is a teacher, learns and acquires knowledge.

There are therefore three stages here which, in rough chronological order of development, are:

(a) A capacity to know that is not yet fulfilled;

(b) A fulfilment of the capacity to know through the agency of a teacher who knows;

(c) A change from the mere possession of knowledge to contemplation of a particular piece of knowledge.

The situation in (i), he says, should not be called teaching or learning; the situation in (ii) presumably should be (417b9–12).[7] And Aristotle also thinks that there is reason not to call the situation in (i) an alteration (*alloiōsis*) or, if it is an alteration, then it is a distinct kind of alteration (417b6–7). The reason for this hesitation is that in the case of the situation in (i) the development is 'to itself and to fulfilment' (εἰς αὐτὸ γὰρ ἡ ἐπίδοσις καὶ εἰς ἐντελέχειαν): a curious phrase that implies that the change from being

---

[6] (1) and (2) both have the capacity for knowing but in different ways. (1) has the capacity in the sense that he can acquire knowledge and contemplate; (2) has the capacity in the sense that, provided that nothing external prevents him, he can exercise his capacity to contemplate some knowledge that he possesses. (1) can acquire knowledge and (2) can, provided that circumstances are right, exercise the knowledge he already has.

[7] Aristotle also considers the metaphysics of learning in *Phys.* 3.3, where he says that when a teacher teaches something to a pupil who learns there is a single change that occurs in the pupil; this fulfilment of the pupil as something changeable is brought about by the teacher as something productive of change.

someone who possesses knowledge to someone actively using that knowl-edge in contemplation is indeed the fulfilment of the knower as such – it brings the knower to his fulfilled state – and is the development of the knower to the state of being what it is by nature. It is a fulfilment of the nature of the knower and perhaps a satisfaction of the universal desire to know trailed at the beginning of the *Metaphysics*.

We can also add to this picture the various distinctions offered in Aristotle's account of memory and recollection. Memory (*mnēmē*) is the preservation of some prior experience or knowledge and is to be distin-guished from the first acquisition of knowledge (*De Mem.* 2 451a20–451b2). Recollection (*anamnēsis*), by contrast, is the retrieval of some previously held knowledge, perception, or state (*De Mem.* 2 451b2–7). We should note, however, that it is also possible for the same person to learn the same thing twice (451b7–8). This last comment is rather important; it shows that just as there is a change that is, so to speak, the opposite of change (i) above, so too there is a change that is the opposite of change (ii) above. Not only can someone cease now to be thinking about some piece of knowledge and nevertheless retain that knowledge but also someone can forget a piece of knowledge and have to re-learn it.[8]

Much of this will be familiar. But I want to draw attention to three aspects of this general account that are important for Aristotle's conception of the relationship between pleasure and knowing and allow him to improve upon the Platonic account discussed in the previous chapter. First, and most basically, there is a set of distinctions that cover the relevant stages: the capacity to acquire, the acquisition, the use, the ceasing to use, and the loss of knowledge. Second, Aristotle identifies a related set of distinct changes involved in the transition from one of these stages to the next, although he signals that in this respect we should not think of all the changes in the same way.[9] Third, we should take seriously the implication that the process of first having a capacity to know, then acquiring some knowledge, and then actively contemplating that knowledge is a teleological process; each step is part of a process of perfecting the nature of the human knower. In so far as

---

[8] Cf. Sorabji 2004, 35–46, who rightly stresses that Aristotle is here responding to various Platonic accounts of learning as recollection.

[9] In the case of the change in (ii), this is a simple exchange of knowledge for ignorance. But it seems that the change in (i) is not the familiar kind in which an underlying subject exchanges one of a pair of opposite properties for another; instead Aristotle signals that it may be a different kind of *alloiōsis* involved in the completion or fulfilment of a capacity. This difference between the two changes is the focus of attention for those interested in the kinds of changes – particularly material changes – that may be involved in perception. See for further detail and discussion: Burnyeat 2002, esp. 48–65; Lorenz 2007; Johansen 2012, 158–69.

they are both progressions towards this goal, the changes in (i) and (ii) are alike. The culmination and goal of the process is for the knower as such to be in a state of fulfilment and to be 'itself'. These guiding notions form the important background of the account of the pleasures associated with learning and knowing that are the focus of Aristotle's attention elsewhere, principally in his ethical and aesthetic works.

Pleasures of thought in the *Nicomachean Ethics*

The assertion of a universal human desire for knowledge in *Metaph.* A.1 stands in contrast with Eudoxus' assertion of a universal desire for pleasure which is the subject of Aristotle's interest in *NE* 10.2 and which introduces some of the important ideas that are developed in Aristotle's own account in the following three chapters. Eudoxus begins his argument with the observation that all animals – both rational and non-rational – aim at pleasure (10.2 1172b9–11) and concludes from this that pleasure is the good. Eudoxus emerges from the chapter as a whole as someone who, in Aristotle's estimation, has hit upon the important truth that pleasure and pain are important indications of an organism achieving or failing to engage in its proper natural activity. But Eudoxus overplays his hand and infers that pleasure itself is the goal of all animal desires rather than the accompaniment of an organism achieving its proper *telos*.[10] Eudoxus also fails properly to take into account the important distinctions to be drawn between rational and non-rational creatures. His assertion that both rational and non-rational creatures prefer pleasure to pain and prefer pleasure to the mere absence of pleasure is not disputed. However, one of the arguments ranged against Eudoxus' strong conclusion is inspired by Socrates' observation in the *Philebus* that we humans would want to live a pleasant life only if it were accompanied by wisdom. Aristotle begins with the relatively weak claim that a life without *phronēsis* at all but with plenty of pleasure would not be so worthy of choice as a life with both (10.2 1172b28–32). This is something from Plato's otherwise deficient analysis of pleasure that Aristotle is happy to preserve: when we consider the place of pleasure in a human life we should never lose sight of the fact that we are rational animals. In the next chapter Aristotle strengthens the claim. He insists not merely that a life of pleasure with reason is 'more choiceworthy' (10.2 1172b29) than a life of

---

[10] For discussion of Eudoxus' arguments, Speusippus' criticisms of them, and Aristotle's partial rehabilitation and defence of the Eudoxan insight see Warren 2009. See also Broadie 1991, 346–53; Rapp 2009, 209–14.

pleasure alone. Now he also claims that no one would choose to live with the intellectual capacity of a child (10.3 1174a1–3: ζῆν παιδίου διάνοιαν ἔχων) for their whole life even if that life were filled with pleasures and free from pains. (This is stronger than the *Philebus'* claim that we would not want to live the life of a mollusc, even if it were filled with pleasures; a child does at least have some intellectual capacities.) And we would choose to see, remember, know, and be virtuous even if none of these ever brought us pleasure. The fact that pleasures do necessarily follow from these activities is irrelevant for the moment; we would choose them even if no pleasures ensued (10.3 1174a1–8).

Nevertheless, Eudoxus is also right to say that pleasure is a good even for rational creatures like us. Aristotle agrees that we should pay attention to the fact that not only non-rational animals but also we rational humans aim at what is pleasant. He thinks, for example, that this fact undermines the argument of those who sneer at any proposed good that is the focus of such widespread pursuit by all animals; true, pleasure is something rather commonly pursued, but it is significant that even intelligent (*phronima*) creatures like us pursue it also (10.2 1172b35–1173a5). The conclusion Eudoxus ought to have drawn, we discover as Aristotle's discussion proceeds, is that each kind of animal is pursuing its own proper natural activity and that this activity is what is accompanied by pleasure; pleasure itself is not the goal (cf. 7.13 1153b25–32: animals and humans all pursue pleasure but perhaps not all the same pleasures).[11]

Negotiating the importance of our human nature as rational animals for the role of pleasure in the good life is therefore part of the very opening arguments in the last book of the *Nicomachean Ethics*. Before Aristotle turns to offer his own account of the nature of pleasure and its relationship to various human activities, he highlights the importance of recognising the ways in which we humans are not only like but also distinct from non-rational animals. It is no surprise, in that case, that our human capacities for various kinds of cognitive and rational activity play a central role when he elaborates on his view in *NE* 10.3–5 and, in particular, explains his dissatisfaction with the idea that pleasure is a kind of change or coming-to-be.

Aristotle criticises the view of pleasure as a coming-to-be in both of the sections of the *Nicomachean Ethics* in which the discussion of pleasure's role

---

[11] Cf. Rapp 2009, 225–9. See also *NE* 10.5 1176a5–8: a horse's pleasure is different from that of a dog or a human; so Heraclitus was right to say that donkeys prefer rubbish to gold.

in the good life comes to the fore, namely 7.11–14 and 10.1–5.[12] In both passages we find a strong interest in the pleasures to be had from various kinds of cognition and it is clear that Aristotle takes the pleasures experienced in perception and thought to be a strong piece of evidence in favour of his opposition to the pleasure-as-*genesis* view. This in turn is part of his series of objections to the view that pleasure cannot be good. In this case, the argument is based on the idea that a coming-to-be cannot be a good because it is essentially incomplete and looks to its goal for any derivative value it might possess. Indeed, Socrates and Protarchus decide that it would be odd for someone who thinks that pleasure is a good to choose a life of 'thinking in the purest way possible' (ὡς οἷόν τε καθαρώτατα) over a life of pleasure and pain, that is, a life of destruction and coming-to-be.[13] Aristotle counters this argument by denying that pleasures are all comings-to-be and cognitive pleasures are his prime piece of evidence. For example, in 10.3 he writes:

ἡ δόξα δ᾽ αὕτη δοκεῖ γεγενῆσθαι ἐκ τῶν περὶ τὴν τροφὴν λυπῶν καὶ ἡδονῶν· ἐνδεεῖς γὰρ γενομένους καὶ προλυπηθέντας ἥδεσθαι τῇ ἀναπληρώσει. τοῦτο δ᾽ οὐ περὶ πάσας συμβαίνει τὰς ἡδονάς· ἄλυποι γάρ εἰσιν αἵ τε μαθηματικαὶ καὶ τῶν κατὰ τὰς αἰσθήσεις αἱ διὰ τῆς ὀσφρήσεως, καὶ ἀκροάματα δὲ καὶ ὁράματα πολλὰ καὶ μνῆμαι καὶ ἐλπίδες. τίνος οὖν αὗται γενέσεις ἔσονται; οὐδενὸς γὰρ ἔνδεια γεγένηται, οὗ γένοιτ᾽ ἂν ἀναπλήρωσις. (*NE* 10.3 1173b13–20)

The same opinion [*sc.* that pleasure is a movement and coming-to-be] seems to have arisen because of the pains and pleasures of nutrition. This is because it seems that those who have become in need and are in pain beforehand take pleasure in the replenishment. But this is not the case for all pleasures; for the pleasures of learning are without pain as are those that come about according to the senses – through smell and from the many things we hear and see – as well as memories and expectations. And of what will these be comings-to-be? For no deficiency has come about of which there would be replenishment.

There are three types of pleasure that Aristotle offers as counter-examples to the replenishment view: the pleasures of learning, of sense perception, and of memory and expectation. For now, that is as much as Aristotle has to say;

---

[12] The details of Aristotle's criticisms of this theory and his own preferred account in terms of activities (*energeiai*) are the subject of a great deal of debate and interest. See Gosling and Taylor 1982, 301–17; Broadie 1991, 339–46; Gonzalez 1991; Frede 1997, 418–27; Bostock 1998; Van Riel 2000, 7–78; Taylor 2003; Heineman 2011; Shields 2011; Strohl 2011; Wolfsdorf 2013a, 114–33; Aufderheide 2013.

[13] Plat. *Phileb.* 55a5–11; see above p. 50. The argument for classifying pleasure as a coming-to-be begins at 54a3. Cf. Arist. *NE* 7.12 1153a7–12. Damascius, *In Phileb.* §§214–22 offers a response to Aristotle's concerns (cf. Van Riel 2000, 145–73, and 2012 on Damascius' interpretation that the *Philebus* is compatible with the Aristotelian view that there are pleasures 'in activity'). On 'purity' used of the objects of thought and of associated pleasures, see below, pp. 64–6.

he merely registers these counter-examples and moves on to debunk the next argument offered by the anti-pleasure camp. But the next chapters elaborate on his preferred conception of the metaphysics of pleasure, and the pleasures of sensing and thinking are again to the fore. Before passing on to look more closely at those chapters, however, we should notice the inclusion here in 10.3 of the pleasures of memory and expectation. Although memory – along, of course, with the sense perception – is something that some non-human animals possess, Aristotle also here includes expectations or hopes (*elpides*) and this points to a capacity that is possessed only by human animals (cf. *PA* 3.6 669a19–21). In that case, since 'memories and expectations' are likely to function as a pair, we should probably think that memory here is not just a general ability to preserve and recall things we have learned but also the specific human capacity for deliberately recollecting one's own past experiences and imagining future ones.[14] The pleasures and pains we experience when considering our own past and imagining our own future have in any case already been the focus of Aristotle's attention in *NE* 9.4 1166a23–9, where the pairing *mnēmai . . . elpides* also occurs.[15]

Throughout the next section of his argument in chapters 10.4 and 10.5 Aristotle makes reference to the pleasures of perception and of cognition. In both cases he is prepared also to distinguish between better and worse or perhaps more and less perfect or complete examples of the two kinds of activity. He also distinguishes between better and worse, or perhaps more and less appropriate, objects for each of those activities. But both perception and thought play an important role in his further defence of the view that pleasure is to be associated primarily with activities (*energeiai*) in Aristotle's own specific sense of the term rather than with changes, comings-to-be, or replenishments. Chapter 10.4 begins with an account of the way in which seeing is something 'complete' or 'perfect' (*teleia*). This notion of 'completeness' or 'fulfilment' works in two ways throughout the argument.[16] It has a chronological sense and also a teleological sense. First of all, seeing is

---

[14] Aristotle might also be gesturing towards Plat. *Phileb.* 39e4–6 and 40a3–4: πολλῶν μὴν ἐλπίδων, ὡς λέγομεν ἄρτι, πᾶς ἄνθρωπος γέμει;

[15] I discuss this passage in Chapter 7 below.

[16] On the question whether there is a shift in the meaning of *teleios* and its cognates in this passage from all cases of seeing being 'complete' to only some cases being 'perfect' see Bostock 1988, 257–9. It seems to me that the adjective *teleios* and its cognate verbs are being used throughout this passage to cover the notions of being 'complete' and of being 'perfect' and that this is best grasped by emphasising the core notion of a completed goal or end-point (*telos*). (See Waanders 1983, esp. §§204, 216.) I do not, however, think that very much of my own discussion hangs on being any more precise than this and so I will use both 'complete' and 'perfect' to render this vocabulary in what follows. Cf. Gonzalez 1991, esp. 151 n. 16; Shields 2011, esp. 209; Strohl 2011.

not a process that takes time. At any moment in an act of seeing, the seeing is complete. We do not have to wait a period of time for the act of seeing to be complete. Seeing is also perfect in the sense that seeing does not have a goal or end-point (*telos*) as, for example, shipbuilding does. Shipbuilding is complete only once the ship is finished: that is the chronological end of the process and it is also the goal or end of the process. Seeing is not like that and that is why seeing is not a change (*kinēsis*). And in this respect pleasure seems to be like seeing (10.4 1174a16–17).[17]

At 10.4 1174b14–16 Aristotle adds something new.

> αἰσθήσεως δὲ πάσης πρὸς τὸ αἰσθητὸν ἐνεργούσης, τελείως δὲ τῆς εὖ διακειμένης πρὸς τὸ κάλλιστον τῶν ὑπὸ τὴν αἴσθησιν·

> All perception involves activity in relation to an object of perception and this activity is active in the most complete/perfect way when the sense is well arranged and is in relation to what is the finest of the things relevant to the sense.

This principle is then generalised for each activity and it is added that in each case when the activity is most complete (*teleiotatē*) it is also most pleasant (10.4 1174b18–20). Although the expression is very abstract and generalised, the central idea is both clear and, I think, familiar from the Platonic account of pleasure in the *Republic*. Aristotle thinks that for each sense we can specify the conditions under which that sense is engaged in its proper activity in the most complete and perfect fashion. For example, I am engaged in seeing in this superlative fashion when not only is my organ of sight in good condition but also it is being trained upon the sort of thing that it is best for me to see: the 'finest thing' that is relevant to that sense.

It is worth pausing to recognise the important background assumptions here: not only the plausible thought about the relationship of the activity of perceiving to the state of the perceiver, but also the assumption that there are better and worse objects for each sense to be trained upon. Aristotle claims that the better the object, the more complete and perfect the activity of seeing will be that is trained upon that object. More noteworthy still is that he chooses to express the property of the object concerned in terms of its beauty or fine-ness (*kallos*). We shall see later in this chapter the importance Aristotle places on the recognition of what is fine in his aesthetic

---

[17] We might think that Aristotle's account of the metaphysics of change and the contrasting cases of activities like seeing is not as accurate as we might wish. He does say, however, that the details are pursued elsewhere (10.4 1174b2–3). For the relation between the discussion of the distinction between *energeia* and *kinēsis* in *Metaphysics* Θ.6 and this section of *NE* 10 see Burnyeat 2008, 265–79; cf. Heinaman 2011, 9–16.

as well as his ethical works and it is evident that Aristotle will have no time for worries about whether it is possible to classify perceptible objects as objectively more or less beautiful or fine. But it is also clear that this beauty and fine-ness is something recognisable only by rational animals. In that case it seems that here we have a good example of Aristotle insisting that our rational capacity has significant effects on our other psychological capacities, including perception. Being rational, we can perceive beauty and fine-ness. What is more, since perception of beauty appears to be directly related to the completeness and perfection of the activity itself, rational animals can engage in perception in a more complete and perfect way than non-rational animals. And, since pleasure is in turn directly related to the completeness of the activity, it will turn out that rational animals take pleasure in their perceptions in a way in which non-rational animals cannot.[18]

Although his general metaphysical account of pleasure is very different from Aristotle's, Socrates offered a similar thought in the *Philebus* when he established that there are 'true and pure' pleasures. His discussion of these is brief, but they seem to include certain pleasures from perception. Socrates suggests that these pleasures are related to 'beautiful colours, shapes, most odours and sounds' (51b3–5) and goes on to explain at 51b9–d3 that his understanding of the beauty (*kallos*) of shapes is not the commonly held account that would say that various living animals or depictions of living animals are beautiful in this way. For Socrates, just as beauty in the case of colour is to be found, for example, in a patch of pure unadulterated white rather than in a variegated colourful scene, so too beauty in shape is found in perfect straight lines or circles and the constructions of these using a compass or ruler. These, he says, have their proper pleasures (*oikeiai hēdonai*).[19] The revisionary Platonic aesthetic views are not accepted whole-sale by Aristotle and we will see that he comes to endorse explicitly the idea that there is a beauty that can be enjoyed in the perception of both living animals and also human imitative depictions.[20] But the underlying point is

[18] Cf. Gonzalez 1991, 153, on *EE* 3.2 1230b21–1231a26, which I discuss below. And compare Taylor 2003, 10–11.

[19] The pair: 'what is straight or round' and 'things constructed from these with a compass etc.' is, I think, supposed to function as an analogue for the pair: 'living thing' and 'depiction of a living thing'. In each pair there is an original item which is the object of a human construction and imitation. Socrates does not here distinguish between the pleasures to be had from one or other member of each pair.

[20] However, at *Sens.* 3 439b31–440a6, Aristotle says that those colours that are most easily expressed in terms of ratios of white and black – apparently these include crimson and purple – will be the most pleasant. The same principle applies for musical concords: τὰ μὲν γὰρ ἐν ἀριθμοῖς εὐλογίστοις χρώματα, καθάπερ ἐκεῖ τὰς συμφωνίας, τὰ ἥδιστα τῶν χρωμάτων εἶναι δοκοῦντα, οἷον τὸ ἁλουργὸν καὶ τὸ φοινικοῦν καὶ ὀλίγ' ἄττα τοιαῦτα (δι' ἥνπερ αἰτίαν καὶ αἱ συμφωνίαι ὀλίγαι), τὰ δὲ μὴ ἐν ἀριθμοῖς τἆλλα χρώματα.

the same in both the *Philebus* and here in the *Nicomachean Ethics*: in the case of perception there are more or less beautiful objects of perception and, the more beautiful the object of perception (however we understand beauty), the more pleasant the act of perceiving it.

The same principle holds in the case of the intellect as well as perception. Aristotle continues:

> καθ᾽ ἑκάστην δὴ βελτίστη ἐστὶν ἡ ἐνέργεια τοῦ ἄριστα διακειμένου πρὸς τὸ κράτιστον τῶν ὑπ᾽ αὐτήν. αὕτη δ᾽ ἂν τελειοτάτη εἴη καὶ ἡδίστη. κατὰ πᾶσαν γὰρ αἴσθησίν ἐστιν ἡδονή, ὁμοίως δὲ καὶ διάνοιαν καὶ θεωρίαν, ἡδίστη δ᾽ ἡ τελειοτάτη, τελειοτάτη δ᾽ ἡ τοῦ εὖ ἔχοντος πρὸς τὸ σπουδαιότατον τῶν ὑπ᾽ αὐτήν· τελειοῖ δὲ τὴν ἐνέργειαν ἡ ἡδονή.
> (*NE* 10.4 1174b18–23)

> In each sense, the activity is best when it belongs to something disposed in the best way and in relation to what is the most powerful of those things that fall in its remit. The same activity would be the most complete/perfect and the most pleasant. For all perception is pleasant, as are both thinking and contemplating, but what is most pleasant is what is most complete/perfect and what is most complete/perfect is what belongs to something in a good state and with relation to the best of the things in its remit. Pleasure completes/perfects the activity.

Intellectual activity, therefore, will be more complete and perfect under the same relevant conditions. It will be most perfect when the knower is in the best state with regard to his capacity for thinking and is thinking of the most excellent objects for that capacity. (Aristotle shifts his vocabulary here away from accounting for the object in terms of beauty to more general terms – *kratiston, spoudaiotaton* – consonant with the move away from cases of perceptual activity.)

The reference to intellectual activities is left without further expansion but they continue in the subsequent exposition to be used as counterpart examples to the initial example of perception (e.g. 10.4 1174b33–1175a3). Both are used to bolster the general account through the explanation of familiar phenomena. The account of the relationship between activity, the completeness or perfection of the activity, and the pleasure that attends on the activity explains why it is not possible to be pleased constantly. Humans cannot engage in constant activity; they get tired (10.4 1175a3–6). It explains why novelties are more pleasant because thought (*dianoia*) is more intensively engaged on something new just as we look more intently on something new. As time passes, the activity diminishes and so does the pleasure (10.4 1175a6–10).

This line of thought continues into the next chapter in which Aristotle supports his account by claiming it makes best sense of the fact that pleasures differ in kind from one another (this is because intellectual activities differ in kind from one another as do perceptual activities) and why it is that people are more likely to do things that they enjoy and their enjoyment in turn makes them more engaged in what they are doing. Again, he uses examples of intellectual and perceptual activity. People who enjoy geometry are the people who become the best geometers and people who love music similarly get better at music because they enjoy it (10.5 1175a21–1175b1). And this also explains how activities might clash with one another – someone who loves flute music might be distracted from a conversation by the sound of the flute – and how pains might destroy an activity – if writing or calculating is painful for someone then they are unlikely to engage in writing or calculating (10.5 1175b3–6, b16–20).[21] The connection between the activity and pleasure is so close, in fact, that some people have mistakenly identified the two (10.5 1175b34–6).

Thus far, Aristotle has been talking mostly in terms of simple differences in kind between activities and their pleasures, although we should not forget his insistence on there being a difference in degree of activity dependent on the state of the agent and the relevant object. From 10.5 1175b36 he returns to marking distinctions in value between activities and it is at this point that the perceptual and intellectual activities begin to come apart from one another. First, perceptual pleasures are ranked in terms of 'purity' (*kathareiotēs*): sight differs from touch and hearing and smell from taste. Their respective pleasures differ accordingly. Next, the pleasures of thought (*dianoia*) differ from all of these and different intellectual pleasures differ from one another (10.5 1175b36–1176a3). So intellectual activities – and therefore their pleasures – are as a kind superior to perceptual activities and their pleasures and there are also further differentiations of value to be made within each of these two classes.[22] What comes next is an argument borrowed again from Plato, since Aristotle rests his account of the relative superiority of the different pleasures on the idea that the guide and judge in these matters is the good person (*spoudaios*, 1176a16). The fact that some people may in fact

---

[21] One of the arguments offered against pleasure being a good at 7.11 1152b16–18 is that pleasure can obstruct thinking. For example, no one can think properly while enjoying sex. At 7.12 1153a20–3 Aristotle counters by saying that this all depends on the pleasure concerned. Pleasure *in general* does not obstruct thinking; in fact, pleasure can enhance learning and contemplating if the pleasure in question is the pleasure of learning or contemplating.

[22] On how fine-grained the differentiation between these activities might be, see Heinaman 2011, 19–40.

enjoy the pleasures of taste over the pleasures of intellectual activity is no reason to lose confidence in the initial classification. Indeed, in a way it confirms it: the preferences of such people are driven by their poor character. Just as the fact that donkeys prefer rubbish to gold makes us humans prefer gold no less, so too the presence of disagreement over the relative values of different pleasures and activities should make us no less sure of the correctness of the good person's ranking. This line of argument continues into the next chapter: tyrants and people who envy the tyrannical lifestyle have no taste for the pleasures that the good person enjoys but what such tyrannical people happen to enjoy gives us no reason to think that they are helpful arbiters of what is good and pleasant or indeed what a good human life is. Rather, Aristotle concludes that the pleasures that complete and perfect the activities of the 'complete and blessed man' are those we should properly call 'human pleasures'. Other pleasures are human pleasures only in a secondary sense, as are the activities that they accompany.[23]

NE 10.6 resumes the topic of human happiness (*eudaimonia*) and establishes that the good man will choose his proper activity, namely virtuous activity; 10.7 then specifies that the best activity will be the intellectual activity of a person's *nous*. This is the most divine thing in us, the best aspect of us, and also what is superlatively human; indeed Aristotle is even tempted to say that each person should be identified with this ruling element (1177a13–17, 1177b26–1178a8).[24] The best activity of this divine part is identified as 'contemplative' activity (*theōrētikē*, 1177a17–18). One of the arguments then offered in support of the conclusion that the best activity of this part is constitutive of a good human life is based on the pleasures associated with this activity.

οἰόμεθά τε δεῖν ἡδονὴν παραμεμῖχθαι τῇ εὐδαιμονίᾳ, ἡδίστη δὲ τῶν κατ' ἀρετὴν ἐνεργειῶν ἡ κατὰ τὴν σοφίαν ὁμολογουμένως ἐστίν· δοκεῖ γοῦν ἡ φιλοσοφία θαυμαστὰς ἡδονὰς ἔχειν καθαρειότητι καὶ τῷ βεβαίῳ, εὔλογον δὲ τοῖς εἰδόσι τῶν ζητούντων ἡδίω τὴν διαγωγὴν εἶναι. (*NE* 10.7 1177a22–7)

---

[23] *NE* 10.5 1176a26–9: εἴτ' οὖν μία ἐστὶν εἴτε πλείους αἱ τοῦ τελείου καὶ μακαρίου ἀνδρός, αἱ ταύτας τελειοῦσαι ἡδοναὶ κυρίως λέγοιντ' ἂν ἀνθρώπου ἡδοναὶ εἶναι, αἱ δὲ λοιπαὶ δευτέρως καὶ πολλοστῶς, ὥσπερ αἱ ἐνέργειαι. The parallel Platonic argument is at Plat. *Rep.* 581c4–583a11. On this and Aristotle's version of the same argument see Taylor 2008. See also Strohl 2011, 260–71. Compare the argument at Iambl. *Prot.* 11, 58.3–13, which concludes in a similar fashion that the philosophical life is the most pleasant. This section is one of those attributed to Aristotle's *Protrepticus* by Hutchinson and Johnson 2005, esp. 265–9.

[24] On the theological aspects of Aristotle's account of the relationship between *nous* and *eudaimonia* see Long 2011.

And we think that pleasure has to be mixed into happiness. Most pleasant of all the activities is, we all agree, activity in accordance with wisdom. So it seems that philosophy offers the most marvellous pleasures both in terms of their purity and security, and it is reasonable that the life of those who know is more pleasant than the life of those who are inquiring.

It is no surprise that this is Aristotle's point of view but he has expressed it in rather precise terms as the culmination of the argument of the previous chapters. We noted that he had earlier ranked activities in terms of purity (*kathareiotēs*, 10.5 1176a1). The same criterion is used now to express the superiority of the pleasures of the life of wisdom, confirming the implication that the activities of such a life are themselves somehow 'most pure'. 'Purity' is not an insignificant term to use. It is not used in the *Nicomachean Ethics* other than in these two passages and it is clearly connected to the theological aspects of the account of the activity of human reason.[25] But it also – particularly when paired with the notion of security (*bebaiotēs*) – looks back to Plato and Socrates' criteria for the superiority of the pleasures from knowing the forms in the *Republic* (584b9, 585b11, 585d11–e5, 586a1–b4).[26] However, Aristotle can also claim to have an account superior to that offered by Socrates because his view can explain easily why we also find it reasonable that the pleasures of those who know should be even better than the pleasures of those who are only inquiring since now we agree that pleasure should be associated with activities and not comings-to-be. After all, knowing – the activity of contemplation – is the goal and completion of a process of inquiry.

Aristotle has now made the case for philosophy itself – understood in a particular sense – as providing the most perfect and pure pleasures. It is a claim that could easily be endorsed by a Platonist too, regardless of the difference of opinion between Plato and his pupil on the precise metaphysical nature of pleasure. Aristotle would presumably take it to be a virtue of his account that it is able not only, to his mind, to give a more reasonable account of all pleasures (including those of perception and cognition) but also can do so while retaining the important insight that there is a specific and special pleasure to be had from philosophical activity in particular and

---

[25] Aristotle also uses the vocabulary of purity when explaining Anaxagoras' notion of *nous*: *De An.* 1.2 405a13–19, *Metaph.* A.8 989b14–16 (cf. *EE* 1.4 1215b6–14, where Aristotle reports Anaxagoras' picture of the best human life. He speculates that perhaps Axagoras thought that the best human life was one lived without pain, unblemished with respect to justice, or sharing in some divine contemplation: αὐτὸς δ' ἴσως ᾤετο τὸν ζῶντα ἀλύπως καὶ καθαρῶς πρὸς τὸ δίκαιον ἤ τινος θεωρίας κοινωνοῦντα θείας, τοῦτον ὡς ἄνθρωπον εἰπεῖν μακάριον εἶναι.).

[26] Van Riel 2000, 70–1. Cf. Plat. *Phileb.* 55a5–8. And see above, Chapter 2.

especially in the highest form of philosophical activity, which is the active contemplation of already-discovered eternal truths. It is this activity which Aristotle famously identifies as 'becoming like god, so far as is possible for a human' (10.7 1177b33–4).[27]

Learning and pleasure in *Rhetoric* 1.11

Outside the *Nicomachean Ethics*, Aristotle discusses the pleasures of learning and knowing in various places. Often the sense of 'learning' involved seems to be of a rather low-level kind not much more elevated than a mere 'recognition' that such-and-such is the case. But this shows that Aristotle accepts that all forms of intellectual achievement are pleasant in a way, even if they fall short of the exquisite and divine pleasures of contemplation, perhaps because these inferior pleasures are all associated with changes or stages that bring us closer to that ideal natural state. Some of the most interesting passages are concerned with explanations of certain forms of aesthetic pleasure that cannot be accounted for by reference to the mere perceptual appearance of an object. Instead, Aristotle is inclined to think that there are also pleasures to be had from recognising the beauty of an object, recognising its being the product of careful design, and also – in certain cases – recognising its being a deliberate imitation of something else. Let us start with a passage in the *Rhetoric* that introduces the general approach and resumes a number of themes we have already found elsewhere:

καὶ τὸ μανθάνειν καὶ τὸ θαυμάζειν ἡδὺ ὡς ἐπὶ τὸ πολύ· ἐν μὲν γὰρ τῷ θαυμάζειν τὸ ἐπιθυμεῖν μαθεῖν ἐστιν, ὥστε τὸ θαυμαστὸν ἐπιθυμητόν, ἐν δὲ τῷ μανθάνειν <τὸ> εἰς τὸ κατὰ φύσιν καθίστασθαι. καὶ τὸ εὖ ποιεῖν καὶ τὸ εὖ πάσχειν τῶν ἡδέων· τὸ μὲν γὰρ εὖ πάσχειν τυγχάνειν ὧν ἐπιθυμοῦσι, τὸ δὲ εὖ ποιεῖν ἔχειν καὶ ὑπερέχειν, ὧν ἀμφοτέρων ἐφίενται. διὰ δὲ τὸ ἡδὺ εἶναι τὸ εὐποιητικόν, καὶ τὸ ἐπανορθοῦν ἡδὺ τοῖς ἀνθρώποις ἐστὶν τοὺς πλησίον, καὶ τὸ τὰ ἐλλιπῆ ἐπιτελεῖν. ἐπεὶ δὲ τὸ μανθάνειν τε ἡδὺ καὶ τὸ θαυμάζειν, καὶ τὰ τοιάδε ἀνάγκη ἡδέα εἶναι, οἷον τό τε μιμούμενον, ὥσπερ γραφικὴ καὶ ἀνδριαντοποιία καὶ ποιητική, καὶ πᾶν ὃ ἂν εὖ μεμιμημένον ᾖ, κἂν ᾖ μὴ ἡδὺ αὐτὸ τὸ μεμιμημένον· οὐ γὰρ ἐπὶ τούτῳ χαίρει, ἀλλὰ συλλογισμός ἐστιν ὅτι τοῦτο ἐκεῖνο, ὥστε μανθάνειν τι συμβαίνει. (*Rhet.* 1.11 1371a31–b10)

And learning and admiring are for the most part pleasant; for in admiring there is a desire to learn, so what is admired is desired. And in the process of learning there is the attainment of a natural state. And benefiting and being benefited are pleasures; for to be benefited is to hit upon what is desired while

---

[27] The claim that contemplation is the most pleasant and best activity is repeated, again in a theological context, at *Metaph.* Λ.7 1072b19–26.

to benefit is to possess something and to have more than enough and these are both things that people aim for. Because conferring a benefit is something pleasant, then it is also pleasant for people to set their neighbours straight and to bring to completion things that are lacking. Since learning and admiring are pleasant, then necessarily also this sort of thing is also pleasant: a product of imitation like a picture, a statue, or some poetry. And everything, in so far as it is a good imitation [is pleasant] even if that which it imitates is not pleasant. For [the audience] is not being pleased by that [which is imitated] but there is a deduction that this [imitation] is that [which is imitated], so a learning of a kind takes place.

Perhaps most striking at the beginning of the passage is the use once again of the notion of learning as the attainment of a natural state. In conjunction with the assertion at the beginning of the passage that pleasure is 'a kind of change in the soul and a complete and perceived return to the underlying nature' (1369b33–5), we might wonder whether this is in conflict with the preferred analysis of pleasure in the *Nicomachean Ethics* as an activity or as an accompaniment of an activity rather than a replenishment. Learning is certainly a change of a kind and can therefore easily be counted as pleasant but we are perhaps left wondering whether it is also possible for knowing to be pleasant if it is not similarly a change.[28] This chapter is more concerned with pleasures related to desires and has nothing to say about the kinds of pleasures that were identified as the most pure and best at the end of the *Nicomachean Ethics*. Even if this chapter were to offer an endorsement of a replenishment model of pleasure, of course Aristotle would not be commit-ted to the idea that a lack of knowledge must be painful any more than Plato before him was committed to the idea that any lack of knowledge must be painful. It might be painful to know that you do not know something – perhaps in order to desire to know something there must be some awareness of one's own ignorance – but the mere absence of knowledge need have no necessary affective accompaniment.

We should also notice a careful use of different aspects of the verb 'to learn'. Aristotle uses both the present-tense infinitive (*manthanein*), which denotes the ongoing process of learning, and the aorist infinitive (*mathein*),

---

[28] See e.g. Pearson 2012, 101 n. 16. Pearson rightly notes in this passage an expanded notion of *epithumia* beyond its more restricted scope of a desire for the tactile pleasures of drink, food, and sex. Frede 1996b, esp. 274–9, insists that the description of pleasure as a *kinēsis* is part of a deliberately Platonising strategy that wants to retain Plato's insight that emotions have a content beyond the mere pleasantness or painfulness of how they feel. Furthermore, since the subject matter of the *Rhetoric* is, to a large extent, human emotions and 'remedial emotions' such as anger in particular, the Platonic account is more appropriate for this inquiry than the activities-based account of the *Ethics*. She takes it to be a virtue of the account in the *Rhetoric* that it does not impose an activities-based account that would have been quite unsuitable.

which signals a complete action. The argument proceeds as follows: it is pleasant both to be learning (*manthanein*) and to be admiring something (*thaumazein*) because to admire something is to desire to learn (*mathein*) and to be learning (*manthanein*) is to be returning to a natural state. In other words, the argument is carefully phrased to respect the position that knowing – the completed action of learning – is the natural state of a human animal and is therefore a state for which we have a natural desire. Coming-to-know – the process of learning – is indeed a move towards a human's good and natural state and is therefore also something we naturally desire.

Aristotle is not insisting that learning is a return to a certain state that did obtain at some time in the past. While the relevant verb (*kathistasai*) can imply a return to a previous state it certainly does not always do so.[29] So we should not think that Aristotle is committed to the idea that every learner was at some previous time in such a state, which he later lost and has now once again attained. There is no reason to detect here a lingering Platonist idea of a pre-natal state of knowledge to which learning might finally return us. It will perhaps be helpful to Aristotle that his account here is compatible with both the more extravagant flights of Platonism and also other views that do not similarly assume a pre-natal state of knowledge. And it is also a virtue of this account that it need not restrict in any way the kind of knowledge that will be relevant. After all, towards the end of the passage it is evident that Aristotle wants to include some apparently rather mundane examples of learning in his account such as recognising that this picture is a picture of, say, Apollo.[30]

There is also an important role played by 'admiration' or 'wonder' in the argument. We have previously been told in this chapter of the *Rhetoric* that people take pleasure in being admired (1.11 1371a23) and after this passage we find out that reversals of fortune (*peripeteiai*) and being rescued from danger at the last moment are both objects of wonder (*thaumasta*, 1371b11). So it seems that something is admired or wondered at because it is impressive or

---

[29] LSJ s.v. καθίστημι A.2. Compare the account of pleasure at the opening of *Rhet.* 1.11 1369b33–5, where Aristotle similarly sets down the claim that pleasure is a change in the soul and a complete perceptible return to an underlying nature (ὑποκείσθω δὴ ἡμῖν εἶναι τὴν ἡδονὴν κίνησίν τινα τῆς ψυχῆς καὶ κατάστασιν ἀθρόαν καὶ αἰσθητὴν εἰς τὴν ὑπάρχουσαν φύσιν, λύπην δὲ τοὐναντίον). For the most part, simple bodily pleasures will indeed be a return to some previously obtaining state but, more generally, we should thnk of pleasure as a movement towards some normative natural state, whether or not the animal in question has ever previously been in that state.

[30] I here assume that the things that can be recollected from pre-natal knowledge according to the *Meno* and *Phaedo* are restricted to eternal truths or certain eternal and intelligible objects (the Forms). In the *Phaedo* Socrates does also recognise a sense in which we might 'recollect' something we have learned through perception and experience while alive, as when we recollect Cebes when we see Simmias or indeed recollect Simmias when we see a picture of Simmias (*Phaed.* 73c5–74a8).

demands our attention and concern. To admire something, then, is to direct one's attention to it on account of its possessing some kind of arresting feature. What is interesting at 1371a32–3 in the passage above is that this admiration is linked closely to a kind of desire and to a desire to learn in particular: presumably a desire to learn about the thing being admired. Perhaps we should think, for example, of dramatic performances since they seem to be what is indicated by the talk of 'reversals of fortune'. We see Oedipus fall from being a strong ruler to a blind outcast and this provokes wonder and demands our attention. Our attention, furthermore, involves a desire of a kind: a desire to learn more about the event and perhaps even to understand how and why such an amazing thing could happen to such a person.

There is an important role for wonder and the associated pleasure of wonder in Aristotle's aesthetic theory in general. Tragedy ought, in Aristotle's view, to strive for the marvellous. In *Poetics* 9 he insists that tragedy should concern events that arouse pity and fear and, what is more, that those events should occur not unexpectedly but as a consequence of one another; in that way the plot will be more *thaumaston* (*Poet.* 9 1452a1–11). Even chance events are more arresting in this sense if there is the appearance of design: it is more marvellous in this sense that Mitys was killed when a statue honouring him fell on him at a public festival. It looked as if there was some kind of purpose to what was in fact a simple accident. So too, we presume, it is more *thaumaston* for events in a tragic plot to unfurl as consequences of one another rather than, for example, for Oedipus simply to discover by brute accident the truth of his paternity.

At *Poet.* 24 1460a11–18 Aristotle restates a connection between what is marvellous or arresting and pleasure. He restates his earlier assertion that tragedy in particular ought to show what is *thaumaston* but warns that this can be difficult on a stage. Epic poetry can describe Achilles' pursuit of Hector, for example, in a way that would be ridiculous in performance. But nevertheless, evidence that the marvellous brings pleasure comes from the fact that we all embellish stories to engage the attention of our audience.[31] This evidence further suggests that wonder is to be associated with close engagement and attention. The added details of the story make no substantial difference to the content of what is being said but they allow the audience to linger over it, savour the narrative, and take pleasure in listening.

---

[31] *Poet.* 24 1460a17–18: 'What is marvellous is pleasant. An indication of this is the fact that people embellish the stories they tell so as to make them more enjoyable' (τὸ δὲ θαυμαστὸν ἡδύ· σημεῖον δέ, πάντες γὰρ προστιθέντες ἀπαγγέλλουσιν ὡς χαριζόμενοι).

The overall lesson seems to be that wonder is a form of engagement in or attention paid to some arresting object. That engaged attention is pleasant because it involves an active cognitive relationship with the object based on some kind of desire to linger over it in our thoughts, pay it greater attention, ponder it or the like because it is an object of such a kind as to deserve close attention. This conclusion is supported by the famous contention in *Metaph.* A.2 that 'both at present and in the past people began to engage in philosophy because of wonder' (διὰ γὰρ τὸ θαυμάζειν οἱ ἄνθρωποι καὶ νῦν καὶ τὸ πρῶτον ἤρξαντο φιλοσοφεῖν, A.2 982b12–13). An initial interest in things close at hand that are 'unusual' (*atopa*) gradually leads us to ponder things that are of greater import. Most importantly:

> ὁ δ' ἀπορῶν καὶ θαυμάζων οἴεται ἀγνοεῖν (διὸ καὶ ὁ φιλόμυθος φιλόσοφός πώς ἐστιν· ὁ γὰρ μῦθος σύγκειται ἐκ θαυμασίων)· ὥστ' εἴπερ διὰ τὸ φεύγειν τὴν ἄγνοιαν ἐφιλοσόφησαν, φανερὸν ὅτι διὰ τὸ εἰδέναι τὸ ἐπίστασθαι ἐδίωκον καὶ οὐ χρήσεώς τινος ἕνεκεν. (*Metaph.* A.2 982b17–21)

> The person who is at a loss and is in wonder thinks that he does not know the answer (hence also the person who loves myth is in a way a philosopher, because a myth is put together from wondrous things). The upshot is that since they took to philosophy because of fleeing from ignorance, it is clear that they were pursuing understanding for the sake of knowing and not for some use.

This rounds off the argument begun at the beginning of A.1 and integrates this sense of wonder into Aristotle's general account of a natural human drive for understanding.[32] Wonder is in some ways close to what we might call 'curiosity' but with the addition of an implied recognition of ignorance about a matter of some importance. Humans feel wonder for something that they want to know or understand and recognise that they do not yet know or understand. Philosophy begins in wonder in the sense that it presupposes the realisation of ignorance about some important matter and involves the desire to know more about the object of wonder.

Learning and pleasure in *Poetics* 4

In *Poetics* 4 Aristotle returns to a theme we have already introduced in the discussion of *Rhet.* I.11, namely the pleasures that humans may enjoy at the

---

[32] See Broadie 2012, 44–53, on the general argument of *Metaph.* A.1–2, and, 62–4, on this passage.

recognition of products of *mimēsis*. In the *Poetics*, as is perhaps to be expected, these pleasures are given a more detailed treatment:[33]

ἐοίκασι δὲ γεννῆσαι μὲν ὅλως τὴν ποιητικὴν αἰτίαι δύο τινὲς καὶ αὗται φυσικαί. τό τε γὰρ μιμεῖσθαι σύμφυτον τοῖς ἀνθρώποις ἐκ παίδων ἐστὶ καὶ τούτῳ διαφέρουσι τῶν ἄλλων ζῴων ὅτι μιμητικώτατόν ἐστι καὶ τὰς μαθήσεις ποιεῖται διὰ μιμήσεως τὰς πρώτας, καὶ τὸ χαίρειν τοῖς μιμήμασι πάντας. σημεῖον δὲ τούτου τὸ συμβαῖνον ἐπὶ τῶν ἔργων· ἃ γὰρ αὐτὰ λυπηρῶς ὁρῶμεν, τούτων τὰς εἰκόνας τὰς μάλιστα ἠκριβωμένας χαίρομεν θεωροῦντες, οἷον θηρίων τε μορφὰς τῶν ἀτιμοτάτων καὶ νεκρῶν. αἴτιον δὲ καὶ τούτου, ὅτι μανθάνειν οὐ μόνον τοῖς φιλοσόφοις ἥδιστον ἀλλὰ καὶ τοῖς ἄλλοις ὁμοίως, ἀλλ᾽ ἐπὶ βραχὺ κοινωνοῦσιν αὐτοῦ. διὰ γὰρ τοῦτο χαίρουσι τὰς εἰκόνας ὁρῶντες, ὅτι συμβαίνει θεωροῦντας μανθάνειν καὶ συλλογίζεσθαι τί ἕκαστον, οἷον ὅτι οὗτος ἐκεῖνος· ἐπεὶ ἐὰν μὴ τύχῃ προεωρακώς, οὐχ ᾗ μίμημα ποιήσει τὴνἡδονὴν ἀλλὰ διὰ τὴν ἀπεργασίαν ἢ τὴν χροιὰν ἢ διὰ τοιαύτην τινὰ ἄλλην αἰτίαν. (*Poet.* 4 1448b4–19)

The following two natural causes seem to account for the existence of poetry in general. First, humans have from childhood a natural affinity with imitation. In this respect they differ from the other animals because of being the most imitative of creatures, the fact that humans' first steps in learning come about via imitation, and the fact that all humans enjoy imitations. Evidence for this is available from the following facts. We enjoy gazing at images that are particularly accurate representations even of the very things that we look upon with distress, for example the shapes of the most lowly beasts and even corpses. The reason for this too is that learning is most pleasant not only to philosophers but to all people in the same way, even if they share in it only fleetingly. That is why they take pleasure in looking at representations, because as they look they learn and reason out what each thing is, for example that this is so-and-so. Because, if the viewer does not happen to have seen the original previously, the imitation will not give pleasure as an imitation but because of its workmanship or some colour or some other reason of that kind.

In part, this passage repeats ideas we have already seen in the last section of the passage from *Rhet.* I.11. Indeed it repeats one interesting piece of evidence that Aristotle has for finding in humans an interest in and enjoyment of considering things that are imitations of something else, namely the fact that we can enjoy looking at something if we are looking at it as an imitation or representation even if what it imitates or represents would itself be unpleasant to perceive. For example, it is perfectly possible to take

---

[33] My understanding of this issue has been helped by discussion with Pierre Destrée. See Destrée 2012 and 2014.

pleasure in looking at a statue of Laocoön and his sons being attacked by serpents. It would be odd, to say the least, to take pleasure in the sight of a father and his sons in fact being killed in this way. The reason for this difference, Aristotle says, is that we humans take pleasure in thinking of the representation as a representation. We recognise: 'This is [a statue of] Laocoön' and therefore we can take pleasure in the workmanship, the lifelike depiction, and so on, as well as the recognition itself of this thing as a representation of something else.

Of course, were we not to know anything of the story of Laocoön, we might still take pleasure in the statue. Aristotle recognises that we might take pleasure in the craft, in the colour, or perhaps in the formal arrangement of the elements. Later, in *Poet.* 7 1450b35–1451a10, he famously insists that all beautiful things must have both a certain orderly arrangement and a certain magnitude, so that a beautiful object takes some time to perceive as a whole. Animals that are too small cannot be beautiful since they are perceived more or less all at once, and those that are too long are not beautiful since it is difficult to perceive them as wholes. Something similar holds, he says, for the plots of good tragedies: they must be neither too brief nor too long.[34] What is worth noting is that there is a certain kind of arrangement that we humans perceive as beautiful which can be viewed as a whole but not in an instant. It is hard to be certain, but the idea might be that it must be possible to perceive the whole as an arrangement of parts and that is why something that is perceived all at once as a unit will not fit the bill, nor will something which is so large that its overall structure cannot be grasped. (A beautiful piece of music is a good example: it cannot be so short as not to be perceived as having a structure at all, nor too long so that the listener cannot keep in mind the recognition of its overall form.) The recognition of this structural beauty will bring a certain kind of pleasure. In so far as recognising such structural arrangements is dependent on a rational appreciation since the fineness and beauty of the structure is related to the good, then this pleasure too will be a kind of rational pleasure.[35] So without knowing whom this statue is supposed to depict, we can

---

[34] Cf. *Poet.* 23 1459a17–21: Aristotle insists that a story must be whole and complete with a beginning, middle, and end so that, like a single and complete living creature, it can generate its own proper pleasure (περὶ δὲ τῆς διηγηματικῆς καὶ ἐν μέτρῳ μιμητικῆς, ὅτι δεῖ τοὺς μύθους καθάπερ ἐν ταῖς τραγῳδίαις συνιστάναι δραματικοὺς καὶ περὶ μίαν πρᾶξιν ὅλην καὶ τελείαν ἔχουσαν ἀρχὴν καὶ μέσα καὶ τέλος, ἵν᾽ ὥσπερ ζῷον ἓν ὅλον ποιῇ τὴν οἰκείαν ἡδονήν, δῆλον).

[35] See Richardson Lear 2006, 122–3, and Moss 2012a, 206–19. In Chapter 7 below I return to this theme and suggest that the virtuous agent has a similarly pleasant appreciation of the arrangement and order of his own life. This may be compared also with Plato's account in the *Philebus* of the good and pious man discussed in Chapter 6.

nevertheless take pleasure in its formal and structural properties as we look at it.[36] Certainly, at *EE* 3.2 1230b36–1231a5 Aristotle notes that although other animals often have rather sharper senses than we humans, nevertheless they do not recognise some pleasant objects of perception that we do. They do not, for example, recognise good order or beauty (εὐαρμοστία ἢ κάλλος, 1231a1–2) and, barring certain very unusual circumstances, are not affected by beautiful sights or sounds as such. This must be a case in which our human capacity for reason allows us to take pleasure in perceiving items as beautiful or as fine in a way that other animals that can hear or see simply cannot.[37]

There is a further pleasure beyond the simple appreciation of beautiful order to be had from our contemplation of imitative art. Were we not to know that this is a statue of Laocoön, we would be missing the additional pleasure of recognising the imitation as such. This enjoyment of imitation as such is taken by Aristotle in this passage of the *Poetics* to be a sign of a general human enjoyment of learning. Quite how it is supposed to instigate the 'first steps in learning' is not made clear, but we might speculate that it is part of a general process of cognitive development that involves seeing how things differ from and resemble one another, drawing general inferences about kinds and the like. What is more, someone who takes pleasure in the statue as a mimetic object also shows some appreciation of the fact that it has been deliberately fashioned in order to resemble something else; recognition of its causal history and its being the product of deliberate rational skill are also involved in enjoying seeing something as an imitation of something else. Aristotle is certain that there is a pleasure to be had just in the recognition of that kind of design. This also provides a second reason for distinguishing two kinds of pleasure available from such works of art. The first argument is the fact that, in the absence of recognition of the imitation we might nevertheless take pleasure in the formal arrangement. The second is the mirror image of the first: even if the object under consideration is not formally or structurally beautiful we might nevertheless take some pleasure in recognising it as

---

[36] This would also allow Aristotle to give an account of the pleasures to be had from non-imitative art.

[37] Compare Plat. *Laws* 653e3–654a3: 'The other animals do not perceive orderliness and disorder in motions – what we call rhythm and harmony – but those same gods we called our companions in the chorus gave this to us as a gift: the pleasant perception of rhythm and harmony' (τὰ μὲν οὖν ἄλλα ζῷα οὐκ ἔχειν αἴσθησιν τῶν ἐν ταῖς κινήσεσιν τάξεων οὐδὲ ἀταξιῶν, οἷς δὴ ῥυθμὸς ὄνομα καὶ ἁρμονία· ἡμῖν δὲ οὓς εἴπομεν τοὺς θεοὺς συγχορευτὰς δεδόσθαι, τούτους εἶναι καὶ τοὺς δεδωκότας τὴν ἔνρυθμόν τε καὶ ἐναρμόνιον αἴσθησιν μεθ' ἡδονῆς). See also Warren 2013a.

an imitation of something else. Something grotesque and ugly might nevertheless be enjoyed as a product of skilful imitative craft.[38] The 'reasoning out' involved here (*syllogizesthai*: the cognate noun is used in the parallel claim at *Rhet.* 1.11 1371b9) is not an onerous cognitive labour and the 'learning' involved is similarly undemanding. The viewer works out what this statue imitates and the product of this working out is something that is learned. The whole process requires the prior knowledge in some sense of what is being imitated and the recognition of the imitation as a deliberate attempt at representation. The viewer must remember what is being imitated, recall it, and perform some basic intellectual operation that concludes with the thought that this particular statue, for example, is an attempt to depict this particular individual.[39] This is all some distance from the pleasures of philosophy, as Aristotle notes, but the fact that everyone can enjoy something of this kind of intellectual achievement, even at the very low level of recognising that this is a statue of a snake, or of Laocoön, or that it depicts *that* passage in *that* poem, shows that there is a common psychological capacity in all humans.[40]

There is a similar kind of pleasure noted at *Rhet.* 3.10 1412a33–1412b3. Aristotle describes a kind of joke or pun that depends on the similar sound in Greek of the phrases 'something bothers you' and 'you are a Thracian slave' said by one Theodorus to Nicon.[41] There is a pleasure in recognising the play on words for anyone who knows also that Nicon is a Thracian and that therefore the double meaning is appropriate. Here too Aristotle describes the relevant pleasure as one of learning (διὸ μαθόντι ἡδύ, 1412b1), where the learning involved is not much more demanding than a certain kind of recognition of the relevance of a possible double meaning. This learning itself depends on a prior background knowledge of the situation but the pleasure of this learning is nevertheless distinct from any enjoyment of that prior knowledge.

The connection between the pleasure of seeing naturally well-arranged items and similarly ordered products of imitative craft is made even closer if we bear in mind Aristotle's general notion that art imitates nature. He makes explicit the connection between natural and imitative design in *PA* 1.5 when

---

[38] See also Plutarch's account of the pleasure to be had in recognising the products of deliberate, rationally guided craft: *Quaest. Conv.* 5.2 673D–E and *De Aud. Poet.* 18B–C. Plutarch too notes that this pleasure may be taken even in objects which imitate things we would not perceive with pleasure.

[39] Recollection too is a kind of *syllogismos*: *De Mem.* 2 453a10–12. Again, compare *Phaed.* 73c5–74a4.

[40] For further discussion of this passage see Halliwell 1992 and 2011, 208–9; Heath 2009, 62–8; Destrée 2012, 98–103.

[41] The phrases are θράξει σε and Θρᾷξ εἶ σύ.

making the case for there being something wonderful (*thaumaston*, 645a17) in all natural things and identifies a pleasure to be had in contemplating even the lower animals. In this case, the pleasure involved might require a prior commitment to a certain kind of philosophical enterprise or, at the least, some capacity to appreciate natural philosophical explanations. But for anyone suitably predisposed, there will be a pleasure in considering natural living things that is perhaps even better than the pleasure we can all enjoy in contemplating the products of human design.

The chapter opens by restating the now familiar idea that the best and most pleasant objects of thought are things that are eternal and ungenerated, although it is likely in this case that what Aristotle means are not necessary truths but eternal perceptible things such as the heavenly bodies. (This seems to be the sense of the parenthetical phrase at *PA* 1.5 644b25–8; cf. 645a4–6.) But the chapter concentrates on making a case for there being pleasures to be had also in the investigation and understanding of corruptible things such as animals and plants (644b20–31). These may not admit of the divine contemplation that the eternal objects do but, in compensation, they are more easily investigated. Indeed, the eternal objects are much more honourable and provide more pleasure even if they are grasped only fleetingly or in part (*kata mikron*). This much is also familiar from the arguments for the superiority and pleasure of contemplation in the *Nicomachean Ethics*. But here in *PA* 1.5 Aristotle adds that there is a pleasure to be had also in considering the perishable natural world and, what is more, the natural world offers much closer and more accessible objects of study. Moreover, there is pleasure and value in considering the full range of natural living things, even those that might initially appear lowly or ugly.

καὶ γὰρ ἐν τοῖς μὴ κεχαρισμένοις αὐτῶν πρὸς τὴν αἴσθησιν κατὰ τὴν θεωρίαν ὅμως ἡ δημιουργήσασα φύσις ἀμηχάνους ἡδονὰς παρέχει τοῖς δυναμένοις τὰς αἰτίας γνωρίζειν καὶ φύσει φιλοσόφοις. καὶ γὰρ ἂν εἴη παράλογον καὶ ἄτοπον, εἰ τὰς μὲν εἰκόνας αὐτῶν θεωροῦντες χαίρομεν ὅτι τὴν δημιουργήσασαν τέχνην συνθεωροῦμεν, οἷον τὴν γραφικὴν ἢ τὴν πλαστικήν, αὐτῶν δὲ τῶν φύσει συνεστώτων μὴ μᾶλλον ἀγαπῷμεν τὴν θεωρίαν, δυνάμενοί γε τὰς αἰτίας καθορᾶν. διὸ δεῖ μὴ δυσχεραίνειν παιδικῶς τὴν περὶ τῶν ἀτιμοτέρων ζῴων ἐπίσκεψιν. (*PA* 1.5 645a7–16)

For also in the case of those animals that are not agreeable to look at, nevertheless nature's craftsmanship provides enormous pleasures to those who contemplate them: those who are able to recognise their causes and are naturally lovers of wisdom ('philosophers'). For it would be paradoxical and odd if, when contemplating representations of these things, we take pleasure in considering the craftsman's skill in painting or sculpture, for example, but do not take more pleasure in the contemplation of those very things that are put together by nature when we are able to survey their causes. Hence we must not grumble like children at the consideration of the less noble animals.

The themes introduced in *Poetics* 4 are brought together here in defence of Aristotle's project of investigating all natural things, including those animals that might be thought less worthy of attention and even perhaps unpleasant to look at. He notes first of all our enjoyment of recognising the art and skill of painting and sculpture and then offers an argument *a fortiori*. He reminds us that there should be more enjoyment in seeing the products of nature's skill, particularly since we take pleasure in looking at depictions in paint or marble of just these same natural things. If someone enjoys looking at a fine and beautiful statue of a deer then there should be no less pleasure to be had in contemplating the fine and beautiful natural design of a deer itself. To be sure, it might take a particular kind of philosophical nature in this case to recognise natural design but the principle is precisely the same as in the case of human arts: recognition of the explanations for the arrangement and construction of the item under consideration is part of taking pleasure in appreciating the item in question. Presumably, this will also be the case even for those animals that were in *Poetics* 7 thought too small to be pleasant to view; in those cases too there might nevertheless be a pleasure to be had in recognising the cunning natural design of an insect's eye or a tiny worm's body.[42]

Conclusions

The differences between the Platonic and Aristotelian accounts of the metaphysical nature of pleasure and their disagreement over the ontological nature of the objects of human thinking and perception should not obscure the similarities between their approaches to the role of pleasure in a good human life. Both are inclined to think that the best things that a human being can do are intellectual activities, and both place these activities at the heart of what makes for an excellent human life. Both are inclined to identify pleasures that accompany such activities and therefore identify a class of superior pleasures that will characterise an excellent human life. Aristotle differs from Plato, however, in expressing in more detailed terms the various differences between processes of learning, recalling, contemplating, and knowing. But he agrees with his predecessor in thinking that all of

---

[42] Cf. Destrée 2014, 8–9.

these are directed ideally at a final goal of possessing and actively contemplating eternal truths. Aristotle also differs from Plato – certainly the Plato of the *Republic* – in the explicit acknowledgement of pleasures associated with a variety of forms of inferior intellectual and cognitive activities and changes, and he is more prepared to find an intellectual accomplishment of a sort – and also an accompanying pleasure – in thinking and learning about the natural perceptible world and the products of human craftsmanship.

CHAPTER 4

Epicurus and Plutarch on pleasure and human nature

Debates over the pleasures and pains of various kinds of learning and knowing continued into the Hellenistic period. To illustrate this, in the present chapter I consider the extent to which the hedonistic school of Epicureanism found room for such pleasures and then how the Epicureans were attacked by Plutarch on the grounds that they demonstrated an insufficient grasp of human rational nature. Plutarch's anti-Epicurean polemic borrows heavily from some of the Platonic texts that were discussed in Chapter 2. It also offers a further perspective on the identification of the proper pleasures of the rational part of the soul that suggests something about the later Platonists' understanding of Plato's own position.

Epicureans on the pleasures of learning and knowing

The Hellenistic Epicureans were hedonists. Since they thought that we humans should aim to live the most pleasant life possible, it is perhaps no surprise that they have a lot to say about the importance of different kinds of cognitive activity for the production and maintenance of pleasure. They certainly claim that it can be *instrumentally* good – and therefore pleasant – to know things and to be good at planning and predicting one's future experiences. For example, at *Ep. Men.* 128 Epicurus insists that maintaining 'unwavering consideration' (ἀπλανὴς θεωρία) of the fact that some of our desires are natural and necessary is essential for making sure we make the correct choices about what we need to pursue and avoid to maintain a pain-free life.[1] (We will come to look more closely at that aspect of their theory in Chapter 8 below.) And he also insists that the proper understanding of the nature of the world and of human mortality is essential

---

[1] On which see Erler 2012: θεωρία and its cognate verb and adjective (sometimes amplified with the addition of the phrase διὰ λόγου) is often used in Epicurus specifically to mean a rational grasp or consideration of some topic or truth. See e.g. *Ep. Hdt.* 35, 47.

for ridding our lives of various kinds of false but painful beliefs. But the Epicureans also emphasise how learning and knowing can be pleasant in themselves. This is perhaps surprising, particularly given the predominantly hostile reaction their philosophy received in antiquity, since most critics of Epicureanism concentrate on painting a picture of a philosophy of life dedicated only to the most basic physical pleasures. A good example of that hostile reaction can be found in Plutarch's essay *On the Fact That It Is Impossible to Live Pleasantly Following Epicurus* (*Non Posse*). But let us turn first to what the Epicurean texts themselves have to say about the pleasures of learning and knowing.

Epicurus himself clearly states that it is important to acquire an understanding of the world through what he calls the 'study of nature' (*physiologia*) because such knowledge is required for living a happy, and therefore pleasant, life. He stresses this towards the end of the *Letter to Herodotus* (78–9) and also at the opening of the *Letter to Pythocles* (85–8). Here it seems that the purpose of such understanding as can be acquired of the nature of the world is to dispel painful fears and superstitions. The essential message is presented in *Kyriai Doxai* 11 and 12: *physiologia* is needed because we tend to be troubled by superstitions concerning natural phenomena we do not understand. In a similar vein, the Epicurean poet Lucretius repeatedly encourages his addressee, Memmius, to pay attention and recognise the benefits of understanding the nature of things. By coming to understand why such things as thunder occur we come to avoid painful anxieties about them; so some knowledge of natural science is necessary for a pleasant and trouble-free life (see e.g. Lucr. *DRN* 6.80–9). Epicurus' own *Letter to Herodotus* begins (35–7) by insisting on the importance of thoroughly understanding the principles of Epicurean natural philosophy and committing the essentials to one's memory so that they can be easily and accurately referred to whenever necessary.[2]

Usefulness for removing pain and anxiety of learning about and understanding the nature of the world is the principal contribution that these intellectual pursuits can make to the production of pleasure. But there are also indications that Epicurus envisaged a more direct relationship between knowledge of the nature of things and pleasure. The best piece of evidence for this is one of the *Vatican Sayings:*[3]

---

[2] The Epicureans set great store by memorisation of the essentials of their philosophy, which led to the composition of epitomes of the larger works, sometimes in the form of letters such as those collected in DL 10, sets of aphorisms such as the *Kyriai Doxai* and the distillation of the essentials of their views in the most concise form: the *tetrapharmakos*.

[3] Körte 1890 assigns this *Saying* to Metrodorus (fr. 47).

ἐπὶ μὲν τῶν ἄλλων ἐπιτηδευμάτων μόλις τελειωθεῖσιν ὁ καρπὸς ἔρχεται, ἐπὶ
δὲ φιλοσοφίας συντρέχει τῇ γνώσει τὸ τερπνόν· οὐ γὰρ μετὰ μάθησιν
ἀπόλαυσις, ἀλλὰ ἅμα μάθησις καὶ ἀπόλαυσις. (*SV* 27)

For other pursuits the reward arrives with some toil once the pursuit is
complete. But in the case of philosophy the joy comes hand in hand with
knowledge; for the pleasure does not come after the learning but pleasure and
learning are simultaneous.

This *Saying* is concerned with pointing out not only that knowledge can be
pleasant but also and more specifically that knowledge and pleasure come
about simultaneously. At the moment I come to know something I
simultaneously enjoy knowing that something. I do not need to wait for
that knowledge to be useful or to lead to some later pleasure; it is pleasant all
by itself and the pleasure occurs as soon as something is known.[4] The
chronological claim is perhaps best understood as a claim about the nature
of the value of knowledge. The *Saying* might well be aimed at dispelling the
idea that the Epicureans think that knowledge – like virtue – is good only in
a crude way because of some later pleasure that it might produce. Instead,
they want to say that knowledge is good because it is pleasant immediately
and all by itself. Knowledge is intrinsically pleasant and therefore valuable;
knowledge does not have to bring about some later pleasure for it to be
valuable.

The Epicureans clearly feel some pressure to recognise a value for knowledge
that is not merely contingent on its producing some later pleasure while still
holding firm to their hedonist axiology. Perhaps the idea is as follows. It is not
pleasant for me to learn and then to know some trigonometry only in the sense
that it will allow me later on to build a house efficiently and live in a secure and
watertight dwelling. Yes, my learning geometry will do that and it will in this
way produce pleasure and prevent pain. But learning and knowing that the
square on the hypotenuse is equal to the sum of the squares on the other two
sides is also pleasant all by itself; I take pleasure in that knowledge. Or, if we
want a more specific example of some Epicurean philosophy, perhaps it is
pleasant to know that lightning is not caused by divine anger not just because
that will allow me to live a life free from superstitious anxieties. Yes, it will do
that.[5] But it is not necessary to wait until the next thunderstorm to derive any

---

[4] Compare Diogenes of Oinoanda fr. 33.VI.11–VII.10 Smith for the idea that the pleasure and the cause
of the pleasure can be simultaneous: we do not eat and then afterwards experience pleasure because of
eating nor do men ejaculate and then later experience sexual pleasure. In these cases what causes the
pleasure and the pleasure itself are simultaneous. See Sedley 2002.

[5] Compare *KD* 12, *Ep. Hdt.* 78–9, and *Ep. Pyth.* 86, which stress the necessity of the understanding of
such things for living a good life.

pleasure from this piece of knowledge; knowing that lightning is caused in such-and-such a way is just pleasant all by itself. It is still the case that the value of knowledge lies in its being pleasant, of course, but its pleasantness is not merely a product of its usefulness.[6]

The *Saying* does not make clear whether it continues to be pleasant to know something after the initial enjoyment of discovery, but it seems likely that the Epicureans would indeed want to make such a claim. To be certain, it will help to determine the precise meaning of *gnōsis* and *mathēsis* in *SV* 27, translated above as 'knowledge' and 'learning' respectively. For example, if *mathēsis* means 'learning' in the sense of the event of coming to know something, then it will not follow that just because this is all by itself pleasant when it happens, it will continue to be pleasant to have learned something. But the sense of the event of coming-to-know something makes best sense of the claim that there need be no time lag between the *mathēsis* and the pleasure.[7] *Gnōsis*, on the other hand, is more likely to mean an ongoing state of knowing or understanding. (See, for example, its use in *Ep. Hdt.* 78–9.) In that case, the combination of the two terms in this *Saying* may be intended to encompass both the claim that coming-to-know something will be immediately pleasant and the claim that a continued comprehension of some truth will continue to be pleasant.

Vatican Saying 41 also offers a generally uplifting picture of the joys of living an Epicurean life:

> γελᾶν ἅμα δεῖ καὶ φιλοσοφεῖν καὶ οἰκονομεῖν καὶ τοῖς λοιποῖς οἰκειώμασι χρῆσθαι καὶ μηδαμῇ λήγειν τὰς ἐκ τῆς ὀρθῆς φιλοσοφίας φωνὰς ἀφιέντας.

> We must laugh at the same time as we philosophise and do our household duties and employ our other faculties and never cease proclaiming the sayings of the true philosophy.[8]

All these activities – philosophy, housework, and the rest – are a source of joy and laughter. Certainly, the Epicureans seem to have thought that philosophical conversations are themselves a source of pleasure besides any instrumental benefit they might provide. Epicurus himself says that he looks back and recalls such discussions with pleasure (DL 10.22).

---

[6] Compare Lucretius' famous experience of *horror ac divina voluptas* at the vision of the boundless universe offered by Epicurean physics (*DRN* 3.27–9).

[7] *Mathēsis* is not a common word in Epicurus; nor is the cognate verb. But compare *SV* 74: 'In philosophical shared inquiry the one who is beaten gains more according to how much more he learns [*prosemathen*].'

[8] Usener 1887 omits γελᾶν in his edition and adds it to the end of *SV* 40. See Bailey 1926, 382, for compelling reasons to retain it.

Epicureans against Plato, Platonists against Epicurus

Plutarch's work *On the Fact That It Is Impossible to Live Pleasantly Following Epicurus* (*Non Posse*) is devoted to showing that the Epicureans are mistaken in their understanding of pleasure, the gods, and death, and therefore fail in their project of offering a recipe for living a pleasant and good life free from irrational fear. Plutarch's demonstration of the Epicureans' failure relies heavily on a set of Platonic assumptions about the body and soul and their respective pleasures, many of them based in a reading of Plato's *Republic*. In particular, Plutarch accuses the Epicureans of failing to install intellectual achievements in their proper place in a good human life.[9] To do so, Plutarch cleverly – albeit sometimes very selectively – uses the Epicureans' own texts and their known anti-Platonic position on a range of philosophical topics as the evidence on which he bases a critical interpretation of these philosophical rivals.

Non Posse is one side of a tit-for-tat Platonist versus Epicurean polemic, whose other side is well exemplified by what we have of Epicureans like Colotes' strong and equally committed reaction to Platonic works. *Non Posse* is explicitly offered as a companion piece to the *Adversus Colotem* (see *Non Posse* 1086c–d) and the Epicurean polemic against other philosophers – in Colotes' case also against various Platonic works including the *Republic* – is the perfect justification, should there really be any need for one, for Plutarch to adopt this robust approach in response. He feels no pressure for the criticisms he offers to be based on a charitable or even-handed interpretation of Epicurus' views. Nor does he feel the need for any serious dialectical engagement with the opposing school's philosophy. Perhaps Plutarch did take that approach elsewhere, however, since the Lamprias catalogue (§129) includes mention of a work *On Epicurean Contradictions* (Περὶ Ἐπικουρείων ἐναντιωμάτων) which might have been somewhat like the surviving anti-Stoic work with a similar title (*De Stoic. Repug.*).[10] But in *Non Posse* Plutarch is perfectly at liberty to write a retaliatory Platonist critique of Epicureanism from a partisan standpoint.

Despite the Epicureans' reputation for being generally uninterested in inter-school dialectic, they were accomplished polemicists and, by

---

[9] While I concentrate on *Non Posse* since it contains Plutarch's most sustained treatment of Epicurean hedonism, it is clear that similar concerns surface in other works. See e.g. *An Seni* 786c, *Lat. Viv.* 1129B (Usener 411, 412).

[10] The situation with the Stoics is complicated further by their philosophical affinity with the Socratic tradition, often drawing on Platonic works, and Plutarch's own preferred account of that same tradition. For a careful and illuminating discussion of this theme in *De Stoic. Repug.*, see Boys-Stones 1997.

Plutarch's time, had long been engaged in criticism of Platonic works. Indeed, the Epicureans had been both interested in and irritated by Plato since the foundation of the school. There is good evidence of a close engagement by Epicurus himself in various aspects of Plato's dialogues, including notably the *Timaeus* and *Phaedo* and also the *Republic*.[11] The first generation of Epicureans also were keen polemicists: Metrodorus appears to have written an *Against the Euthyphro* and *Against the Gorgias* and Polyaenus wrote *Against Plato* (DL 10.25). Colotes, in particular, seems to have warmed to this theme. As well as the general work to which Plutarch's *Adversus Colotem* is a response, Colotes wrote works *Against the Lysis* and *Against the Euthydemus*. And, most interesting for current purposes, he was keen to criticise Plato's *Republic*; at least, we know from Proclus' commentary on the Platonic work that he was keen to offer criticisms of the myth of Er.[12] Proclus even dubs him 'the enemy of Plato', something which would in all likelihood have pleased him greatly.[13] Proclus, we might also notice, writing more than seven hundred years after Colotes, still feels it important to offer a rebuttal of the Epicurean's accusations. And he notes that Porphyry before him had felt a similar need to respond to Colotes (Procl. *In Plat. Rem Pub.* vol. 2: III.6ff. Kroll).

Although the evidence is not particularly rich, there is every reason to think that the period in which Plutarch was writing the *Non Posse* saw the continuation of a general vein of polemic between the two schools. There is, to be sure, little explicit polemic surviving between Epicureanism and Platonism in later Hellenistic and early Imperial times, but there is no reason to think it disappeared in the period between Colotes and Plutarch; there are certainly in our sources some traces which might support such a case.[14] The second-century evidence is nevertheless much clearer. As well as Plutarch's evident interest in Epicurean theories of pleasure, we have Aulus Gellius' report of the – admittedly peculiar – view that all subsequent philosophical accounts of pleasure are dependent on one or other of

---

[11] See also Warren 2006 for a discussion of Epicurus' engagement with the *harmonia*-theory of soul and its refutation in the *Phaedo*. Epicurus' *On Nature* book 14 (*PHerc.* 1148) discussed the physical theory of the *Timaeus*. See Leone 1984.

[12] See Procl. *In Plat. Rem Pub.* vol. 2: 105, 23; 109, 12; III, 6ff.; 113, 9; 116, 19; 121, 24 Kroll. Cf. Warren 2002b, 204–5, for how Proclus plays Colotes against his atomist predecessor Democritus. For more information on Colotes' works see Westman 1955, 26–107.

[13] See Procl. *In Plat. Rem Pub.* vol. 2: 113, 9–10 Kroll.

[14] The question of Lucretius' interest in non-Epicurean philosophy in general is rather complicated. I offer some thoughts on how the didactic nature of his poem may suppress complex inter-school dialectic in Warren 2007. Philodemus clearly had an interest in the Academy and wrote a history of the school (*PHerc.* 1021 and 164).

Plato's descriptions of pleasure's various forms.[15] One of the views mentioned prominently in this connection is the Epicurean conception that the highest good is pleasure and that this is a 'well balanced state of the flesh' (τὸ σαρκὸς εὐσταθὲς κατάστημα), for which Gellius uses the same Epicurean tag that also appears in Plutarch at 1089D and 1090A.[16] This short phrase therefore appears to be a favourite touchstone for this kind of anti-Epicurean criticism, precisely because of the prominence it offers to the state of the flesh rather than the soul.[17] (The phrase is also quoted by Clement at *Strom.* 2.119 and 131. It could well be another phrase made notorious by Timocrates' selective quotation.) For his part, the second-century Platonist Calvenus Taurus seems to have been particularly attached to an anti-Epicurean and anti-hedonist agenda of an extreme kind. Certainly, the terms of his attacks on Epicurus reported by Gellius are uncompromising:

> Taurus autem noster, quotiens facta mentio Epicuri erat, in ore atque in lingua habebat verba haec Hieroclis Stoici, viri sancti et gravis: ἡδονὴ τέλος, πόρνης δόγμα· οὐκ ἔστιν πρόνοια, οὐδὲ πόρνης δόγμα. (*Noct. Att. 9.5*)

> But our own Taurus, whenever he made mention of Epicurus would have on the tip of his tongue this phrase of the Stoic Hierocles, a pious and serious man: 'That pleasure is the goal of life is the dogma of a whore; that there is no providence is not even the dogma of a whore.'

The details remain obscure, but it is enough for my purposes to show that there was an ongoing debate between the two schools. This debate, furthermore, points towards two features which are relevant to the interpretation of this work by Plutarch. First, the report from Gellius shows that, whether in the case of Calvenus Taurus' abusive dismissal or in the more sober attempt to undermine Epicurean innovation by pointing to an original Platonic source, there was heated discussion or polemic over the true nature of pleasure and its precise role in a good human life. Second, as the evidence from Proclus suggests, discussion between Platonists and

---

[15] See Aul. Gell. *Noct. Att.* 9.5. The whole of this section is often attributed to Calvenus Taurus; it appears, for example as 18T Gioé, §10 Lakmann and cf. Lakmann 1995, 98–113. There are, however, reasons to doubt that the whole of the report concerns Calvenus Taurus' views, rather than Gellius' own. See Tarrant 1996, esp. 187–93 and cf. Annas 1999, 138–9 and n. 5. For more on Taurus see Tarrant 2007, 456–60.

[16] Aul. Gell. *Noct. Att.* 9.5.1: *Epicurus voluptatem summum bonum esse ponit; eam tamen ita definit*: σαρκὸς εὐσταθὲς κατάστημα.

[17] Usener 1887 prints as fr. 68 the entire sentence from Plut. *Non Posse* 1089D: τὸ γὰρ εὐσταθὲς σαρκὸς κατάστημα καὶ τὸ περὶ ταύτης πιστὸν ἔλπισμα τὴν ἀκροτάτην χαρὰν καὶ βεβαιοτάτην ἔχει τοῖς ἐπιλογίζεσθαι δυναμένοις. (I return to discuss this sentence in Chapter 8.) On the use of εὐστάθεια in Plutarch see Albini 1993, 62.

Epicureans sometimes included discussion of Plato's *Republic*, perhaps instigated by an early critical work by the Epicurean Colotes.[18] Plutarch's *Non Posse* fits neatly into both of these strands of Platonist–Epicurean debate. For Plutarch, it would have seemed entirely natural to reach for the *Republic* as a source for material to wield against the Epicureans and their conception of pleasure. Indeed, it would have seemed perfectly apt for him to do so given Colotes' famous hostility to Plato and to this dialogue, and also the obviously fertile material in *Republic* for producing not only alternatives to the Epicurean view but also diagnoses of their mistakes. In casting the hedonist and empiricist Epicureans as subject to the very failings which Socrates finds in both the 'lovers of sights and sounds' in book 5 and also the patients and gluttons in book 9, *Non Posse* offers an object lesson in the creative use of a Platonic text for the purposes of inter-school polemic some five hundred years after the *Republic* was written.[19]

Plutarch's Platonist attack on Epicurean pleasures

Plutarch's most striking use of Plato's *Republic* comes at *Non Posse* 1091D–E:

τὸ γὰρ ἀναγκαῖον οὐκ ἀγαθόν ἐστιν, ἀλλ᾿ ἐπέκεινα τῆς φυγῆς τῶν κακῶν κεῖται τὸ ἐφετὸν καὶ τὸ αἱρετὸν καὶ νὴ Δία τὸ ἡδὺ καὶ οἰκεῖον, ὡς Πλάτων ἔλεγε, καὶ ἀπηγόρευε τὰς λυπῶν καὶ πόνων ἀπαλλαγὰς ἡδονὰς μὴ νομίζειν, ἀλλ᾿ οἷόν τινα σκιαγραφίαν ἢ μῖξιν οἰκείου καὶ ἀλλοτρίου, καθάπερ λευκοῦ καὶ μέλανος, ἀπὸ τοῦ κάτω πρὸς τὸ μέσον ἀναφερομένων, ἀπειρίᾳ δὲ τοῦ ἄνω καὶ ἀγνοίᾳ τὸ μέσον ἄκρον ἡγουμένων εἶναι καὶ πέρας· ὥσπερ Ἐπίκουρος ἡγεῖται καὶ Μητρόδωρος, οὐσίαν τἀγαθοῦ καὶ ἀκρότητα τὴν τοῦ κακοῦ φυγὴν τιθέμενοι καὶ χαίροντες ἀνδραπόδων τινὰ χαρὰν ἢ δεσμίων ἐξ εἱργμοῦ λυθέντων ἀσμένως ἀλειψαμένων καὶ ἀπολουσαμένων μετ᾿ αἰκίας καὶ μάστιγας, ἐλευθέρας δὲ καὶ καθαρᾶς καὶ ἀμιγοῦς καὶ ἀμωλωπίστου χαρᾶς ἀγεύστων καὶ ἀθεάτων.

For what is imposed by necessity is not good; the object of our aspiration and choice lies beyond the escape from ills; yes, and so too does what is pleasant

---

18 Epicurus himself was no less graphic than Calvenus in his dismissal of opposing views. Epicurus famously is supposed to have said: 'I spit on the fine (τὸ καλόν) and those who vacantly gawp at it, whenever it produces no pleasure' (Athenaeus 547a (Usener 512)). It is possible that this is an anti-Platonic jibe. (And see above for Plutarch's assertion of a φιλόκαλον aspect of the human soul.)

19 Cf. Hershbell 1992, 3362. For a more sophisticated discussion of Plutarch's interest in Colotes' work see Kechagia 2011, 19–45, who notes the Platonic atmosphere of the discussion related in *Adv. Col.* and the explicit Platonist sympathies of at least some of the participants. Aristodemus, in particular, is a real Plato enthusiast (*Adv. Col.* 1107E). Much of her discussion could, with little modification, be equally applied to *Non Posse*.

and appropriate, as Plato said, who forbade us to regard riddance from pain and discomfort as pleasure, but as instead some trick of perspective as it were or blend of what is appropriate with what is alien to us, like a blend of white and black, which occurs when people ascend from a lower to a middle region, and suppose, in their lack of any expertise or knowledge of the higher region, that the middle is the summit and the end. So Epicurus supposes, and Metrodorus too, when they take the position that escape from harm is the reality and upper limit of the good; and thus their delight is that of slaves or prisoners released from confinement, overjoyed to be annointed and bathed after the cruel treatment and the flogging, but knowing neither the taste nor the vision of a free man's delight, pure, untainted, and bearing no scars from the lash (trans. B. Einarson and P. H. De Lacy, modified).

Commentators rightly point out that in this passage Plutarch borrows heavily from Plato's *Rep.* 584d–585a, which is an obvious passage for Plutarch to have in mind.[20] There, Socrates outlines two criticisms which are taken by Plutarch to apply to the Epicureans' account of the ideal pleasant life. Plutarch finds ammunition to use against his principal target in this very section of *Republic* book 9 and can therefore point to clear Platonic authority for his anti-Epicurean polemic: the Epicureans are just as misguided as the poor opponents whose misconceptions Socrates dismisses.

Plutarch thinks he can find good evidence in the Epicureans' own words of this turn away from the soul to the pleasures of the body and, more specifically, of the stomach. Indeed, it is announced early on that his criticisms will be aided by what the Epicureans themselves have to say. This is not to say that the conversation is properly dialectical in the sense that it is working from and wholly within Epicurean premises to uncover some sort of internal inconsistency or flaw. Rather, the polemic will quote Epicurean sources – selectively, no doubt – and show how the grounds of the criticism to be offered can be located in authentic Epicurean texts.[21] And it is certainly true that some of the passages Plutarch cites, particularly a passage from a letter from Metrodorus to his brother Timocrates at 1098c–d (previewed at 1087d), give a strong impression of the reprehensible outlook Plutarch wishes to emphasise since they do indeed appear to highlight above all the pleasures of a full stomach. (These also contrast, we might note, with

---

[20] Cf. H. Adam 1974, 36 and n. 73; Zacher 1982, 208–10; Hershbell 1992, 3373; Albini 1993, 34–5.
[21] *Non Posse* 1087D: νῦν δὲ χρήσομεθα τοῖς διδομένοις ὑπ' αὐτῶν. Compare Roskam 2005, 360: 'For here too [*sc.* in *Non Posse* as well as *Adv. Col.*], the whole discussion is conditioned by a specific polemical strategy, viz. the technique of attacking the philosophical opponent from the inside. Such a strategy of course implies that one starts from the premises of the opponent himself. Accordingly, Plutarch always introduces his reflections by a reference to Epicurus' own convictions (1097A, 1099D, 1099F–1100A).'

various Epicurean claims about the relative unimportance of bodily pleasure introduced 1088B–C.) Timocrates is a very helpful source for a writer like Plutarch since he seems to have cast himself as the victim of some persecution by the first generation of Epicureans and even as the object of a long attack by Epicurus himself (Cic. *De Natura Deorum* 1.33). Whatever the cause of the original disagreement, Timocrates is perfect for Plutarch's needs: an Epicurean insider who can cite with plausibility various claims by the early Epicureans which make them appear to be gluttons and hypocrites, confirming Plutarch's portrait of the school with unimpeachable first-hand evidence.[22] The picture of Epicureanism suggested by this evidence is then subjected to various criticisms inspired by Platonic texts, especially book 9 of the *Republic*.

In book 9 Socrates argues that the absence of pain is a distinct state from the experience of pleasure. In other words, he tries to dispel the notion that the relief from pain is truly a pleasure and instead wishes to show that it is a mere false pleasure, a shadow of the true and original pleasure (*eskiagraphēmenē* in Plato at 583b5, cf. *skiagraphia* in Plutarch at 1091D). Given the Epicureans' famous insistence that the greatest magnitude of pleasure is indeed the absence of pain, it is no surprise that Socrates' argument might appear helpful in an anti-Epicurean text. Plutarch enjoys quoting from both Metrodorus' *Against the Sophists* (fr. 28 Körte) and an un-named work by Epicurus (Usener 423) to show that the Epicureans did indeed think that the greatest joy comes from the absence of evil (1091A–B). From Socrates' perspective this is merely a false or illusory pleasure and should be contrasted with true, positive, pleasure; this true pleasure is not simply comparatively better than some previous or subsequent state of pain. To expose the error, Socrates mounts a dialectical argument aimed at some opponents who claim that the state of pain-free health is in fact the most pleasant state possible, but that this is only evident once someone is no longer in that state and is instead suffering some kind of sickness (583c10–d2). In response, Socrates sets about convincing his opponents that, on the basis of their own assumption that one's proper hedonic state might be incorrectly evaluated because of current experiences, they should think that a general state of health is in fact merely an intermediate state – neither

---

[22] See also DL 10.6–7 for more of Timocrates' claims. DL 10.4 says that Timocrates wrote a work impugning Epicurus' Athenian citizenship. In short, Timocrates seems to have been 'extraordinarily successful . . . in contaminating the biographical tradition about Epicurus and Metrodorus' (Sedley 1976, 127–32; cf. Roskam 2007, 43–9; Gordon 2012, 14–37). Compare also Timon of Phlius fr. 7 Diels for wording very like what is found at Plutarch *Non Posse* 1098C–D.

pleasant nor painful – and not, as in their sickened state they currently claim, the highest pleasure.

Further, Socrates goes on to use as an illustration of the kind of mistake he wants to expose some people who think they have climbed to a 'higher' region when they have simply lifted themselves out of some kind of depression (584d1–e5; cf. *Phaed.* 109aff.); they think that they have ascended to somewhere elevated but in reality have merely made it back up to ground level. Plutarch is quick to work this same comparison into his brief summary. For Plutarch, the Epicureans are much like those people in the *Republic* whom Socrates describes as 'sick' (583c10). These people – like the Epicureans – mistakenly consider the absence of pain to be a pleasure because, in their illness, they wrongly overvalue their previous health in comparison with their present state. It is not coincidental that a consequence of this illusion is that the sick people deny that there is any intermediate state between pleasure and pain.[23]

This leads to Socrates' second argument, which was discussed at some length in Chapter 2 and which is based on the hypothesis of there being certain perfect intelligible objects of knowledge to which human reason naturally ought to tend and which best satisfy human rational desires. In ignoring these perfect intelligible objects – 'the Forms' – and concentrating on the satisfaction of bodily needs, in Plutarch's eyes the Epicureans are clearly attempting to offer as the goal of life something which, considered rightly, is at best only an illusory or false pleasure.

In this same passage at *Non Posse* 1091D–E there are indications that Plutarch may also be looking outside the argument specifically concerning misconceptions of pleasure in *Republic* book 9 for material he can usefully deploy. For example, Plutarch here compares the state of the Epicurean who knows only the cessation of pain and mistakes this for pleasure to the state of a slave or prisoner who has been released from painful torture and bondage (1091E). The prisoner may feel, comparatively, free. But he is nevertheless still in no position to experience true pleasure; he may have been freed from his bonds but he remains a prisoner. His present state may be good in comparison with his former misery but it remains inferior to the pleasures of a free man who has never been held prisoner or beaten. Given the immediately preceding direct reference to the *Republic* it is not implausible that we are here meant to think of the central arresting metaphor in book 7 of that work: the simile of the cave and the imagined release from bonds of one of the cave's prisoners who is then able to learn the true nature of things and

---

[23] For more on this argument in the *Republic* see Warren 2011b and Wolfsdorf 2013b.

experience true pleasures.[24] The crucial notions of (metaphorical) ascent and of being mistaken about one's true epistemological and hedonic state are clear enough in both the cave simile and the extended discussion of pleasure in book 9 of the *Republic*; it is perfectly reasonable for Plutarch to think that they should be read together.[25]

To his mind, the Epicureans find themselves in the position of the prisoners in the cave of *Republic* book 7 or the sick of *Republic* book 9, concentrating overly in their misery on bodily and perceptible objects of pleasure and failing to recognise that the cessation of pain that they seek is merely a pale imitation of something much better and more stable. And this failure is linked to a general failure to recognise the existence of permanent intelligible things independent of the perceptible and bodily world. Indeed, much of Plutarch's discussion of the Epicureans' errors turns on the metaphysics of pleasure: what its proper objects are and how this is related to a proper conception of human nature. There is obviously a lot of good material for building such a case to be found once again in the *Republic*, specifically in the argument at 585a–e, where Socrates uses the overall metaphysical vision of Forms and particulars to distinguish between the pleasures of the soul, whose objects are pure, true, and stable (i.e. the Forms) and which are registered by something which is itself everlasting (i.e. the soul) and the pleasures of the body whose objects are changeable, impure, and so on, and which are registered by an impure and changeable body. These latter pleasures, says Socrates, cannot properly satisfy a person. In ignoring these perfect intelligible objects and concentrating on the satisfaction of bodily needs, in Plutarch's eyes the Epicureans are again clearly attempting to offer as the goal of life something which, considered rightly, is at best only an illusory or false pleasure. Time and again, Plutarch characterises the Epicurean pleasures as unstable – *abebaioi* – which is often coupled with the claim that they are also untrustworthy – *apistoi*: 1090A, 1090B, 1090D, 1091A, 1092D, 1104F – both of which are watchwords of the original Platonic account (see 585e3–5). The Epicureans are attempting vainly to achieve satisfaction and painlessness by filling something which is by nature changing and cannot be stably satisfied with objects that are themselves

---

[24] Zacher 1982, 211 also compares Plat. *Phaedr.* 258e2–5.

[25] Even if this specific reminiscence is not intended, Plutarch surely is offering a more general reminiscence to the Platonic theme of the *sōma sēma* and to the notion that a preoccupation with bodily pleasure merely enslaves and further binds the soul to the body. Certainly, when later in the work Plutarch adds to his discussion the mistaken Epicurean idea that death is annihilation, he returns to that general theme: 1105D.

unstable and unreliable guides to what is of true value. And this has a further consequence for their chances of living a good human life.

Just a little further on in the *Republic* there is another passage which clearly underlies Plutarch's Platonist position:

> οἱ ἄρα φρονήσεως καὶ ἀρετῆς ἄπειροι, εὐωχίαις δὲ καὶ τοῖς τοιούτοις ἀεὶ συνόντες, κάτω, ὡς ἔοικεν, καὶ μέχρι πάλιν πρὸς τὸ μεταξὺ φέρονταί τε καὶ ταύτῃ πλανῶνται διὰ βίου, ὑπερβάντες δὲ τοῦτο πρὸς τὸ ἀληθῶς ἄνω οὔτε ἀνέβλεψαν πώποτε οὔτε ἠνέχθησαν, οὐδὲ τοῦ ὄντος τῷ ὄντι ἐπληρώθησαν, οὐδὲ βεβαίου τε καὶ καθαρᾶς ἡδονῆς ἐγεύσαντο, ἀλλὰ βοσκημάτων δίκην κάτω ἀεὶ βλέποντες καὶ κεκυφότες εἰς γῆν καὶ εἰς τραπέζας βόσκονται χορταζόμενοι καὶ ὀχεύοντες, καὶ ἕνεκα τῆς τούτων πλεονεξίας λακτίζοντες καὶ κυρίττοντες ἀλλήλους σιδηροῖς κέρασί τε καὶ ὁπλαῖς ἀποκτεινύασι δι᾽ ἀπληστίαν, ἅτε οὐχὶ τοῖς οὖσιν οὐδὲ τὸ ὂν οὐδὲ τὸ στέγον ἑαυτῶν πιμπλάντες. (*Rep.* 586a1–b3)

Therefore those who have no experience of wisdom and virtue but spend their time always in feasts and the like, are – so it seems – carried downwards and hardly even make it back up to the middle. And they wander back and forth like this for their whole life, never making it up to what is truly above nor looking up nor being taking up to it. They would never be filled with what really is, nor would they ever taste stable and pure pleasure. But they are always looking downwards and, bent over towards the ground like cattle, they scoff from tables, grow fat, and mount one another. In order to get more of this than anyone else they kick and butt one another with iron horns and hooves. And they kill one another out of a lack of satisfaction because they are trying to fill with things that are not something that is not and is not watertight.

Two further themes central to Plutarch's account are prominent here. First, Socrates ends with a reference to a familiar metaphor of pleasure as a kind of filling. People who concentrate on bodily pleasures are like people trying to fill up a leaky jar: the satisfaction they seek is forever unattainable because they have failed to attend to an underlying fault in their souls. The image is expanded more fully and famously in Plato's *Gorgias* (493a–494a) with reference to the myth of the Danaids, but it is certainly being invoked here in *Republic* too and Plutarch makes prominent use of it early in *Non Posse* at 1088E–1089A and 1089D–E. The first of these is an elaborate reworking of the Platonic model which is designed also to take a swipe at the Epicureans' notorious claim that present pain might be offset mentally by either anticipating some future pleasure or recollecting some past pleasure.[26]

---

[26] I will return to the Epicureans' use of the pleasures of memory and anticipation in Chapter 8 below.

εἰ δ᾽ ἀκούεις αὐτῶν μαρτυρομένων καὶ βοώντων, ὡς ἐπ᾽ οὐδενὶ ψυχὴ τῶν
ὄντων πέφυκε χαίρειν καὶ γαληνίζειν πλὴν ἐπὶ σώματος ἡδοναῖς παρούσαις
ἢ προσδοκωμέναις, καὶ τοῦτ᾽ αὐτῆς τὸ ἀγαθόν ἐστιν, ἆρ᾽ οὐ δοκοῦσί σοι
διεράματι τοῦ σώματος χρῆσθαι τῇ ψυχῇ, <καὶ> καθάπερ οἶνον ἐκ πονηροῦ
καὶ μὴ στέγοντος ἀγγείου τὴν ἡδονὴν διαχέοντες ἐνταῦθα καὶ παλαιοῦντες
οἴεσθαι σεμνότερόν τι ποιεῖν καὶ τιμιώτερον; καίτοι γ᾽ οἶνον μὲν χρόνος
διαχυθέντα τηρεῖ καὶ συνηδύνει, τῆς δ᾽ ἡδονῆς ἡ ψυχὴ παραλαβοῦσα τὴν
μνήμην ὥσπερ ὀσμὴν ἄλλο δ᾽ οὐδὲν φυλάσσει· ζέσασα γὰρ ἐπὶ σαρκὶ
κατασβέννυται, καὶ τὸ μνημονευόμενον αὐτῆς ἀμαυρόν ἐστι καὶ κνισῶδες,
ὥσπερ ἑώλων ὧν τις ἔπιεν ἢ ἔφαγεν ἀποτιθεμένου καὶ ταμιεύοντος ἐπινοίας
ἐν ἑαυτῷ καὶ χρωμένου δηλονότι ταύταις προσφάτων μὴ παρόντων. (*Non
Posse* 1088E–1089A)

But when you hear their loud protest that the soul is so constituted as to find
joy and tranquillity in nothing in the world but pleasures of the body either
present or anticipated, and that this is its good, do they not appear to you to
be using the soul as a decanter of the body, and to imagine that by decanting
pleasure, like wine, from a worthless and leaky vessel and leaving it to age in
its new container, they are turning it into something more respectable and
precious? Yet there is a difference: the new vessel preserves the wine that has
settled in the course of time and improves its flavour, whereas in the case of
pleasure the soul takes over and preserves the memory of it, as it were the
bouquet, and nothing else; for the pleasure effervesces in the flesh and then
goes flat, and what is left of it in recollection is faint and greasy, as though a
man were to lay away and store up in himself the thoughts of yesterday's food
and drink, resorting to these, we must suppose, when nothing fresh is at
hand (trans. Einarson and De Lacy).

It is not hard to see why Plutarch might have taken up this image so eagerly.
In addition to the Platonic background, Plutarch can draw additional
support for his use of this analogy from the fact that the Epicureans
themselves prominently used the very same image in order to make
clear their claim that the highest pleasure is the absence of pain and can
offer a stable and lasting hedonist *eudaimonia* (see e.g. Lucr. *DRN* 3.935–46,
6.9–27).[27] No doubt, the Epicureans are in part responding to Plato's
attacks on hedonism by recasting the Platonic image and this is what in
turn provokes Plutarch to offer a Platonist response. (This is a recurrent
theme: Plutarch takes up Platonic arms against Epicureans in response to
their original attacks on Plato.) The philosophical disagreement between
the Epicureans and Plato over the relationship between pleasure and desire

---

[27] See for further discussion Görler 1997. The Epicureans also used the image of the body as the
container of vessel of the soul (see Epicurus, *Ep. Hdt.* 65–6 and Lucr. *DRN* 3.433–44), perhaps in
order to emphasise the dependence of the proper functioning of the soul on a functioning body.

is complex but, in brief, the Epicureans agree with Socrates that a 'leaky jar' can never properly be filled but disagree with the assumption that pleasures are always associated with processes of filling rather than states of plenitude. They want there to be a kind of pleasure – indeed the highest pleasure – which is precisely a state of plenitude and not a process of filling. What we need, in that case, is to set a limit to desires and in this way make sure the jar remains watertight (see e.g. Lucr. *DRN* 6.9–34). For his purposes, Plutarch can again draw on the metaphysical argument at *Rep.* 585a–e and insist that the body is irredeemably porous, so to speak, since it is a changing and impermanent item and the objects of the pleasures it is able to enjoy are themselves unstable and impermanent.

Plutarch avoids any detailed engagement with the fine-grained interpretation of Epicurean conceptions of the nature of pleasure; perhaps rightly so: it is far from clear whether we can make genuine and satisfying philosophical sense of this notion of 'katastematic pleasure'.[28] Indeed, Plutarch makes no attempt to offer much of an argument at all against the Epicureans rather than simply rejecting their view on the basis of a restatement of a Platonist standpoint. But he does make great capital from the possibilities of imagining the soul and body as two vessels, particularly the idea of being able to decant pleasures from one vessel to the other. Plutarch's use of the image of the vessel is clever, in that case, because he can combine the general point about the impossibility of lasting bodily satisfaction with a further criticism of the Epicureans' own notions that remembered or anticipated pleasures may be used to counteract physical pains. Putting the two together allows Plutarch to show the absurdity of the operation of pouring from one leaky vessel to another and back again as a means of trying to store pleasures over time.[29] Of course, Plutarch's preferred understanding of the relationship between the soul and body which underpins his polemical approach to this – admittedly implausible – Epicurean idea is quite unlike the Epicureans' own. Their distinction between what is physical/bodily and what is psychic, given their general physicalist approach to the soul, is rather different from Plutarch's Platonic dualism. But once again, Plutarch makes no attempt to tailor his criticisms to be particularly sensitive to the details of Epicurean psychological theory. There is no attempt, for example, to consider the Epicureans' distinction

---

[28] For my discussion of this difficulty, with reference to Cicero's criticisms in *De Finibus*, see Warren, forthcoming a.

[29] The most celebrated example of this was Epicurus' own insistence on his deathbed that the recollection of prior pleasant philosophical conversations could be set against the pain of his terminal disease (DL 10.22). Plutarch is not impressed: 1099D–F.

between the rational and non-rational soul or their own preferred account of the relationship between a body and a soul. Evidently, the Epicureans' own reputation for slander and polemic licenses their being paid back in kind (1086E).

The second, and related, theme taken from the Platonic cue at *Rep.* 586a1–b3 is the notion that the Epicureans – deliberately or not – persuade themselves to live a somehow bestial life and, in presenting us with a picture of the supposedly good human life which is in fact somehow bestial, would therefore reduce the rest of us to their subhuman level. This motif has been foreshadowed towards the close of *Adversus Colotem*, at 1124D–1125C, where Colotes is reported to have argued that the great early lawgivers lifted humans out of a bestial form of life. In reply it is suggested that it is the Epicureans who mistake the proper role of law in human societies and would be unable to salvage a recognisably human life were their contractual laws to be undermined. In fact, when considered properly their position holds that the laws provide only a fragile veneer to mask the essentially bestial nature of Epicurean societies.[30] The point here is not, of course, that the Epicureans are bestial simply because they pursue pleasure; rather, the particular kinds of pleasures they pursue – in Plutarch's eyes, the pleasures of bodily gratification and pain avoidance – are not appropriate to our nature as rational thinking souls. Their hedonism is therefore based upon an impoverished view of human nature. Socrates' arresting image in the *Republic* makes such people into animals bent over a feeding trough, looking to fill their stomachs and satisfy their appetites rather than properly tend to their rational natures. This fits perfectly with a common strand in anti-Epicurean polemic which compares them with pigs in particular or beasts in general, concerned with full stomachs and nothing more.[31] It is, moreover, a criticism of the Epicurean view which has already been voiced at *Adv. Col.* 1108C, but now that Plutarch's focus is more directly on the Epicureans' own positive account of the pleasant life these concerns can be given free rein and a much more expansive exposition. Plutarch can now seize the perfect opportunity to rehearse those well-known anti-Epicurean charges once again, with the full backing of his Platonic source. Certainly, he appears to be enjoying himself in recalling on a number of occasions the motif of the bestial Epicurean life. At *Non Posse* 1091C Epicurean happiness is compared with that of 'pigs or sheep' (cf. 1094E). The same charge

---

[30] For more on the close of *Adv. Col.* see the remarks in Kechagia 2011, 157–60.
[31] For a more extended discussion of the theme and some possible Epicurean responses see Warren 2002a, 129–49.

reappears at 1092A–B: Epicurus perversely wants to lead us to the state in which brute animals are placed by nature; and it is prominent once more at 1096C–D: the Epicureans covertly 'turn the whole person into flesh' (σαρκοποιεῖν τὸν ἄνθρωπον ὅλον), fail to recognise the proper concentration on and identification of oneself with one's soul, and instead 'think it right to play swineherd to the soul with the pleasures of the body' (ἀξιοῦσι τὴν ψυχὴν ταῖς τοῦ σώματος ἡδοναῖς κατασυβωτεῖν).[32] Indeed, Plutarch repeats a familiar criticism of the Epicureans: their view in fact results in the absurd conclusion that non-rational animals are better placed than humans for living a good life since humans have to be rid of false beliefs to attain a carefree, 'ataraxic', view of the gods, death, and other supposed sources of misfortune; in contrast, non-rational animals are fortunate not even to be able to form any such false beliefs and cannot therefore suffer any mental anxiety as a result (1092B–D).[33] Once again, the overall message is that the Epicureans fatally misunderstand what humans essentially are. In particular, they fail to recognise the superiority of the human rational soul and its pleasures and, as a result, cannot provide an account of a proper human life, let alone a pleasant human life. (That final point is made most clearly at 1096D–E.)

Plutarch and the pleasures of reason

Plutarch is working with a clear set of identifications: the Epicureans are like the misguided fools who mistake the absence of pain for pleasure and, worse still, are so fixated on the body, bodily pleasures, and other sensible objects of pleasure that they are in danger of betraying their rational natures and bestialising themselves. But there is an even stronger case to be made against their philosophy. The Epicureans do not, it appears, dedicate themselves even to the more usual cognitive delights of human existence, at least not those of the more refined kind. They are famously distrustful of culture and *paideia* and, whether or not this is a fair representation of their stance, in Plutarch's eyes, at least, it suggests that they fail even to enjoy the best pleasures to be had by way of the senses: they turn away from music, poetry, and other literary arts.

---

[32] Also cf. θηριώδη at 1089C and 1094A.

[33] For similar concerns in other writers and for a discussion of the proper Epicurean response to such charges see Warren 2002a, 129–42, where I also suggest that Plutarch's work *Bruta ratione uti* (or *Gryllus*) may be related to this debate.

The argument progresses by elaborating in turn the various pleasures which the Epicureans ignore. Clearly, they know nothing of the exquisite pleasures of coming-to-know the perfect and eternal Forms. But they are also guilty of failing to cultivate other, perhaps less refined, pleasures of the better part of our souls. When Plutarch comes to offer his preferred characterisation of the pleasures appropriate to a rational human soul, his discussion implies that he is prepared to soften the restrictive account found in *Republic* book 9. There it is quite clear that Socrates wants true and pure pleasures, strictly understood, to be focussed only on those objects which always are and are always unchanging. Most obviously, this is a reference to the Forms – the objects of knowledge of the true philosopher-ruler – but perhaps a case might also be made for pure pleasures of this kind being generated by contemplation of mathematical objects of some sort. Plutarch, however, describes a significantly more expansive notion, including among his list of appropriate sources of pleasure not only mathematics and astronomy but also the study of literature, history, and the like (1092D–1095B).[34] For Plutarch, we take pleasure in learning the truth even in the case of truths related to contingent facts about things that might be otherwise (1093A–C). Plutarch is in fact prepared to say that we take pleasure in hearing some news even when that news relates something painful. And we certainly take great pleasure in listening to Herodotus' *Histories* or Homeric poetry (1093B–C). All these possible pleasures, we are asked to agree, are rejected by the Epicureans as part of a blanket rejection of cultural and intellectual pursuits in favour of a concentration on the most basic physical needs.[35]

This expansion in the scope of pleasures assigned to the rational soul is perhaps allowed by Plutarch's particular understanding of the dual nature of that aspect of human psychology. Plutarch is not terribly explicit about his own conception of the different faculties of the soul, although we might expect him to be indebted in general terms to the Platonic and Aristotelian tradition.[36] There are some important hints, however, here and there. In this very work, for example, he gives a reasonably clear indication that he sees the working of the rational soul as being turned to two separate but related functions. At 1092E he describes two general types of pleasure which a human ought properly to pursue, neither of which is grasped by the

---

[34] This is noted by Albini 1993, 35–9.

[35] At *Quaest. Conv.* 674A–B Plutarch also claims that the Epicureans are in a worse position than the Cyrenaics when it comes to accounting for the pleasures of viewing the products of mimetic craft. (Here Plutarch seems to be indebted to Aristotle's view in *Poet.* 4, discussed above.) See Warren 2013b.

[36] See Opsomer 2005, 180–3.

appetitive and bestial soul emphasised by the Epicureans. Pleasures from anticipations of bodily delight are not only unstable and empty but also vulgar and immodest. The pleasures which we ought to pursue instead are described as pure, that is, neither preceded nor followed by pain, and attributed to the rational soul.

ᾶς δ᾽ ἄξιον καὶ δίκαιον εὐφροσύνας καὶ χαρὰς νομίζεσθαι, καθαραὶ μέν εἰσι τοῦ ἐναντίου καὶ σφυγμὸν οὐδένα κεκραμένον οὐδὲ δηγμὸν οὐδὲ μετάνοιαν ἔχουσιν, οἰκεῖον δὲ τῇ ψυχῇ καὶ ψυχικὸν ἀληθῶς καὶ γνήσιον καὶ οὐκ ἐπείσακτον αὐτῶν τἀγαθόν ἐστιν οὐδ᾽ ἄλογον, ἀλλ᾽ εὐλογώτατον ἐκ τοῦ θεωρητικοῦ καὶ φιλομαθοῦς ἢ πρακτικοῦ καὶ φιλοκάλου τῆς διανοίας φυόμενον. ὧν ὅσας ἑκάτερον καὶ ἡλίκας ἡδονὰς ἀναδίδωσιν, οὐκ ἄν τις ἀνύσειε διελθεῖν προθυμούμενος. (*Non Posse* 1092E)

But what properly deserve to be called 'delights' and 'joys' are pure of any taint of the opposite, have no element of aching or stabbing pain, and bring no regret; the good in them is proper to the soul and really 'psychic' and genuine and not adventitious or irrational but rational in the truest sense since it comes from the theoretical or learning-loving part of the mind or else the action-guiding and beauty-loving part. The pleasures yielded by each of these are so many and so great that with the best will in the world no one could tell the whole story (trans. Einarson and De Lacy, with modifications).

Plutarch is correcting the Epicurean understanding of pleasure and does so by offering the correct understanding of 'delight' (*euphrosynē*) and 'joy' (*khara*). Both of these terms were used by the Epicureans themselves, although it remains controversial whether there is a clear and precise distinction to be made between these two concepts in Epicurean hedonism.[37] However the Epicureans understood these notions and however Plutarch understood the Epicureans' view, Plutarch offers in place of the Epicurean view a correct account in which these are pure (*katharai*) pleasures that belong to the rational soul. The classification of these preferred pleasures as 'pure' is familiar from both Plato's and Aristotle's discussions of the best kinds of pleasures we rational humans can enjoy. Plutarch offers

---

[37] They appear in the fragment of Epicurus' work *On Choices* cited at DL 10.136: ἡ μὲν γὰρ ἀταραξία καὶ ἀπονία καταστηματικαί εἰσιν ἡδοναί· ἡ δὲ χαρὰ καὶ ἡ εὐφροσύνη κατὰ κίνησιν ἐνεργείᾳ βλέπονται. There has been extensive discussion of this fragment since it promises to help in the interpretation of Epicurean hedonism, in particular whether there was a distinction between 'katastematic' and 'kinetic' pleasure and, if there was, how this should be understood. But the interpretation, translation, and even the text itself is the subject of considerable dispute. See, for more recent contributions to the discussion: Purinton 1993, Wolfsdorf 2009 (and, for Prodicus' distinctions between these and other pleasure terms: Wolfsdorf 2011), Warren forthcoming a. *Khara* also appears in the fragment from Epicurus' *On the Telos* cited at *Non Posse* 1089D (discussed further below) and in the scholion to *Ep. Hdt.* 66. Cf. DL 2.89, where it appears during a report of the differences between Cyrenaic and Epicurean hedonism.

two reasons for the superiority of these pleasures. First, he specifies that these are pleasures that are neither preceded nor followed by any pain; second, they are the pleasures that belong to the best part of the soul. The precise psychological picture which Plutarch has in mind is nevertheless unclear. There is some doubt whether the alternatives mentioned in the passages – 'the theoretical or learning-loving part of the mind or else the action-guiding and beauty-loving part' – correspond to two aspects (or even parts) of the rational part of the soul – one theoretical and the other practical – or alternatively to the rational and 'spirited' parts of the soul understood more or less on the model of the tripartite soul of Plato's *Republic*. This is related to the wider question, of course, whether Plutarch adopts a full-blown tripartite psychology along the lines of that found in the *Republic* or is more inclined to work for the most part with a simpler two-part division. That question cannot be settled definitively, in part because the evidence to be found in *Non Posse* is not conclusive. In favour of the view that at 1092E we are offered two complementary roles for the rational soul, producing 'delights' and 'joys', is Plutarch's preceding comment that the good he is discussing is the good appropriate to the soul – the truly 'psychic' good – and has no mixture of pain and the like, all of which suggests that this is somehow still meant to capture the essence of the pure rational pleasures which Socrates discusses in the *Republic*. In that case, when Plutarch characterises these alternative aspects of 'thinking' (*dianoia*) he intends them to be two faculties of the rational part of the soul or, perhaps, the rational soul viewed as acting in two different spheres, one theoretical and the other practical.[38] This interpretation would also appear to give a more satisfying overall coherence to his view, since the pleasures he goes on to list at 1092F onwards would be difficult to assign to the spirited part of the soul as described in the *Republic*. Instead they are, broadly speaking, aesthetic and cultural pleasures which are concerned nevertheless with particular stories, works, or occasions. They are therefore just the class of items which, on the one hand it would be hard to assign to the theoretical aspect of reason, if that is conceived as concerned exclusively with necessary and eternal abstract objects and truths; but, on the other hand, they are certainly related in some sense to a rational appreciation and a general love

---

[38] Plutarch's use of the term διάνοια elsewhere is not easy to pin down. It may be used simply as a synonym for ψυχή but on other occasions has a more restricted reference to the rational or 'hegemonic' part of the soul (*Virt. Mor.* 441C, cf. 451B; *De Fato* 571D; *De Soll. Anim.* 960A, 960C, 963D, 969C, *Quaest. Plat.* 1001D, 1002A). Cf. Opsomer 2012.

of acquiring true beliefs and information, albeit about particular or contingent facts.

Support for this view might also come from *De Animae Procreatione in Timaeo*, which describes reason (*logos*) in terms which suggest that it is a single faculty able to operate on both intelligible or universal and also perceptible or particular objects (see 1024E–1025A and 1025D–E).

Consider this passage:

καὶ μὴν θεωρητικῆς γε τῆς ψυχῆς οὔσης ἅμα καὶ πρακτικῆς, καὶ θεωρούσης μὲν τὰ καθόλου πραττούσης δὲ τὰ καθ' ἕκαστα, καὶ νοεῖν μὲν ἐκεῖνα ταῦτα δ' αἰσθάνεσθαι δοκούσης, ὁ κοινὸς λόγος ἀεὶ περί τε ταὐτὸν ἐντυγχάνων τῷ θατέρῳ καὶ ταὐτῷ περὶ θάτερον ἐπιχειρεῖ μὲν ὅροις καὶ διαιρέσεσι χωρίζειν τὸ ἓν καὶ τὰ πολλὰ καὶ τὸ ἀμερὲς καὶ τὸ μεριστόν, οὐ δύναται δὲ καθαρῶς ἐν οὐδετέρῳ γενέσθαι διὰ τὸ καὶ τὰς ἀρχὰς ἐναλλὰξ ἐμπεπλέχθαι καὶ καταμεμῖχθαι δι' ἀλλήλων. (*De An. Procr. in Tim.* 1025E)

Now, as the soul is at once contemplative and practical and contemplates the universals but acts upon the particulars and apparently cognizes the former but perceives the latter, the reason common to both (ὁ κοινὸς λόγος) as it is continually coming upon difference in sameness and upon sameness in difference, tries with definitions and divisions to separate the one and the many, that is the indivisible and the divisible, but cannot arrive at either exclusively, because the very principles have been alternately intertwined and thoroughly intermixed with each other (trans. H. Cherniss).

This is clearly a Platonist attempt to make sense of the relationship between theoretical understanding and practical reasoning based upon a metaphysical account of the relationship between universals and particulars. The details are more difficult to tease out, but what is important for present purposes is that theoretical understanding and practical reasoning are most emphatically understood to be two related uses of a single and shared faculty of reason (and a similar account can be found at *Virt. Mor.* 443E, which further identifies the virtue of the theoretical use of reason as wisdom, *sophia*, and of the practical use of reason as prudence, *phronēsis*).[39] It would be reasonable, given this view, to think that there could be rational pleasures associated with both the cognition of universals and the learning

---

[39] There are also evident Aristotelian influences on this general view, and a strong Peripatetic influence throughout *Virt. Mor.* (Compare, for example: *NE* 6.2 1139a5–15.) The passage at 443E is, admittedly, a little odd since it appears to make part of theoretical wisdom a grasp of truths concerning not only heavenly bodies but also, more surprisingly, the sea. In contrast, thoughts about what is good will belong to practical wisdom only. Nevertheless, the general point is clear: Plutarch is not averse to offering reason differing spheres of activity and tends to discriminate these by positing different kinds of object upon which a single rational faculty operates.

or appreciation of particulars. Perhaps we might argue that by reference to this more expansive notion of the remit of the reason, Plutarch can conceive of a range of objects appropriate for the pleasures of reason that is broader than we might have suspected solely from reading Plato's *Republic*.

On the other hand, concerns about the pleasures appropriate to a sense of self-worth, reputation, and the like, all of which might be associated with the *Republic*'s spirited part of the soul, are also discussed in *Non Posse*. Plutarch is evidently also concerned to show that Epicureanism fails properly to acknowledge the natural sense in which humans take pleasure in fame and a good reputation and therefore to continue his gradual reduction of the Epicureans' pleasures to the most basic ones available to human experience. Much of the discussion of 1098E–1100D, for example, is designed to show not only that there are examples of men who have taken proper pleasure in their noble achievements but that there is a general desire for and enjoyment of such pleasures among humans. Indeed, Epicurus himself is criticised for being inconsistent on this score: his own concern for a particular reputation is what drove him to disown and then slander his teachers but enjoy the reverence paid to him by his followers (1100A–C). In the terms of Plato's *Republic*, these would indeed appear to be the pleasures of the spirited part of the soul (see, for example, 581a9–b5). However, there is no clear evidence in *Non Posse* that Plutarch is committed to a strong notion of psychic tripartition including the existence of a separate spirited part of the soul. To be sure, when Plutarch concludes the work he offers a summary of the various pleasures and goods which the Epicureans omit from a human life. And there he tells us that Epicurus made 'the love of learning of the theoretical aspect of us and the love of honour of the action-guiding aspect of us' (τοῦ θεωρητικοῦ τὸ φιλομαθὲς καὶ τοῦ πρακτικοῦ τὸ φιλότιμον) blind to their due pleasures (1107C). Nevertheless, my suspicion is that, just as at 1092E, these two are both considered to be aspects of *dianoia*, which is itself the rational part of the soul, rather than distinct soul parts.[40]

In any case, it is important to note that the pleasures of the broad range of intellectual and social pursuits canvassed by Plutarch in 1093A–C certainly do not correspond, strictly speaking, to the exquisite cognitive pleasures of the philosopher-ruler imagined by Socrates in the *Republic*. Whether they are meant to be thought of as still, in a sense, pleasures of our rational natures or are somehow linked also to a spirited part of our souls, Plutarch can nevertheless use them as part of his *a fortiori* argument: the Epicureans

---

[40] For example, contrast the distinction between the rational and non-rational soul at *De Adul.* 61D.

not only reject the best pleasures of the intellect; they even try to recommend a life which omits the pleasures which the majority of educated readers might take to be their most intellectual or stable objects of enjoyment. Not only do the Epicureans, in that case, fail to recognise the most pleasant life possible because they do not admit the pleasure of contemplation of perfect eternal object; they also recommend that we jettison the best pleasures that most of our lives currently contain.

There may even be another inconsistency in Epicurean theory since, as Plutarch notes at 1095C, Epicurus claimed in his work *Diaporiai* that a sage would be a 'lover of spectacle' (*philotheōros*) and enjoy more than anyone else the sounds and sights of Dionysian performances.[41] For a reader already alert to Platonic echoes, this will surely recall another famous passage from the *Republic* – the discussion with the 'lovers of sights and sounds' beginning at *Republic* 475d – and further consolidate the Platonic image of the empiricist Epicureans as falling far short of the correct standards of knowledge, true pleasure, and the good life. And this – albeit passing – reference is yet one more example of a motif we have seen emerging already: the charge of inconsistency is Plutarch's riposte to a hostile Epicurean reaction to Plato's *Republic*. There is some reason to think this part of *Republic* book 5 was in Epicurus' mind when rejecting the Platonic dissociation between philosophers and lovers of spectacle.[42] And, in any event, it is not implausible that Plutarch should make this connection since this passage in *Republic* book 5 has a number of close similarities with the discussion with the patients in *Republic* book 9, which, as we have seen, he most surely does have in mind. Structurally, both involve a twofold discussion: Socrates and Glaucon agree independently on the basis of some previously agreed premises – themselves involving reference to what we can recognise as 'Forms' – what the true nature of pleasure and knowledge is; they also undertake a dialectical discussion with an opponent attempting to show the same conclusion but on the basis of commonly held, non-proprietorial assumptions. Further, in both passages, the reader is alerted to the mistake made by these opponents by the comment that they are 'sick' or somehow hold unhealthy opinions (584e7, cf. 476e2). Finally, it is just the objects that are of prime interest to the lovers of sights-and-sounds which are revealed in *Republic* book 9 as the sources of imitation or false

---

[41] Cf. DL 10.120.
[42] Cf. Asmis 1995, 18–21, who argues that this is part of Epicurus' general reaction to Platonic concerns about poetry. He and Plato agree that the content of poetry is often to be criticised. But he and Plato differ sharply about the proper nature of the philosophy which ought to take the place of traditional education. For more on the Epicureans' attitude to the arts see Blank 2009.

pleasures – unstable objects enjoyed by the unstable and impermanent body – while the objects of knowledge are the sources of true and genuine pleasures of the soul. Whether or not Plato intended such a close link to be drawn between these two sets of characters, it is clear that they are in various ways analogous in the content and reasons for the false beliefs they uncover. It is also not at all implausible for a reader of the *Republic* such as Plutarch to reach for both passages in an attack on a school of empiricists and hedonists such as the Epicureans.[43]

It certainly suits Plutarch's anti-Epicurean polemical purposes to be able to draw on Socrates' characterisation – at various points of the *Republic* – of the kinds of people who are overly impressed by and fixated on what they can experience and enjoy through sense perception: the empiricist Epicureans, who famously insisted that 'all perceptions are true', can hardly announce that they are unconcerned with the perceptible world. But, according to Socrates and Plutarch, an unfortunate consequence of this concentration on the perceptible and physical world is that it prevents access to what is truly and properly pleasant for humans. Epicureans therefore cannot live a pleasant life since, in failing to recognise their true, rational human nature, they fail to recognise what is properly pleasant. And since they identify pleasure and the good, they cannot – even by their own standards – live a good life.

Conclusions

Plutarch reasserts many of the concerns and commitments about pleasure and human nature that Socrates elaborated in the *Republic*. He agrees that there are proper human pleasures associated with the proper exercise of the very best part of our nature: our rational souls. He appears, however, tempted to include among those pleasures the enjoyment of a wider range of intellectual activities than those of coming-to-know the Forms. He is no hedonist, of course, and therefore strongly resists what he sees as the dangerous Epicurean attempt to reduce human nature to mere animal desire-satisfaction and allow no room for the more valuable activities of learning, knowing, and contemplating. The disagreement between the

---

[43] Another possible connection is Plutarch's choice of wording at 1091F. He is expanding on the notion that the Epicureans restrict pleasure to mere absence of pain and connects this with the idea that Epicurean pleasure is somehow subhuman; they put joy into a tiny and closed pen where it is forced to twist and turn (ἐν ᾧ στρέφεται καὶ κυλινδεῖται). Although this verb is not uncommon in Plutarch, this is the only time he uses this form. Perhaps it is meant as an allusion to the nature of the 'many beautiful things' at Plat. *Rep.* 479d4.

Platonists and Epicureans is therefore not just a disagreement over whether pleasure is the *telos*. It is, perhaps more importantly, a disagreement over some fundamental claims about human nature. The place and role in our human lives of rational activities is a central bone of contention in that more fundamental disagreement, and both sides, in their approach to their opponents' views, are guilty of exaggerating and distorting the other's position for polemical effect. The Epicureans' approach to the role of reason in securing and maintaining the good and pleasant life is certainly more nuanced than Plutarch will allow. And I shall return to consider their account in more detail in Chapter 8 below.

CHAPTER 5

Measuring future pleasures in Plato's
Protagoras and Philebus

Towards the end of Plato's *Protagoras*, Socrates and Protagoras discuss our ability to choose between possible courses of action or possible objects of pursuit by comparing respective levels of pleasantness and painfulness. Socrates outlines a means by which someone can ensure that he makes the right decision by having an accurate measure of the pleasantness and painfulness of the various options available and then comparing them appropriately. Socrates promises that this is a means by which we might maximise our pleasures and minimise our pains through the use of our rational capacities.

This is another way in which our ability to think is related to our ability to experience pleasure and pain and, moreover, to our general preference for pleasure over pain. Of course, in this case our ability to reason, measure, and compare is first of all a means by which we can ensure that our lives overall are as pleasant as possible and the pleasures involved might be pleasures of any kind. Although they might include pleasures from learning, thinking, and the like, they can also include pleasures of eating, drinking, competition, and so on. Some of this material will be relatively familiar but it is worth our while to set out in some detail Socrates' proposal and the various assumptions on which it must depend since in doing so we have a clear model against which we can compare other similar discussions of the procedure of prudential reasoning and of anticipating future pleasures and pains. Considering in detail this section of the *Protagoras* and the various questions that Socrates' proposals provoke will provide a helpful background to the discussion in each of the subsequent chapters.

First, the *Protagoras* suggests one way in which human reasoning and the consideration of future experiences might be subject to misleading appearances and mistaken anticipations of future experiences. Our opinions about the pleasantness and painfulness of an object of pursuit might be false because the objects appear to be more or less pleasant or painful than they really are. Second, it shows how correct reasoning and evaluation of future experiences can be a means of maximising the pleasure and minimising the pain in a life taken as a whole. Similar recommendations for accurate and reliable prudential reasoning also appear in Epicureanism. Third, the *Philebus* builds on these two thoughts to consider the way in which such planning and anticipation might also be a source of pleasure and how this pleasure itself might also be subject to misleading appearances and evaluated accordingly. According to Socrates in the *Philebus*, we anticipate pleasures in order to consider and choose between courses of action, and our anticipation of future pleasure and our present evaluation of different possible future pleasures might also be pleasant or painful. Therefore, the activity of reason in the service of prudential planning can itself have important and interesting affective aspects. What is more, those affective aspects can in turn influence – or distort – our capacities for prudential planning and our comparative evaluations of future pleasures and pains.

Finally, by considering the discussion in the *Protagoras* we begin to consider how the manner in which an agent looks forwards and backwards through his or her own life reveals important – and often morally significant – things about the agent's character: its consistency, predictability, and stability. In Chapter 6 I argue that this connection between anticipation and character is a central aspect of the account of the false pleasures of anticipation at *Phileb.* 40a. In Chapter 7 I show how Aristotle uses notions of regret, and recollection and anticipation of pleasure as markers of a person's moral character. The *Protagoras*' interest in prudential hedonic reasoning and the importance of the character and consistency of the agent concerned are also both echoed in the philosophy of the Hellenistic period; those echoes are the topic of Chapter 8.

Weighing and measuring

There are many puzzling aspects of the argument in Plato's *Protagoras* in which Socrates tries to persuade the famous sophist that all the virtues are somehow unified. Socrates attempts to persuade Protagoras of this view in a roundabout fashion, part of which involves what has now come to be known as a denial of *akrasia* ('incontinence' or 'weakness of will'). Socrates invites Protagoras to join him in objecting to a common view that it is possible for someone, thinking that one course of action open to him is better, nevertheless to choose an alternative course of action that is thought worse. The view held by 'the many' ascribes this failure to the intervention of some kind of passion or to the enticement of pleasure. Socrates focusses our attention on the idea of pleasure as the cause of this phenomenon and proceeds, with Protagoras in support, to argue instead that if there is any failing in such cases then it must in fact be a failure of some kind of rational calculation and evaluation. And since it is a kind of rational failure then it can be remedied with some appropriate rational education. Here, Socrates proposes that there is in fact a 'skill of measurement' – a *tekhnē metrētikē* – which, once acquired, will prevent such errors and remove the possibility of the phenomenon that is commonly thought of as *akrasia* but which has now been revealed to be an intellectual mistake. Socrates' account makes significant use of a rational power of correct estimation and comparison, to be contrasted with a simple acceptance of 'appearances', and it is this rational procedure that promises to result in the recommendation of choices that will lead to a better life overall, where a better life is at least for the moment understood to be a life that is more pleasant and less painful.[1]

Socrates offers two distinct analogies in his general description of the kind of procedure that he envisages. The first analogy concerns the weighing of pleasures against pleasures, pains against pains, and pleasures against pains. The second analogy concerns the proper estimation of size, taking into account problems of perspective caused by different distances from the person carrying out the estimation. The weighing analogy addresses the question of how to recommend one of a set of possible courses of action both in terms of deciding whether, for a given course of action, the agent will experience more pleasure than pain overall and, for pairs of courses of action, which of the pair will produce more pleasure or which of the pair will produce less pain.[2] The measuring analogy, on the other hand, addresses the question of how to assess the value of a given course of action and its consequences accurately and without the distorting effects of, for example, relative temporal proximity.[3] It will be necessary for the agent first to measure up the various options and then to weigh them against one another. But Socrates begins at 356a5 by outlining the weighing procedure,

---

[1] This brief summary skates over a number of important interpretative controversies. For an introduction to some of the important issues and recent scholarship see Russell 2005, 239–48, and Evans 2010.

[2] Given a presumption of some form of psychological hedonism, the agent must choose the course of action that appears more pleasant (hence the occurrence of words connoting obligation: *prakteon* 356b8–c1). Cf. Moss 2006, 506.

[3] Richardson 1990, 32, emphasises how the measuring art by itself will provide accurate accounts of value rather than choices between options: 'The science of measurement in the Protagoras plays the fact checker's role of assuring a precise estimation of consequences, not the decision theorist's role of presenting a precise criterion of choice.'

perhaps because he can in this way familiarise us with the notion of the commensurability of pleasures and pains that his model requires, before moving on to the measuring procedure which will be the principal element in his insistence on the power of reason over the potentially disruptive power of mere appearances.

The principal aim of the art of measurement is to produce an accurate account of something's size or value which is not distorted by factors that are irrelevant. The example offered of such an irrelevant factor is the physical proximity of an object. This might give a misleading impression of a given object's size: distant objects appear smaller than they really are. And this might lead someone to think mistakenly that a nearer but in fact smaller object is larger than a more distant but in fact larger object. Proper measurement will counteract this misleading appearance. This phenomenon caused by physical proximity is then taken to be an analogue for a similar phenomenon caused by temporal proximity in the case of the estimation of the value of some potential object of pursuit: things further in the future sometimes appear less valuable than they really are when compared with things in the nearer future. But Socrates also talks as if the measuring art itself involves a degree of comparison between different objects, and this comparative aspect of the measuring seems to usurp the principal point of the weighing analogy. So he talks of the art itself – the 'salvation of life' – showing whether something is larger than, smaller than, or equal to something else (357a5–b3), whereas this comparative conclusion must be the result of the measuring art being trained on more than one object and then the results being subjected to a comparative assessment. Of course, it is easy to see why this comparative procedure might naturally be assimilated to the measurement. After all, the measurement itself might be of a comparative kind, as it is when we measure a quantity in terms of multiples of an agreed standard unit amount of that quantity.[4]

At *Prot.* 356a8–c1 Socrates uses the metaphor of weighing to describe how we make choices between different possible courses of action on the basis of the pleasure or pain involved in each. The courses of action being weighed

---

[4] It is certainly true that it is hard to think of a method that would provide some kind of quantitative precision in measurement of the pleasure or pain of a given object. (What would the relevant quantity be? Cf. Taylor, 1991, 197: 'There can be no numerically specifiable unit of measurement of pleasures and pains, since the ability to describe an object in quantitatively precise terms implies that the description is inter-subjectively true.') And it is therefore more plausible to think in terms of relative assessments, perhaps nevertheless using some agreed reference example against which other pleasures and pains may be compared. But for an example of such a system see Hall 1966–7.

against one another will each often include both pleasures and pains. The ways in which pleasures and pains may vary are:

355d8–e1:   larger/smaller and more/fewer (μείζω/σμικρότερα πλείω/ ἐλάττω)

356a3–5:   larger/smaller, more/fewer, and more/less (μείζω/σμικρότερα, πλείω/ἐλάττω, μᾶλλον/ἧττον)

The precise meaning of each pair of opposing variables and how each pair relates to the others is not spelled out in full but it is not difficult to imagine that we are faced with choices between pleasures and pains that vary according to duration, frequency, intensity, and perhaps also extent (how much of a person is pleased or pained). There is no reason to think that Socrates here is pointing to the incommensurability of pleasures and pains, particularly since the remainder of his theory seems to commit him to their commensurability.[5] There is no room here for pleasures and pains differing in value according to their proximity or their certainty. These two – proximity/remoteness and certainty/uncertainty – are related to one another; generally speaking, the more remote a good the less certain an agent can be of attaining it. And there have been versions of a hedonistic calculus that include one or both of these variables in the criteria for assessing the value of a pleasure or a pain.[6] Socrates omits them both and instead asserts a form of temporal neutrality. The temporal position of a good or bad is irrelevant to its value.

---

[5] Nussbaum 1986, 89–121, for example, takes Socrates to be assuming commensurability. Richardson 1990 argues that Socrates' position does not assume commensurability (although it is compatible with it) (25): 'The disjunctions vary, and sometimes Socrates pairs a positive element from one disjunct with the negative one of another. This disarray is slightly easier to understand on the hypothesis that he was trying to allow for the complexity of incommensurably different types of pleasure than it would be on the supposition that he had in mind a precise model of maximising homogeneous pleasures.' Richardson then claims (21) that if two pleasures compared are indeed incommensurable, the preference for one rather than another cannot be a case of *akrasia* 'since there is no unique answer' and therefore does not endanger Socrates' thesis.

[6] Jeremy Bentham, *An Introduction to the Principles of Morals and Legislation* (1789), chapter IV: 'Value of a lot of pleasure or pain, how to be measured', lists various characteristics used to assess the pleasure experienced, considered 'by itself': intensity, duration, certainty or uncertainty, and propinquity or remoteness (IV.II). (In the case of multiple subjects these four are supplemented by an additional factor: extent.) On this account a more distant pleasure is less valuable than a less distant pleasure, and a more certain pleasure is more valuable than a less certain pleasure. Sidgwick 1907, 124 n. 1 (cf. 381), allows that intensity and duration are relevant factors for assessing pleasures but rejects Bentham's factor of 'proximity': '[P]roximity is a property which it is reasonable to disregard except in so far as it diminishes uncertainty. For my feelings a year hence should be just as important to me as my feelings next minute, if only I can make an equally sure forecast of them. Indeed this equal and impartial concern for all parts of one's conscious life is perhaps the most important element in the common notion of the *rational* – as opposed to the merely *impulsive* – pursuit of pleasure.'

Having assessed the relevant pleasures and pains according to these criteria the various possible courses of action are then evaluated comparatively. Socrates mentions three tests and gives a recommendation for each based on the outcome.

Test 1. Weigh pleasures against pleasures (356b3–4).

Here, the right thing to do is to choose the option with the most pleasures.

Test 2. Weigh pains against pains (356b4–5).

Here, the right thing to do is to choose the option with the fewest pains.

Test 3. Weigh pleasures against pains (356b5–c1).

Here, the right thing to do is explained in two conditional claims: for a given course of action (*praxis*), if pleasures outweigh pains then choose this course; if pains outweigh pleasures then do not choose this course.

The question settled by Test 3 is different from the questions addressed in Test 1 and Test 2. The first two Tests are concerned with ranking options, all of which are apparently being considered as possible courses of action. In Test 3, however, it is being decided whether a course of action should be taken or not. Many courses of action will pass Test 3; it judges only whether we would be better off doing a given action than not doing it.

Consider someone who is a maximising hedonist. He is trying to choose the best course of action available to him. He first gathers up the pleasures and pains for a particular action and weighs the pleasures against the pains. (He submits a proposed course of action to Test 3.) Let us imagine that the pleasures win out. That course of action is therefore given a preliminary recommendation. He will perhaps also consider other courses of action and retain all and only those for which their respective pleasures outweigh their pains and for which he therefore has a similar preliminary recommendation. But now what does he do? He needs to rank the options in order to choose the one in which there is the greatest preponderance of pleasure over pain since he is a maximiser. But the procedures in Test 1 and Test 2 will not individually allow him to settle this question. Imagine that two courses of action are being considered: A and B. Both A and B have both pleasures and pains associated with them. For both A and B, moreover, it is the case that the pleasures outweigh the pains (so both pass the Test 3). But how will the good-maximiser choose between A and B? For example, course of action A may have more pleasure associated with it than course of action B (A will beat B in

Test I) but course of action A may also have more pains associated with it than course of action B (A will lose to B in Test 2). The procedure will be unable to adjudicate between such cases since Test I and Test 2 register only the fact of one set of pleasures being greater than another or one set of pains being greater than another.[7] Similarly, we can imagine a range of options in which the choice with the greatest net result of pleasure minus pain is neither the choice with the most pleasure (since at least one other choice involves more pleasure but also more pain) nor the choice with the least pain (since at least one other choice involves less pain but also less pleasure).

This interesting omission comes about because the analogy of weighing used throughout is one in which we use a pair of scales to determine which, if either, quantity is the larger.[8] The procedure will not tell us with any degree of accuracy by how much the quantity in one pan is greater than that in the other pan. True, if one outweighs the other by only a very small amount then perhaps we would see its pan descend rather slowly, but for any significant discrepancies between the two amounts the larger quantity will cause its side of the scales to sink immediately. Furthermore, both pleasures and pains are being considered, as it were, to have positive weight. This should be contrasted with a view in which pleasures and pains are thought to be in some sense opposed in the manner of positive and negative amounts of some common quantity or as, respectively, credits and debits in some kind of ledger. This is helpful for Socrates because it allows the procedure in Test 3: pleasures can be weighed directly against pains such that a larger quantity of pain will outweigh a smaller quantity of pleasure. But it prevents us from considering the 'net' weight of a given course of action as being the combination of the positive value of pleasures and the negative value of pains.

Imagine again two courses of action available to a given agent which are being evaluated in the manner outlined at *Prot.* 356a8–c1. Imagine also that course A will produce eight units of pleasure while course B will produce six. (So: A beats B in Test I.) And imagine that course A will produce six units of pain while B will produce five. (So: A loses to B in Test 2.) Nevertheless, both course A and course B will pass Test 3 since in both there is more pleasure than pain produced. The three tests outlined so far will not suffice to show which alternative course of action ought to be chosen. In order to generate the desired determinate action-guiding result, a new procedure is

---

[7] Richardson 1990, 18, argues: 'This passage suggests the possibility that each disjunct [i.e. larger and smaller / more and fewer] might operate separately, according to its own "scale". What would make this necessary besides the difficulty of incorporating temporal nearness and remoteness, would be the incommensurability of pleasures.' Cf. Russell 2000, 325.

[8] Cf. Rudebusch 1999, 89–91.

required. For example, we might imagine a fourth test in which the pleasures of course A are combined with the pains of course B in one pan of the scales and weighed against the pleasures of course B combined with the pains of course A in the other pan. The winning course of action is the one whose pleasures are in the lower pan.[9] But Socrates makes no explicit reference to any such additional test in the description here.

The procedure outlined at *Prot.* 356a8–c1, in that case, does not amount to a full recipe for pleasure-maximisation. The three tests will, if followed correctly, prevent someone from choosing to pursue a course of action that produces more pain than pleasure overall. And they will, if followed correctly, allow a person to rank as clearly as possible the available courses of action either in terms of the respective amounts of pleasure involved or in terms of the respective amounts of pain involved. But that is all. The three tests will not allow an agent to classify the available courses of action in terms of their overall net goodness, where net goodness is understood as a sum of pleasures minus pains. In short, the tests will be able to prevent gross errors but will not provide a reliable recipe for the overall maximisation of pleasure.

At this point Socrates changes the metaphor he uses from one of weighing pleasures and pains to one of measuring pleasures and pains. This will help him to imagine assigning values to pleasures and pains that will allow them to be ranked comparatively rather than merely tested to see which set of pleasures or which set of pains is the greater.

Measurement, illusion, and prudentialism

Socrates stresses that the art of measurement he has in mind is a means of correcting our estimation of future pleasures and pains. (Since he is concerned with such evaluations as the basis for choices and actions, he is unconcerned with our estimation of past pleasures and pains.) Here he draws the analogy between our thinking of pleasures and pains and our perception of sizes of items that are at different distances away. Things further away may mistakenly be thought to be smaller than they really are and often smaller than things that are closer but in fact smaller.[10]

---

[9] Since if $Pleasure^A + Pain^B > Pleasure^B + Pain^A$, then $Pleasure^A + Pain^B - Pain^A > Pleasure^B$, and $Pleasure^A - Pain^A > Pleasure^B - Pain^B$. Denyer 2008 notes the need for such a procedure in his commentary *ad* 356b1.

[10] Socrates makes an analogous claim about sounds (356c6–8) and also thicknesses and pluralities (356c6–7). The last of these is a little puzzling. Presumably, the idea is that we underestimate the number of a group of things that are far away. If this is true, it must be because some of the distant things are just too far away to be seen at all or perhaps seen as distinct members of the collection. It seems equally possible that sometimes things are too close to count accurately.

Socrates argues that rather than being 'overcome by pleasure', when people act against their best interests and favour a present pleasure over a longer-term goal, they are committing a cognitive error. This error is then diagnosed as caused by the 'bias towards the near'. Consider the diagram below (after Parfit 1984, 159), which tracks the varying strength of an agent's desires for two goods over time. One good is greater but later than the other. Assume that obtaining the lesser good precludes the agent from going on to obtain the greater good. Also, assume that the two goods are both certainly attainable.

For the majority of the time, the agent has a greater desire for the greater than the lesser good (see Figure 1). This is a rational preference based on the relative values of those goods. However, the fact that the lesser good is obtainable earlier than the greater good affects this preference as time progresses. As the object of desire approaches so the concern for that object increases. This indicates the 'bias towards the near' described by Plato (although it does not demonstrate that such a bias is irrational). There is a point at which the two lines cross. This occurs at the moment when the desire for the lesser good equals that for the greater good. When the two lines diverge again, the preference changes. Now for the first time the lesser good is preferred to the greater. This preference remains until such a time as the earlier good is past and then the agent reverts to a desire for the greater good which, since it is indeed for a greater good, eventually becomes greater than the desire for the lesser good ever was. Since we stipulated that the two goods are mutually exclusive, any agent who obtained the lesser good will now regret doing so since this has prevented him from obtaining the greater good which he now desires more.

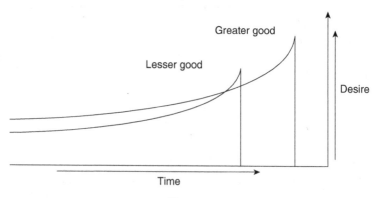

Figure 1

Socrates argues that this change of preference is irrational. The only proper criterion of choice is the greater versus the lesser good and the relative temporal distance of the goods and bads in question is irrelevant.[11] Moreover, if the agent is adversely affected by an irrational bias to the near and acts on the new preference for the lesser good he will do himself harm by preventing himself from going on to obtain the greater good at a later time. Socrates argues that rather than such changes in preference being caused by some sort of *pathos*, specifically 'being overcome by pleasure', the preference of a closer but lesser good over a more remote but greater good is produced by an error of calculation caused by a kind of illusion.[12] Were the agent in possession of a true account of the relative values of the relevant goods then it would be impossible to prefer the lesser over the greater good.

The 'power of appearance' that misleads the agent and prevents him from seeing the true relative values of the objects of choice might be described in various ways. Most commonly the relevant factors are expressed as psychological biases and there are various different such biases:[13]

Bias towards the future (F-bias):	a future good is overvalued in comparison with an equal past good.
Bias towards the perceived (P-bias):	a good that is perceived is overvalued in comparison with an equal but unperceived good.
Bias towards the near (N-bias):	a good that is nearer (temporally or spatially) is overvalued in comparison with an equal but more remote good.

Since Socrates is considering only rankings between future goods, F-bias is not directly relevant here. It is relevant, however, in discussions of more general forms of temporal neutrality. Socrates does not distinguish between P-bias and N-bias, perhaps because he accounts for temporal N-bias in terms of a perceptual illusion. The two are nevertheless distinct: I might conceive a greater desire for the cake I can see at the opposite end of the room than for the similar cake hidden from view in the cupboard nearby.

---

[11] Parfit 1984, 164: 'A mere difference in when something happens is not a difference in its quality. The fact that a pain is further in the future will not make it, when it comes, any less painful.' Cf. Taylor 1991, 188: 'Rational calculation of one's own interests requires that one abstract oneself from one's present situation in space and time and give equal weight to one's desires, feelings etc. at future times.'

[12] Parfit 1984, 161.

[13] For these distinctions and a detailed discussion of which if any can be justified see Persson 2005, 195–234. These biases can be combined: it is possible to be biased towards goods in the near future (NF-bias).

Socrates proposes an art of measurement that will counteract these various biases. A measurement of the values of the available goods will provide a sound basis for choice. Having emphasised how the appearance of relative value might be misleading, Socrates does not make clear, however, just how things appear once an unbiased measurement has been obtained. Most likely, the appearance will persist: I know that the old Cavendish laboratory is taller than St Bene't's church but still the church appears to be larger from where I sit looking out of my window. Reason and measurement do not dispel the appearance but they can make the appearance powerless (*akuron*, 356d8). They do this by revealing the truth (356d8–e2).[14] Socrates insists that this persisting appearance will not generate any problems that might lead the agent back into choosing a lesser good over a greater good. The knowledge provided by the measuring and weighing will win out and will continue to win out. The agent no longer desires what merely appears to be the greater because this appearance has been rendered impotent by the knowledge that something else is in fact the greater good. Socrates accepts that we will desire whatever we think provides the greater pleasure but adds the claim that knowledge will trump appearance in persuading us which pleasure is greater. In that case, desire will follow knowledge even if the knowledge is inconsistent with mere appearance. Only in the absence of knowledge will desire and choice follow mere appearance.[15]

Socrates' recommended procedure requires the agent to be able accurately to assess the size of different future pleasures, regardless of their relative distances from the present. Leaving aside the worry that the future in general may not be sufficiently predictable, it also faces the difficulty that the agent's own future preferences in particular may not be sufficiently predictable. For, in order to assess correctly the future pleasures and pains

---

[14] Note how Socrates insists that the soul will stick to the truth once it has been revealed. Cf. Rudebusch 1999, 87–8.

[15] Moss 2006, 510, raises concerns over Socrates' confident optimism: 'Reasoning can make optical illusions "lose their power" over a person's judgment, but not over her vision: her eyes will see the nearer object as larger even when she knows that it is not. If desires for pleasure are really analogous to perception, then we should expect that reasoning can make pleasure-illusions lose their power over a person's judgment, but not over her desires for pleasure: she will still desire the nearer object even when she knows that she should not.' Compare Sidgwick's similar lack of optimism (1907, 141). Indeed, Sidgwick enlists Plato himself in support of his objections: '[our habitual comparison of pleasures and pains] is liable to illusion, of which we can never measure the precise amount, while we are continually forced to recognise its existence. This illusion was even urged by Plato as a ground for distrusting the apparent affirmation of consciousness in respect of present pleasure. Plato thought that the apparent intensity of the coarser bodily pleasures was illusory; because these states of consciousness, being preceded by pain, were really only states of relief from pain, and so properly neutral, neither pleasant nor painful – examples of what I have called the hedonistic zero – only appearing pleasant from contrast with the preceding pain.' (He probably has in mind the discussion beginning at *Phileb.* 43c.)

the agent must be able to predict what will and will not bring him pleasure in the future, including even the remote future. It would be absurd to think that an agent should now give equal weight to desires he once had but no longer possesses. So it is likely that, in the future, at least some of the desires he possesses now will in retrospect be viewed in a similar fashion. Just as his past desires may be incompatible with his present desires, an agent's future desires might be wholly incompatible with his present desires. In that case how can an agent consider future pleasures and pains and produce a maximising strategy?[16] We know that our preferences will change over time but we are not able with any confidence to predict just what our future preferences will be. But without any guide to what one's future preferences will be, it is impossible to form any assessment of possible future pleasures and pains to allow the comparison of different possible courses of action.[17]

Some attempts to deal with these difficulties involve the demarcation of different stages of a life. We should be temporally neutral within each stage but we need not be neutral between stages. For example, a person's life can be viewed as falling into a number of different 'life stages', for example: childhood, adolescence, adulthood, old age. Each of these stages has a set of appropriate desires and aspirations and prudential reasoning should function in the way suggested by the notion of temporal irrelevance only within each stage.[18] However, the division into life stages may look arbitrary and is always susceptible to further division.[19] Also, the insulation between life

---

[16] Cf. Parfit 1984, 149–58. There he canvasses various alternative models. Suppose I think that as I grow older I become wiser. Then I should have good reasons for preferring desires in the further future to those in the present or nearer future. Alternatively I might decide that as I age I lose touch with the proper ideals which I held as a youth. Then as an old man I should have reasons for preferring my past desires over my present and more recent desires. For another reaction to such worries see Williams 1976, 205–7, who discusses these questions against the background of Parfit's own treatment of personal identity. William concludes that (206): 'If it is indeed true that this man will change in these ways, it is only by understanding his present projects *as the projects of one who will so change* that he can understand them even as his present projects . . .' Empirical research suggests that most people are unable to give proper weight to the fact that their preferences will change since, no matter what their current age, people tend to think that they will change less in the next n years than they think they have changed in the past n years. See: Quoidback, Gilbert, and Wilson 2013.

[17] Nagel 1970, 39–40, argues that such problems are endemic in any system which makes it a necessary condition of acting to further future interests that the agent should have a present desire to foster those same future interests. Indeed, Nagel's objections are against any analysis of prudential reasoning which makes such thought processes dependent on a 'prudential desire'. Cf. Cockburn 1997, especially 21–34.

[18] See Slote 1983. He is criticised by Vorobej 1987, 407–23.

[19] At the limit this will collapse into a form of aprudentialism, which holds that it is rational to pursue only present pleasure. For an outline of aprudentialism see Trebilcot 1974, who also tries to answer some of Nagel's worries about whether an aprudentialist can retain a conception of himself as a single, persistent individual. Cf. Cockburn 1997, 192–202.

stages makes it less easy to see how they can be knitted together to form a single and continuous life. Some psychological continuity must surely be reintroduced between any adjacent temporal sections of a life, and as a result the desired 'insulation' is once again breached.[20]

The salvation of life

Before we move on to the *Philebus*, we should pause to notice that in the *Protagoras* Socrates more than once refers to this art – perhaps to the combined exercise of both measuring the correct value of a given pleasure or pain and weighing it against alternatives – as the 'salvation of life': *sōtēria tou biou* (356d3, 356e2, 356e8–357a2). What does this mean? Consider two possible roles that Socrates' weighing and measuring might be held to play in one's life. On one view, the procedure is intended to be applied constantly and in a thoroughgoing manner to all decisions; at each and every moment of choice we should properly measure and then weigh up the possible outcomes in terms of pleasure and pain. Call this the Measure Every Choice (MEC) view of the Socratic *tekhnē*. In so far as the measuring art here ought to be closely associated – if not simply identified – with virtue itself, this is an argument in favour of MEC. We would expect a virtuous agent to be behaving virtuously continuously and thoroughly.[21]

Alternatively, we might imagine that the skill is invoked only at certain points of one's life or for certain decisions. For the most part we are able to make do without invoking the full procedure of measuring and weighing. But on other occasions we will need to use it if we are not to make an error and suffer some damage to our wellbeing as a consequence. Call this the Measure Only Some Choices view (MSC). Think again of the analogy Socrates draws with comparing sizes of objects located at different distances away. Often, there is no need to expend any effort in deciding that the church tower over in the next village, for example, is in fact taller than the pencil I am holding up as I try to sketch it. Even though there is a sense in which the pencil appears larger, I am never in any doubt about the true comparative sizes of the two. But we can imagine harder cases than this. Is the church tower in the next village taller than the church tower just along

---

[21] Such a view invites its own concerns. The calculation, for example, is itself likely to be of some hedonic cost in so far as it requires time and effort and, even if it is not itself a painful activity, precludes the performance of some other potentially more pleasant activity. Indeed, perhaps the procedure is sufficiently demanding that it will be better overall in hedonic terms sometimes not to engage in it and instead to make a choice based on much less accurate consideration.

the road here? I cannot tell for sure and I realise that the appearance might not be a reliable guide. I need to do some measuring and comparison of those measurements to come up with a sound answer. If the *tekhnē* plays a role such as this, namely as a 'saviour of life' in testing circumstances or in circumstances in which there is a *prima facie* difficulty, then we need not imagine even the virtuous person always using the art for every choice that is made. Rather, for the majority of the time there is no need to engage the art since there is no hard choice to be made. Most choices are sufficiently obvious so as not to mislead even the most unreflective person or, perhaps, the agent is sufficiently experienced in similar situations to recognise the right answer even when others might be misled.

As an illustration of this last point we might consider the Müller-Lyer illusion that is sometimes discussed in relation to Socrates' proposal. It is sometimes noted that the two lines in the illusion still appear to the perceiver to be of different lengths even once that perceiver has measured them and knows that they are equal. But having seen and measured and recognised the truth, that perceiver is able to recognise similar situations in the future and, if presented with the same illusion again, will not need to measure the two lines to avoid being misled by the appearance. MSC is therefore both less and more demanding of the agent than MEC. It is less demanding in that it allows that for many choices no measurement will be needed at all. It is more demanding in that it requires the agent to have built up a set of experiences which allow him or her to forgo the need for measurement in all but the more difficult cases. MSC imagines a two-stage procedure. A given choice will first be compared with past experiences and only if these are not enough to determine what we need to do to maximise the overall good will it be necessary to deploy the *tekhnē*. So it envisages an important role for knowledgeable experience in addition to the art since experience will determine many choices and the art will be needed only for cases which experience cannot settle.

It is hard to determine whether MEC or MSC is the dominant view.[22] Socrates and Protagoras are initially interested in ruling out cases of what we might term significant error: cases which the many are tempted to call 'being overcome by pleasure' or 'being overcome by anger' and in which it seems that the agent acts in such a way as significantly to compromise his

---

[22] A quick glance at the use of the term *sōtēria* elsewhere does not settle the matter. In tragedy *sōtēria* is often something wished for; it is simple survival in the face of a particular threat (e.g. Eur. *Or.* 778, 1173). A similar use can be found in Thucydides (e.g. Thuc. 1.65.3, 3.20.4). A broader meaning of 'preservation (*sc.* of one's current good state)' can be found elsewhere, including elsewhere in Plato (e.g. *Laws* 960d1–4).

overall wellbeing. The cases are not those in which an agent merely falls just short of maximising pleasure. On the other hand, it seems that, once acquired, this art of measurement could be applied as and when the agent thinks fit and, as Socrates comments, if our wellbeing did depend on counting correctly then this art would indeed determine the goodness of our lives (357a5–b3).

Commentators have wondered whether the measuring skill is suggested to Protagoras in part because it allows Socrates cheekily to allude to the sophist's most famous pronouncement that 'man is the measure'.[23] But Socrates' use of the term coupled with the description of its being the 'salvation of life' is also an allusion to another Protagorean idea. As part of his great speech earlier in the dialogue, Protagoras told a story of how Epimetheus set about arranging a division of powers between the various new species of living creatures.

1. 320e3: To some animals he gave claws or horns and to others he gave some other means for their *sōtēria*.
2. 321b6: Those species that were preyed upon by others he made more numerous for the *sōtēria* of the species.

And mankind too received some assistance. Prometheus saw that they were struggling to survive and stole gifts for them from Hephaestus and Athene.

3. 321c7ff.: Seeing that they had been left without any other means of *sōtēria*, Prometheus gave to mankind fire and technical wisdom (*entekhnos sophia*). This is later referred to as 'wisdom concerning life' (*peri ton bion sophia* 321d4) and distinguished from the political skill which Zeus grants to humans, again because otherwise humans seemed doomed to extinction (322c1–3).

Here, *sōtēria* seems also to mean survival or preservation and sometimes it means the survival of the species rather than the survival of any given member of the species. Some animals have claws in order not to starve; other animals are numerous so that the species does not become extinct through predation. Humans were able to survive despite their lack of physical defences against predation and the elements thanks to intellectual abilities and skills. And yet, even with these gifts human life was precarious. Humans were able to cultivate crops but were as yet ill-equipped to ward off wild beasts (322b1–6). Seeing the danger that humans might still be wiped out, Zeus sent Hermes to distribute to all humans a form of political skill – part of which is the skill to make war, which is necessary to ward off wild animals (322b5) – and the means to organise themselves into cities,

---

[23] E.g. Denyer 2008, 192; cf. Rowett 2013.

form friendships, and the like. It is possible, in that case, that a full account of the *sōtēria tou biou* as illustrated in this mythological narrative would include not only the skills brought by Prometheus that allow humans to cultivate the land, make clothes, and so on, but also the political skills granted by Zeus that allow humans to form societies and cities.[24]

The possession of sharp teeth does not allow each and every lion to live the best leonine life possible. Rather, the teeth prevent the lion from starving to death or, perhaps, the teeth that lions have ensure that lions as a species do not become extinct. A similar case might be made for the *sōtēria tou biou* which humans receive as the gifts of first Prometheus and then Zeus. One might say that for humans these technical abilities and political associations are necessary means for the preservation of a life or the preservation of the species and are therefore necessary conditions for a good life. But they are evidently not sufficient conditions for any given human living a good life and perhaps not even sufficient conditions for the survival of any particular human individual.

If that is the sense of *sōtēria* we should carry across to our reading of Socrates' weighing and measuring art then we should conclude that the measuring art is intended to prevent us from falling prey to our own ignorant or unthinking appraisal of goods; without the measuring art we could not possibly manage to live or perhaps would live only in a precarious fashion. The presentation of the role of the measuring art does indeed make it a means for avoiding a certain kind of peril, namely the errors which a reliance on the mere power of appearance might generate. Socrates, in that case, is cleverly turning the possibility of *akrasia* into a threat to our lives as pressing as the threat of hunger, cold, thirst, and the attentions of naturally much better-armed creatures.

Philebus 41e–42c

At *Phil.* 41e–42c Socrates returns to something like the problem addressed in the *Protagoras*. In both dialogues Socrates is interested in exploring ways in which people might be mistaken in the evaluation of future pleasures and pains. However, in the *Philebus* but not in the *Protagoras* Socrates wishes to classify the pleasure experienced by someone who is committing the error in question as a false pleasure. It is possible, Socrates contends, to be misled by appearances and experience a false pleasure in the act itself of making the comparative evaluation. This is a significant addition to the overall

---

[24] See also Nussbaum 1986, 100–6.

account of what goes on in such cases of deliberation: the *Protagoras* had nothing to say about the affective aspect of the comparative procedure itself but concentrated solely on the pleasures and pains of the various possible courses of action being compared. The *Philebus*, in contrast, is interested in the pleasures that are involved in the comparative evaluation and brings to bear a much more developed account of the psychology of desire and deliberation to shed light on the affective aspect of practical deliberation.[25]

The *Protagoras* makes no use of a distinction between true and false pleasures, instead treating all pleasures as classifiable relative to one another solely in terms of size or intensity. In the *Philebus* Socrates connects the difficulties involved in these comparative evaluations between pleasures and pains with the fact that pleasure and pain are both classified as belonging to 'the unlimited' (*to apeiron*): one of the four categories of things introduced earlier in the dialogue.[26] Just what that means is itself a disputed matter. For now, it suffices to note that this means that both pleasure and pain 'admit of the more and the less' (41b8–9) and therefore there can be relative comparisons between pleasures and between pains. The fact that pleasure and pain vary in this way is just what generates the problems of choosing between pleasures and between pains because, for example, one of a pair of pleasures might be more pleasant than the other (41e2–6). This prompts Socrates to reach once again for an analogy between evaluating the relative intensity of pleasures and evaluating the relative size of visual objects, and this in turn invites an analogy between relative distance in the case of the visual objects and relative temporal distance in the case of pleasures. Socrates explains:

ΣΩ. τί οὖν; ἐν μὲν ὄψει τὸ πόρρωθεν καὶ ἐγγύθεν ὁρᾶν τὰ μεγέθη τὴν ἀλήθειαν ἀφανίζει καὶ ψευδῆ ποιεῖ δοξάζειν, ἐν λύπαις δ' ἄρα καὶ ἡδοναῖς οὐκ ἔστι ταὐτὸν τοῦτο γιγνόμενον;

ΠΡΩ. πολὺ μὲν οὖν μᾶλλον, ὦ Σώκρατες.

ΣΩ. ἐναντίον δὴ τὸ νῦν τῷ σμικρὸν ἔμπροσθε γέγονεν.

ΠΡΩ. τὸ ποῖον λέγεις;

ΣΩ. τότε μὲν αἱ δόξαι ψευδεῖς τε καὶ ἀληθεῖς αὗται γιγνόμεναι τὰς λύπας τε καὶ ἡδονὰς ἅμα τοῦ παρ' αὐταῖς παθήματος ἀνεπίμπλασαν.

ΠΡΩ. ἀληθέστατα.

---

[25] Gosling and Taylor 1982, 444–8, argue that Plato fails to produce here a category of false pleasure distinct from the preceding false pleasures of anticipation. (For my discussion of that first category of false pleasure, see Chapter 6.) It seems to me that close attention to the experiences involved in comparative evaluation itself rather than to the simple fact that the pleasures and pains are in the future does provide a distinct category of false pleasures in this case.

[26] The account of 'the unlimited' is at 24a1–25a4. Pleasure and pain are assigned to this class at 27e2–28a4. Cf. Cooper 1999a.

ΣΩ. νῦν δέ γε αὐταὶ διὰ τὸ πόρρωθέν τε καὶ ἐγγύθεν ἑκάστοτε μεταβαλλόμεναι θεωρεῖσθαι, καὶ ἅμα τιθέμεναι παρ' ἀλλήλας, αἱ μὲν ἡδοναὶ παρὰ τὸ λυπηρὸν μείζους φαίνονται καὶ σφοδρότεραι, λῦπαι δ' αὖ διὰ τὸ παρ' ἡδονὰς τοὐναντίον ἐκείναις.

ΠΡΩ. ἀνάγκη γίγνεσθαι τὰ τοιαῦτα διὰ ταῦτα.

ΣΩ. οὐκοῦν ὅσῳ μείζους τῶν οὐσῶν ἑκάτεραι καὶ ἐλάττους φαίνονται, τοῦτο ἀποτεμόμενος ἑκατέρων τὸ φαινόμενον ἀλλ' οὐκ ὄν, οὔτε αὐτὸ ὀρθῶς φαινόμενον ἐρεῖς, οὐδ' αὖ ποτε τὸ ἐπὶ τούτῳ μέρος τῆς ἡδονῆς καὶ λύπης γιγνόμενον ὀρθόν τε καὶ ἀληθὲς τολμήσεις λέγειν.

ΠΡΩ. οὐ γὰρ οὖν. (*Phileb.* 41e9–42c4)

SOC.: Well, then. Is it the case that in viewing, seeing magnitudes from near and far off clouds the truth and makes us make false judgements, but in pleasures and pains the same phenomenon does not arise?

PROT.: No, Socrates, it happens more so.

SOC.: So that's the opposite result to what we said just now.

PROT.: What do you mean?

SOC.: Then it was true and false opinions that filled pleasures and pains straightaway with their own state.

PROT.: Very true.

SOC.: But now, because of the fact of being seen from nearby and then far away in turn and, at that same time, being set against one another, the pleasures appear greater and more intense when compared with pain, while the pains seem the opposite when compared with pleasures.

PROT.: Yes, it must be that that sort of thing happens for those reasons.

SOC.: So, to the extent that each of these appears greater and smaller than they really are, separating off this amount from each which is merely apparent and not real, you will not say that this appearance is correct, nor will you ever dare to say that this portion of the pleasure and pain that arises is correct and true.

PROT.: Not at all.

The differences between this passage and the *Protagoras* are best shown by carefully analysing the complex situation which Socrates outlines at *Phileb.* 42b2–6. First of all, we are asked to imagine comparisons between pleasures and pains. As a result of these comparisons, pains tend to look more moderate than they really are in comparison with pleasures and pleasures tend to look larger and more intense than they really are in comparison with pains (42b4–6). It is not made clear why the comparison should be between pleasures and pains and not, as in the *Protagoras*, between pleasures near at hand and those far away or between pains near at hand and those far away. Most likely, Socrates is interested in cases in which an agent is faced with a choice which involves a pair of pleasures and pains: perhaps a near-at-hand pleasure together with a consequent pain or a near-at-hand pain together with a consequent pleasure. The second point to remember is that Socrates is here interested not in how judgements might affect experiences of pleasure and pain but instead in how experiences of pleasure and pain are affected by differences of perspective and may lead to distorted judgements about their relative values.

The most important difference between the interests of the two dialogues is that the *Protagoras* is concerned with the correct evaluation of alternative courses of action in terms of the pleasure and pain involved and with offering a means to ensure that such evaluations are correct and free from the distorting effects of temporal perspective. The *Philebus*, by contrast, is interested in the correct experience of pleasure and pain and in discriminating between cases in which the pleasure itself is 'true' and those in which it is 'false'. Of course, there is a complicated relationship involved between the pleasure itself and some form of judgement and Socrates wishes to insist, notoriously, that we should say that the pleasure itself is true or false and not merely that some underlying judgement is true or false; the best accounts of his view insist that the pleasure itself has some kind of propositional content so it can have a truth value. But, however we understand the notion of 'true' and 'false' pleasures, we must remember that Socrates and Protarchus are here concerned with the possible distorting effects of relative temporal proximity because they are interested in deciding which pleasures might be candidates for inclusion in the mixture that will constitute the best human life. Socrates and Protarchus have already discarded the notion that the maximisation of pleasure and the minimisation of pain is the goal of all our choices.

In the *Protagoras* Socrates is interested in offering a means to gauge correctly which of two alternative courses of action will, overall, produce the greatest pleasure by avoiding the potentially distorting effects of the available pleasure of one course of action being closer in time than the other. What matters is that the agent is capable of determining accurately which of the alternatives is the better choice overall, since Socrates insists that the agent will always choose the option that he thinks is better overall, where 'better overall' is understood in terms of maximising pleasure and minimising pain. In the *Philebus*, by contrast, the problem is not how to determine which alternative is better and therefore to be pursued. Rather, Socrates is more interested in how perspectival distortions may adversely affect the present experience of pleasure or pain and, in turn, an agent's judgements about his current and likely future affective states. His attention is not directed towards mistaken evaluations of pleasures and pains because such mistakes lead to incorrect hedonic prudential choices and actions. Instead, he is interested in the affective aspect of the mistaken evaluations as such.

In the *Protagoras* 'the many' think that people sometimes make bad choices because of being overcome by pleasure, or anger, or love, or some such: our feelings and emotions can distort our decisions and choices. Socrates offers the alternative diagnosis that people make such choices because of a rational misevaluation of the relative values of the relevant available objects. At *Phileb.* 42a5–9, however, Socrates introduces this second kind of false pleasure by drawing a contrast with the first kind: the false pleasures of anticipation. In the case of false pleasures of anticipation, he says, true and false opinions filled up the pains and pleasures with their own condition. In the second case, by contrast, the false pleasure or pain somehow infects an opinion with its own condition.[27] The cause of the error is a certain kind of pleasure or pain which is then held responsible for a mistaken belief. In both the *Philebus* and the *Protagoras*, then, the ultimate cause of any error is an appearance of some sort. But in the *Philebus* the appearance causes a false pleasure, let us say, which is then responsible for a false belief and, in turn, this is responsible for an action.[28]

Lastly, it is also worth noting that just a few pages earlier in the *Philebus* Socrates has already been interested in the difficulties of making correct judgements based on viewing things from a distance. At 38c Socrates is trying to persuade Protarchus that just as there can be true and false judgements, there can also be true and false pleasures. Protarchus is understandably resistant to the idea and thinks instead that we should say that the judgement that gives rise to a pleasure is true or false. Socrates has insisted that the structure of taking pleasure in something is analogous to that of making a judgement about something; in both there is the act of taking pleasure or judging, there is the object of the pleasure or judgement, and there is the content of the pleasure or judgement: 'what is enjoyed or judged' (37a–38b).[29] Next Socrates asks us to think of judgements and pleasures as a kind of internal statement in the soul. He imagines someone looking at a figure in the distance and trying to work out what the figure is. The verb used is *krinein* (38c6): the person is trying to decide what the figure is or perhaps distinguish whether the figure is a human or a statue. He asks himself: 'Is that a human or a statue?' and must make a choice – a *krisis* – between the alternatives. If in company, the person might announce out

---

[27] Compare the interpretations of Delcomminette 2006, 406–7, and Gosling and Taylor 1982, 447–8.

[28] The account of this kind of false pleasure in the *Philebus* is therefore close to the interpretation of Aristotle's account of akratic action defended in Moss 2012a, 100–33, which emphasises the role played by illusory appearances of some object as pleasant and good.

[29] See Delcomminette 2003.

loud 'That's a human.' If alone, the person might say it silently to himself. In either case the person is making a judgement.

At 41e a similar situation is imagined: the problem at hand is again one of making a choice or discrimination (*krisis*, 41e2, 41e8). We should think of the situation as one in which the internal dialogue is provoked by a question: 'Is this pleasure greater or less than this pain?' or 'Is this pleasure greater or less than that pleasure?' (This is the counterpart of the question: 'Is that figure in the distance a human or a statue?' but the question is comparative because we are dealing with pleasures and pains and they belong to the class of the *apeiron*.)[30] A response to this question is given in the form of the internal statement which is the judgement the agent makes. Just as in the case of the identification of the figure, things are much harder if the object of the choice is further away. And, what is more, it is harder still to answer comparative questions about whether A or B is larger when A and B are at different distances away.

In his diagnosis of the problem that gives rise to this new class of false pleasures, Socrates describes two contributing factors (42b2–6). The first concerns the alternate viewing of pleasures and pains first at a distance and then close up. The second concerns the simultaneous viewing of pleasures and pains in comparison with one another. Somehow the combination of these two factors leads to the acceptance of a false appearance of a particular pleasure or pain as being greater and more intense or smaller and less intense than it really is. The thought is rather compressed and, unlike in the case of false pleasures of anticipation, Socrates does not give an example of a situation of the kind envisaged.

As an example of what Socrates might have in mind at *Phileb.* 41b, consider the following situation. John is about to leave a party when John's friend tries to persuade him to stay for another drink. John has to decide whether to stay or to head home now and he begins to wonder what to do. He thinks about the pleasure of another drink and the pain of a sore head. As Socrates has insisted, the anticipation of a pleasure or a pain can itself be pleasant or painful and John will experience such pleasures and pains as he considers his options, thinking now of the pleasure and now of the pain. His attention shifts from one to the other: from the pleasure of drinking now to the expected pain tomorrow and back again. The

---

[30] Cf. Delcomminette 2006, 400–1. Delcomminette goes on (401–12) to argue that in the remainder of the passage it is the nature of the pleasures and pains as *apeira* that causes the difficulties of misleading appearances and not their relative temporal distance from the present. It seems to me that both factors are significant.

anticipated pleasure of the drink is closer and the anticipated later pain of a sore head is more remote. Perhaps John is still thirsty and this desire also contributes to the way in which he pictures the alternative courses of action.

We can see in this example what Socrates means by pleasures and pains 'being seen first from nearby and then far away in turn': John thinks about the pleasure of the drink (nearby) and the pain of the next morning (further away) and turns his attention from one to the other. But he is also thinking of two things side by side, as it were, comparing side by side the pleasure of a drink and the pain of a sore head. John also experiences pleasure and pain in anticipating the future pleasure and pain. The result of this complicated series of comparative assessments of the two is that John 'over-enjoys' the prospect of another drink: he takes greater pleasure in it than it genuinely warrants. Perhaps he also is 'under-pained' by the prospect of the sore head tomorrow.[31]

We can explain why John over-enjoys the anticipated pleasure: he takes too great a pleasure in anticipating the nearby drink just because it is nearer at hand and the associated pain is further away. Perhaps this exaggerated pleasure then leads him to form the false belief that it would, all things considered, be better to stay. The extent to which the appearance is greater than the reality is the extent to which the pleasure is a false pleasure. As we should expect, given the detailed psychological picture that has been assembled in the dialogue up to this point, the situation involves a very close connection between John's experiences of pleasure and pain and John's beliefs about the relevant pleasures and pains he is experiencing or expects to experience. In John's case, the contrast and comparison between the near-at-hand pleasure and the more remote pain affects the present pleasure itself. The appearance of the nearer pleasure being more intense than it really is ensures that John takes more pleasure in considering it than it really merits and also forms a false belief about its value as a result.

Socrates' analysis could remain neutral about the relative effects of pleasure and pain in such situations. We can imagine cases in which someone is over-pained by anticipating a nearer over a more remote pain such that perhaps we would say that a false pain is being experienced. (Someone might mistakenly be so pained by the thought of a dental procedure that he

---

[31] This example requires some extrapolation from what we have in the text. In particular, it is not stated explicitly that the pleasure and pain being considered in these cases are to be linked as they are in John's case where the future pain is taken to be caused by the nearer pleasure. Nevertheless, this appears to be a reasonable addition and will make best sense of what Socrates has to say. Compare Frede 1992b, 447: on Esau: 'Driven by hunger . . . Esau was induced to overrate the worthwhileness of filling himself with a dish of lentils to the point where he thought the pleasure was worth the price of his primogeniture, that is, the future pain of its loss.' Also see Wolfsdorf 2013a, 84–7.

forms the false belief that a lesser pain awaits from neglecting one's dental health.) But Socrates claims that in a situation of this sort pleasures, when set alongside pains, tend to appear greater and more intense than they are and pains, when set beside pleasures, tend to appear 'the opposite' (42b4–6). This might be taken to mean that nearer pains tend to seem less intense than they are when set beside later pleasures. But this is not very plausible. More likely, by 'the opposite' Socrates means that pains appear more intense than they are, imagining that a more intense pain is the opposite of a more intense pleasure.[32] Perhaps we might agree that, carried away by the moment and the pleasures at hand, we enjoy the current experience more than it really warrants. But the same might be said for pains. We sometimes experience the closer pain more intensely than it really warrants just because it is nearer at hand. We sometimes fail to see accurately the later pleasure that will come from this present pain and experience the nearer pain more intensely in comparison. At the limiting case, we experience present pain more intensely just because it is present; it is what we are feeling now.[33]

Why the bias to the near? To secure assent to the existence of false pleasures, Socrates needs to claim only that perspectival distortions can adversely affect our evaluations, not that they affect them in a particular way. For example, it seems that I might well feel less pain than I otherwise would at some present or near-at-hand distress if I am bearing in mind some later pleasure that will be a consequence of the present or near-at-hand distress. If I bear in mind, as I struggle through sleeting rain on the journey home that I am undergoing my present discomfort in order to get home and dry off by the fire with a nice cup of tea, then the present discomfort may itself not feel as bad as it warrants. Present physical discomfort might be lessened if I have in mind throughout some later pleasure or relief that it will bring about. In these cases, therefore, either the present pleasure is overvalued or the present pain is undervalued, just as Socrates maintains. The relevant bias in these cases is not a bias to the nearer over the further future, but a bias towards the pleasant – whether in the nearer or further future – over the painful.

---

[32] This was pointed out to me by Mehmet Erginel. He suggests parallel passages at *Rep.* 586c1–2, 584a7–10, and 584e8–5a5.

[33] Cf. Gosling 1975, 219–20. Damascius comments at *In Phileb.* §187: 'Just as in sense perception the same things are seen larger when near and smaller when far away, so it is also with things pleasant and painful: what is present always appears greater than what is absent: pain greater than pain, pleasure than pleasure, pleasure than pain, and pain than pleasure' (trans. Westerink) (ὅτι ὡς ἐπὶ τῶν αἰσθητῶν τὰ μὲν ἐγγύθεν ὁρᾶται μείζω, τὰ δὲ πόρρωθεν ἐλάττω, τὰ αὐτὰ ὄντα, οὕτω καὶ ἐπὶ τῶν ἡδέων καὶ ἐπὶ τῶν λυπηρῶν· τὸ γὰρ παρὸν ἀεὶ μεῖζον εἶναι δοκεῖ τοῦ ἀπόντος, καὶ <λυπηρὸν> λυπηροῦ καὶ ἡδὺ ἡδέος καὶ ἡδὺ λυπηροῦ καὶ λυπηρὸν ἡδέος).

Elsewhere, Socrates considers cases in which present pain makes some-one overvalue the past or future mere absence of pain, sometimes to the extent that the absence of pain is thought to be the ideal state. One such case is that of the sick people at *Rep.* 583c–585a who, because of their current painful illness, are led to argue that there is no intermediate state between pleasure and pain: the absence of pain – their prior healthy state – now appears to be the greatest pleasure possible. This is an interesting case because the patients appear now to have a distorted and false evaluation of a prior state because of a present pain, although they are also no doubt looking ahead to a longed-for return to health.[34]

There is no particular reason why Socrates could not have considered a case in which a pleasure is false because it is undervalued as a result of a comparison with a later pain. Perhaps I fail to enjoy the last day of my summer holiday as much as is genuinely warranted because I am also thinking about my painful first day back at work.[35] This is a simple omission that could be easily remedied. But it does point to two interesting character-istics common in Plato's discussions of pleasures and pains. First, there is not much interest in cases in which something is enjoyed less than it should be. There seems to be a background assumption that we humans are prone to overestimating pleasures much more than we are to underestimating them. True, perhaps we tend not to think pleasurable at all some things that are in fact extremely pleasant. For example, people who are not philosophers simply cannot see the pleasures involved in the rational part of the soul grasping its proper intelligible objects. But there is relatively little interest in cases in which an agent takes pleasure in something, but to a lesser degree than it truly deserves. Second, there is an overwhelming concentration on pleasures rather than pains. There is no discussion in the *Philebus* of false pains, nor whether we should prefer our pains to be true or false.

Conclusions

Both the *Protagoras* and the *Philebus* are interested in the ways in which our human ability to think ahead and to consider our future experiences of

---

[34] For my account of this argument see Warren 2011b; cf. Wolfsdorf 2013b, esp. 111–19. Compare *Phileb.* 43c13–44a11, where Socrates considers the view that the absence of pain is itself a pleasure.

[35] And consider the possibility that a pleasure is false because it is undervalued as a result of a comparison with a later pleasure: I fail to enjoy my delicious starter as much as is genuinely warranted because I am thinking about the even more delicious main course. Compare also the Cyrenaics' practice of *praemeditatio mali*, discussed in Chapter 8 below. There, the idea is that focussing one's attention on a future pain will help to diminish its harm when it comes.

pleasure and pain may lead us into errors of various kinds. And they also note how this same ability can be harnessed and corrected to ensure that we make the best choices and live overall the best lives possible. They agree that considering future experiences is an activity prone to being misled by appearances and they explore the nature of the illusion both in terms of the adoption of a false belief that a worse course of action is preferable to a better course of action and also in terms of the experience of a false pleasure in the overenjoyment of a chosen course of action.

In both cases the advice offered for avoiding these errors is the cultivation of a clear and reliable standard of evaluation that is not distorted by misleading appearances. A good agent will take an appropriate view of the whole of a life – or at least will do the best to take a view of as much of a life as is possible – and try to make sure that it is as good as possible without being unduly swayed by what goods and bads or pleasures and pains happen to be nearer at hand. This ideal stance makes use of the same human capacities for anticipation and evaluation that can easily otherwise be misled; the same capacity for anticipation that is prone to illusion and error can, if properly directed, either – according to the *Protagoras* – maximise the pleasure in the whole of a life or – according to the *Philebus* – avoid the experience of this kind of false pleasure. Ideally, the agent will not regret any choices and will retain a consistent evaluation of the various pleasures and pains he experiences throughout his life.

CHAPTER 6

Anticipation, character, and piety
in *Plato's* Philebus

In Chapter 2 I suggested that we can use insights from the discussion of certain kinds of pleasures and pains in Plato's *Philebus* to assist in resolving a puzzle about the pleasures and pains of the philosophical life as it is described in the *Republic*. And in Chapter 5 I suggested that the *Philebus* also contains an elaboration of the pleasures and pains involved in the comparative assessment of alternative courses of action and builds on the idea of misleading appearances explored in the *Protagoras*. Here I turn to consider yet another aspect of the *Philebus*. It famously contains a discussion of what we can call 'the pleasures of anticipation'. These are used by Socrates in his first example in support of the controversial thesis that there are false pleasures. The pleasures of anticipation are interesting here for two reasons. First, coming to understand Socrates' account of these pleasures will once again require us to come to grips with the complex relationship in a human life between the activities of *logismos* and the experience of pleasure. Second, Socrates frames his account of the pleasures of anticipation with remarks that point to a connection between an agent's character – specifically, some notion of piety – and the likelihood of his pleasures of anticipation being true or false. This connection between memory, anticipation, character, and pleasure is an example of a theme that we shall also find in Aristotle and the Hellenistic hedonists and that will be explored further in Chapters 7 and 8.

Anticipation and false pleasure

At *Phileb.* 40a9–12 Socrates and Protarchus consider a case of a person taking pleasure in anticipating the future pleasure of coming into a lot of money. Socrates uses the example to try to win Protarchus' approval for the claim that there are such things as false pleasures. Protarchus initially thinks that pleasures cannot be false while Socrates thinks that they can. Roughly speaking, the most plausible explanation for Socrates' view is that he thinks that pleasures involve some kind of propositional content. For Socrates, in cases where the content is false, the pleasure is false. It is not clear whether Protarchus says that pleasures cannot be false because he thinks that it is incorrect to assign a truth value of any sort to pleasures or because he thinks that all pleasures are true. If the former, Protarchus thinks that pleasures are not 'truth-apt' but accepts that the beliefs which are in many cases the object or cause of a pleasure are true or false. If the latter, Protarchus is happy to think of pleasures as being 'truth-apt' but thinks that it is sufficient to guarantee the truth of the pleasure that one is indeed pleased.[1] We can call the thesis that all pleasures are true 'Protagorean hedonism', after the sophist who is credited with the claim that 'all beliefs are true'.[2]

Plenty has been written about the case of false anticipated pleasure. Less often remarked upon is the fact that, immediately prior to this famous example, Socrates claims without much explanation that the kind of false pleasures he is about to discuss, for the most part, is not experienced by those who are just and pious (39e10–11). And, immediately after the example, he and Protarchus agree swiftly that for good men, the hopes, anticipations, and pleasures they have 'painted in the soul' are for the most part true because of their being loved by the gods, offering a clear explanation of the truth of the pleasures he experiences by the fact of a person's possession of a certain kind of divinely approved character (διὰ τὸ θεοφιλεῖς εἶναι, 40b3–4). These passages are sometimes thought to be merely ancillary to the main point of the example.[3] But they are not: they indicate a significant

---

[1] Harte 2004, 118: 'In sum, what Protarchus thinks, I suggest, is this: a pleasure is true insofar as that in which it is taken is truly pleasant; and a thing being truly pleasant is a function of my finding it so.' She also points out that the distinction between the two interpretations of Protarchus' view is not particularly important (118): 'While Protarchus' position is not that pleasure is not truth-apt, his position has an underlying affinity with this view, although, for reasons of space, I will not be exploring it. (As a quick alternative, one may note that Protarchus' position quickly collapses into the other, by making talk of the truth of pleasure redundant at best.)' Cf. Teisserrenc 1999, 272–3.

[2] Cf. Delcomminette 2003, 219–20. (I return to Protagorean hedonism below.)

[3] E.g. Mooradian 1996, 98: 'The argument is brought to a close with the help of an auxiliary point that good men are friends of the gods, while bad men are their enemies.' Gosling 1975 ad loc. dubs this a 'moralistic digression'. Hackforth 1945, 73, comments: 'Plato is doubtless hinting at false value-judgments, which spring not from the weakness of our bodily eyes but from the blindness of our spiritual vision. The man who is θεοφιλής, and therefore blessed with true judgment, is one who like Socrates himself has followed after God by "tending his own soul" so as to heal himself of spiritual blindness.' Cf. Frede 1985, 167 n. 34, who lists other Platonic claims that those who are loved by the gods are successful: cf. *Prot.* 345c; *Symp.* 212a–b; *Phdr.* 273e; *Tim.* 53c; *Laws* 730c. Teisserrenc 1999, 288–93, is a notable exception to the general disregard. See also Delcomminette 2006, 391–6. The most expansive discussion of these passages is Carpenter 2006 (cf. Carpenter 2011, 88).

aspect of Socrates' conception of the good, virtuous, and – importantly – pious life that runs throughout the dialogue. Understanding that conception in turn helps us to understand the puzzling example of false pleasures of anticipation. Furthermore, it helps us to understand what Socrates has in mind as the most important factors determining how various different kinds of human agents anticipate their respective future experiences and, more generally, the way in which memory and anticipation are important for questions of the pleasantness and goodness of a life as a whole.

Here is the example which Socrates offers in an attempt to persuade Protarchus that there are false pleasures:

καί τις ὁρᾷ πολλάκις ἑαυτῷ χρυσὸν γιγνόμενον ἄφθονον καὶ ἐπ᾽ αὐτῷ πολλὰς ἡδονάς· καὶ δὴ καὶ ἐνεζωγραφημένον αὐτὸν ἐφ᾽ αὑτῷ χαίροντα σφόδρα καθορᾷ. (*Phileb.* 40a9–12)

And someone often pictures himself coming into the possession of a large amount of gold and obtaining many pleasures as a result. Moreover, he contemplates himself in this internal picture being particularly pleased with himself.

This example has given rise to a number of competing interpretations, partly because it leaves a number of important aspects under-determined. Although it is evident that this is offered as a possible case of 'false pleasure', Socrates himself does not make clear precisely where any falsehood enters into the imagined situation. We presume that something goes wrong and the imagined scene of enjoying a future windfall does not correspond with what in fact turns out to be the case, but this mismatch between anticipation and outcome can arise in a number of different ways. The differences between interpretations of the example will affect the interpretation of the framing comments on the relationship between character and false pleasure and vice versa.

At 40a9–12 the following picture is offered: a person is pleased because he views, as it were, an internal picture of himself at some time in the future enjoying new-found wealth. A complex set of attitudes is being described, which can be split into present attitudes and future attitudes. Most importantly, two episodes of pleasure are involved in the example, the first experienced in the present and the second imagined taking place at some time in the future. The person in question not only imagines the future possession of wealth; he also imagines the many pleasures that this will bring about and pictures himself rejoicing at some future time.

The picturing falls into the general class of what Socrates calls 'hopes' (*elpides*), a class which seems to include any imagining of some future state of affairs or, perhaps more restrictedly, imaginings which involve the person in question in picturing themselves and their future hedonic state.[4] Discussions of memory sometimes distinguish a class of 'introversive' experiential memories: memories concerned with the past experiences of the person doing the remembering. Introversive memory is what we engage in when we are recalling our own past propositional attitudes, including attitudes taken towards past experiences. Examples of introversive memory include, for example, remembering how much I enjoyed my last birthday party or how I was afraid as a child when I watched a particular film. Socrates evidently has in mind in this example a mirror image of this kind of memory; the anticipation being considered is what we can call 'introversive anticipation'. And just as it is a familiar fact that when we recall introversively we often experience certain affective states (for example, being pleased when we think back to a past pleasure) so too something similar can happen in the case of introversive anticipation. Thus, what Socrates calls 'hopes' appears to include cases of feeling not only 'pre-pleasure' (*to prokhairein*) but also 'pre-pain' (*to prolupeisthai*), not only pleasure at anticipating a future pleasure but also pain at anticipating a future pain (39d3–4). Although Socrates does not seem to notice this, in fact the pair of related present and future experiences need not be both painful or both pleasant. It is possible to think of cases in which imagining in this introversive way some future experience of pleasure could be the object of a present experience of pain.[5] For example, someone attempting to give up smoking might find painful in the present moment the picturing of some future time when he is enjoying a cigarette. Or he might take pleasure in the present at the thought of some later time when he finds cigarette smoke disgusting. In both of these cases there is an important sense of a discontinuity between the present and future character and desires of the person concerned. This notion of continuity will become more important as the discussion progresses but let us continue for the moment with the case at hand, namely that of the person who pictures himself enjoying at some later time the acquisition of a lot of money. This imagined future state is the object of his present prospective pleasure. Consider the following example:

> *John and the anticipated lottery win.* On Monday John imagines winning the next mid-week lottery. He pictures himself accepting on Wednesday a

---

[4] Compare *Laws* 644c9–d3, where fear (*phobos*) and 'confidence' (*tharros*) are species of *elpis*. For discussion see Meyer 2012.

[5] Just as it is possible to anticipate with pleasure someone else's pleasure, it is also clearly possible to anticipate with pleasure someone else's pain or anticipate with pain someone else's pleasure.

cheque for millions of pounds and imagines the pleasure he will feel in doing so. Imagining this on Monday gives him a great deal of pleasure.

There are two episodes of pleasure in this example. First, there is a present pleasure, a pleasure experienced on Monday. This is a pleasure experienced in the present but which is generated by the internal impression of a future state of affairs; it is what Socrates refers to as 'pre-pleasure', *to prokhairein*.[6] That future state of affairs is: the person himself in possession of a large amount of money and, as a result, experiencing a great deal of pleasure. Socrates takes care to draw attention to this last point; what is being pictured, or – as Socrates might say – depicted by the painter in the soul, is some future experience of pleasure (40a10) and not just some future acquisition of wealth. Second, there is this future pleasure which, in John's case, is the pleasure thought to occur on Wednesday. This is the pleasure being depicted in the imagining and is the object of Monday's present pleasure; it is what Socrates refers to at 40a9–12 as the 'many pleasures' which the person sees himself 'pictured as enjoying'.

Socrates wishes to argue that John's pleasure on Monday is a false pleasure. But just why that pleasure is false is less clear. We might explain the overall structure of this kind of anticipation as follows. It involves two important relationships: the first is the relationship between the content of the anticipation (the content of John's anticipation on Monday) and the anticipated attitude (the anticipated Wednesday pleasure). The second is between the anticipated attitude and the object of that anticipated attitude (the anticipated Wednesday attitude and the actual state of affairs on Wednesday). There are therefore two ways in which the anticipation may be false since each of the two relationships may not display the required kind of 'fit'.

It is perhaps easier to understand this structure if we consider instead a case of remembering, since we are comfortable with the assumption that 'remember' is a success word; in many ways, the conditions necessary for an instance of remembering will be analogous to the conditions necessary for an instance of 'true' anticipation. And although Socrates concentrates on anticipation, it is evident that he thinks a similar analysis can be offered of pleasures taken in past or present states of affairs. It is possible, in that case, for there to be true and false pleasures taken in past and present states of affairs.[7] Recall that the relevant kind of memory is 'introversive' memory:

---

[6] On the account given here of such internal representations, see the helpful discussion in Delcomminette 2003.

[7] Cf. Frede 1992b, 446.

memory of the person's own past including, importantly, past attitudes.
Consider the following example:

> *John and the remembered lottery win.* On Friday John remembers winning the
> Wednesday mid-week lottery. He pictures himself accepting on Wednesday
> a cheque for millions of pounds and recalls the pleasure he felt in doing so.
> Recalling this on Friday gives him a great deal of pleasure.

For John on Friday to enjoy remembering enjoying going to pick up the
cheque on Wednesday it must be the case both that on Friday John has the
belief 'I enjoyed going to pick up the cheque on Wednesday' and also that
on Wednesday John did in fact enjoy picking up the cheque. The relationship between the memory and the past must hold in two ways. First, when
John thinks 'I enjoyed picking up the cheque on Wednesday' it must be the
case that he did pick up the cheque on Wednesday; there must be sufficient
content preservation. And second, it must also be the case that he did enjoy
picking up the cheque on Wednesday; therefore there must also be sufficient *attitude preservation.* If both of these obtain we might say that John's
memory is *authentic.*[8] If, on the other hand, John takes pleasure on Friday in
thinking that he enjoyed picking up a winner's cheque on Wednesday but
either he did not pick up a cheque on Wednesday or he did pick up a cheque
on Wednesday but did not enjoy doing so, then this experience on Friday is
a false pleasure.

The conditions necessary for someone to 'enjoy remembering' in this
authentic fashion are the counterparts of the conditions necessary for
what Socrates will call a 'true pleasure of anticipation'. For John authen-
tically to enjoy anticipating on Monday that he will enjoy winning the
lottery then it must be the case that (i) on Monday John enjoys thinking
that on Wednesday he will enjoy winning the lottery, (ii) on Wednesday
John wins the lottery, and (iii) on Wednesday John enjoys winning
the lottery. Socrates thinks that an authentic anticipation of a pleasant
experience will be pleasant and that an inauthentic anticipation of a
pleasant experience might be pleasant too. The latter kind will be a false
pleasure.

---

[8] Cf. Bernecker 2010, 213–17; 214: 'The direction of fit of memory is twofold: mind-to-world as well as
mind-in-the-present-to-mind-in-the-past. Just as the faithful reproduction of a false proposition
doesn't qualify as memory, neither does the inaccurate reproduction of a true proposition. For this
reason there needs to be a content condition and past representation condition in addition to the
truth-condition.' He discusses the important notion of attitudinal identity later in the same chapter,
focussing on the claim that the psychological attitude attributed to one's former self need only be
sufficiently similar to the past attitude for authenticity to hold (231–9).

The twofold condition shows clearly the two possibilities that might prevent this anticipation from being authentic in the desired way and therefore lead to there being a false rather than a true pleasure of anticipation. First, it might be false that John comes into a lot of money on Wednesday ((ii) is false). Alternatively, perhaps it is not true that new-found wealth will generate pleasure; perhaps when it arrives it generates anxiety ((iii) is false). In that case, although it is true that John wins the lottery, the pleasure on Monday he had in imagining how much he would enjoy it is false. The two possible reasons for the existence of a false pleasure point to two possible interpretations of how we should explain the presence of such false pleasures in terms of the general moral character of the agent in question. Assessing the relative plausibility of those explanations might then give us a means to decide between the competing reasons for the falsehood of the anticipated pleasure.

Interpretation 1
John is experiencing false pleasure in the present because John will not become rich. As a result he will feel no future pleasure. The imagined event of winning the lottery simply does not occur. Any present pleasure taken in the imagination of this future pleasure is therefore, according to Socrates, false. The failure, in this case, is in predicting what will or will not happen and so is a failure of 'content preservation'. The person takes pleasure in anticipating enjoying an event which never in fact takes place.[9]

Interpretation 2
John is experiencing false pleasure in the present even though it is true that some of what he anticipates does in fact occur. It is true that John will win the lottery, but there is nevertheless a reason for the pleasure taken in the present anticipation of enjoying that event to be false. The pleasure is false because, although John does in the future come upon some new wealth, it is not the pleasant experience he imagined it to be and, remember, part of what John anticipates on Monday is later his taking pleasure in the wealth. (Perhaps the new-found wealth merely creates anxiety and unwanted attention.) John takes pleasure in the present thought 'I will enjoy winning the lottery' but, when the wealth comes, finds that in fact it brings no pleasure. So, the present anticipated pleasure is false. The failure in this case is a failure of 'attitude preservation'. The pleasure in the present is false because it is based

---

[9] See e.g. Hackforth 1945, 72–3; Penner 1970; Frede 1985; Ogihara 2012 and cf. Williams 1959, Gosling 1975, 111–12. Thein 2012, 132 n. 40, also appears to favour this view, while noting the important connection with character: '[S]ome persons, in virtue of their moral qualities, are good at calculating the future course of those events that concern their own well-being.' Evans 2008 offers qualified support for what he calls the 'Old School' view and a helpful guide to the dispute.

on the mistaken description as pleasant of some future event which, when it arrives, is not in fact pleasant.[10]

Both interpretations note an absence of the future pleasant experience which is the object of the present pleasure.[11] Socrates is not in this example interested in the pleasures of anticipation, if this means the pleasure we might take in the very prospect of some future state of affairs.[12] However, the two interpretations differ in the explanation they give for the absence of that future pleasure. While Interpretation 1 finds fault with a person for taking anticipated pleasure in an event which will not in fact happen, Interpretation 2 finds fault with a person for taking anticipated pleasure in an event which, although it will happen, will not turn out to be the pleasant event it was imagined to be.

True and false pleasures and piety

Immediately before the example at 40a9–12 Socrates and Protarchus agree to some important premises (39e10–40a1):

ΣΩ. δίκαιος ἀνὴρ καὶ εὐσεβὴς καὶ ἀγαθὸς πάντως ἆρ᾽ οὐ θεοφιλής ἐστιν;
ΠΡΩ. τί μήν;
ΣΩ. τί δέ; ἄδικός τε καὶ παντάπασι κακὸς ἆρ᾽ οὐ τοὐναντίον ἐκείνῳ;
ΠΡΩ. πῶς δ᾽ οὔ;

SOC.: A just and pious and overall good man is loved by the gods, isn't he?
PROT.: Of course.
SOC.: And the unjust and altogether bad man? Isn't he the opposite of this one?
PROT.: How not?

These two characters – the all-round good man and the altogether bad one – return at 40b2–c2, immediately after the example:

ΣΩ. τούτων οὖν πότερα φῶμεν τοῖς μὲν ἀγαθοῖς ὡς τὸ πολὺ τὰ γεγραμμένα παρατίθεσθαι ἀληθῆ διὰ τὸ θεοφιλεῖς εἶναι, τοῖς δὲ κακοῖς ὡς αὖ <τὸ> πολὺ τοὐναντίον, ἢ μὴ φῶμεν;
ΠΡΩ. καὶ μάλα φατέον.
ΣΩ. οὐκοῦν καὶ τοῖς κακοῖς ἡδοναί γε οὐδὲν ἧττον πάρεισιν ἐζωγραφημέναι, ψευδεῖς δὲ αὗταί που.

---

[10] Cf. Lovibond 1989–90; Harte 2004, 121 and 125–8; Russell 2005, 181–2 and n. 26; cf. Moss 2012b, 269 n. 21.

[11] Delcomminette 2003, 229: 'Actually, even though the anticipatory pleasure and the anticipated pleasure are not strictly identical, the falsity of the latter necessarily implies that of the first. For, as we have seen, the anticipated pleasure corresponds to the *content* of the anticipatory pleasure.'

[12] Harte 2004, 120–4. Cf. Russell 2005, 179–80.

ΠΡΩ. τί μήν;

ΣΩ. ψευδέσιν ἄρα ἡδοναῖς τὰ πολλὰ οἱ πονηροὶ χαίρουσιν, οἱ δ᾽ ἀγαθοὶ τῶν ἀνθρώπων ἀληθέσιν.

SOC.: Of these depicted images, should we say or not that for the most part those set before good men are true because such men are loved by the gods, but those before bad men are mostly the opposite?

PROT.: We certainly should say that.

SOC.: So also, the depicted pleasures which are present to bad men are no less pleasures, but they are false in some way.

PROT.: Yes.

SOC.: Therefore, wicked men mostly rejoice in false pleasures, but good men in true pleasures.

These framing passages ought to help us to understand the example of false pleasures which they surround. However, both interpretations of the example of anticipated wealth can claim to be compatible with the framing passages. For Interpretation 1, the frame should be read as follows: wicked people generally conjure up improbable or unlikely states of affairs and take pleasure in them. Because the states of affairs they imagine are false, they will not experience any future pleasure, and therefore any present pleasure taken in the contemplation of such future states of affairs is false. On this view, the mistake is in predicting various external states of affairs: the person mistakenly predicts the occurrence of some state of affairs in the future which he will find pleasant. He enjoys in the present imagining that state of affairs and the pleasures it will bring and, in doing so, derives pleasure in advance. However, the fact that the imagined future state of affairs turns out not to be true casts a shadow over the pleasure felt in the present at imagining it. (John, for example, is just a daydreamer. He spends his time imagining the pleasure that a lottery win will bring, but he never in fact wins the lottery.)[13]

This interpretation seems to me to be the less plausible of the two. It offers an unsatisfactory reason to cast doubt on such pleasures since it holds that the mistake involved is not a specifically ethical failure in the person's character so much as a simple mistake in his expectations about what is and

[13] See e.g. Mooradian 1996, 98 n. 10: '[A]ccording to Plato's conception of a good person, this may be appropriate. The intense, mixed pleasures are connected with folly and this type of pleasure is the object of present prognostication. It is also unclear what evidence the person would have for this hope. Hence, Plato is probably connecting the false anticipatory pleasures with folly as well. This would not be impossible either, since, at the very least, folly would interfere with sober and careful thinking.' Ogihara 2012, esp. 304–8, argues similarly: good people tend to hope for things that are more easily realized and also have a genuine concern for what is anticipated; bad people have no genuine concern for what they conjure up in their imagination and also often day-dream about very unlikely states of affairs.

is not likely to happen to him in the future. Wicked people, after all, are not necessarily poor planners and predictors in this very general sense; in fact, their ability to plan and scheme is often rather good and that is why they can cause such harm to themselves and others.[14] The people in question here in the *Philebus* who are most likely to experience false pleasures of anticipation are not 'bad' in some vague or unspecified way; in fact, Socrates – crucially, it will turn out – is careful to spell out that the good people he has in mind are 'just' and 'pious', so we can assume these bad people are not only 'unjust', as Socrates makes clear, but also 'impious'. But it is not at all clear why impiety should be connected with a propensity to anticipate states of affairs that will not in fact occur.[15] It may well be true that good and pious and just people tend to think with pleasure about things that are not very far-fetched and are not unlikely to occur. But there is no sign in the text that the example at 40a9–12 is of a kind of pleasant anticipation that a good and just and pious person either could not or will not enjoy. Socrates does not commit himself to the claim that anyone who experiences pleasure in predicting a future enjoyment of new wealth must be one of the 'wicked' people mentioned in the frame. The case in 40a is meant rather as one in which the pleasure could be false, not one in which the pleasure must be false and the weaker thesis is enough for Socrates to answer Protarchus. Socrates specifies that hopes such as the one described in the example at 40a9–12 will be true in the case of good and pious people and false in the case of unjust and impious people (τούτων, 40b2), so the content of the hope in the example is itself, we might say, neutral with regard to the character of the person whose hope it is.[16] We should not infer that since the picture's being imagined is somehow 'unlikely' to happen then it points to some kind of day-dreaming or otherwise unrealistic set of hopes that should be assigned to people of dubious

---

[14] For example, the oligarchic man in the *Republic* has a badly corrupted set of desires and has a rational part of the soul subservient to the appetite for making money. But he is able to make clear and consistent plans to this unfortunate end (553a–555a); see Lorenz 2006a, 46–7.

[15] Cf. Gosling 1975, 112 (*ad* 39e8–40c2): 'It may still be that reliance is being put on the fact that the gods' favourites will not be affected with many false hopes, while at the same time Plato is relying on normal piety to insert a point in favour of justice. Alternatively, Plato is taking it that he can show ordinary virtues to be part of a man in good working order, and clearly a man in constant error is not in good working order.' Carpenter 2006, 9–14, rightly insists on the close association between reason and divinity and on the possibility that there is a strong connection between divine favour and reasoning about one's future pleasures realistically, accurately, and perspicuously, and with a sure and consistent appraisal of oneself.

[16] This is noted well by Carpenter 2006, 11. Perhaps it is also true that good and pious and just people have a better grip on what is genuinely valuable for a human than do their bad and impious and unjust counterparts. But this points towards the truth of Interpretation 2 below: the failure in that case is not one of simply taking pleasure in an event which is assumed to be going to take place but in fact does not; the failure is rather in thinking that a certain event will bring pleasure when in fact it does not.

character or whose expectations are insufficiently guided by a proper rational grasp of how the world works.[17]

And finally, the imagined situation of coming upon the money, while perhaps not likely, is not impossible. What will we say if it turns out that a wicked person, having anticipated with pleasure the pleasant discovery of this wealth, does indeed come upon the money? Interpretation 1 leaves us no alternative than to say that in this case the anticipated pleasure was a true pleasure since it locates the determination of its truth or falsehood solely in the occurrence or not of the event of coming upon the money. So, had he found a treasure chest or won the lottery then even the wicked person's earlier imagining would have been a true rather than false anticipated pleasure. Interpretation 1 would leave the determination over the truth or falsehood of the anticipated pleasure to external contingencies; there would be no direct and necessary connection to the character of the agent concerned.

For Interpretation 2, the framing passages should be read as follows: wicked people generally conjure up states of affairs which, if they do come to be, do not produce the pleasure they had imagined. Because there is no future experience of pleasure, any present pleasure taken in the thought of such future enjoyment is false. On this view, the mistake is not one of failing accurately to predict external states of affairs. Instead the mistake is in imagining some future state of affairs to be pleasant. This makes better sense of the surrounding context, since such misconceptions about what is in fact pleasant might well be a plausible symptom of some sort of failing in one's character. On this view, John's mistake is in failing to see that his current imagination of what will be pleasant may not in fact be consistent with what he will find pleasant when it finally occurs. Perhaps he has a poor grasp on what he does in fact enjoy. Or perhaps between the moment of his imagining and the occurrence of the imagined event his priorities and preferences have changed sufficiently to make the once anticipated pleasant experience no longer the sort of thing he enjoys.[18] John's preferences and

---

[17] Carpenter 2006, 7–8, notes that it is not hard to imagine that Plato's audience might see a link between a case of new-found wealth and some sort of divine favour even if it is implausible to see a regular and reliable correlation between moral character and fortune of this sort.

[18] Cf. Carpenter 2006, 12–13, who argues that a wicked person is unable to anticipate what attaining the imagined future will be like phenomenologically. I think this is right in the sense that the wicked person cannot properly anticipate what, for example, finding all this gold will feel like, that is, whether or not it will indeed be pleasant as imagined. It does not mean, I think, that he mistakenly anticipates how a future *pleasure* will feel. Carpenter is certainly right to point out that the wicked person's failure is tied to a failure in some form of self-consistency. She expands the notion of consistency in terms of 'mental holism' (16–18); for my account, see below.

pleasures are sufficiently mutable that he first enjoys the thought of something which, when it later occurs, he does not in fact enjoy. Compare the 'tyrannical man' imagined by Socrates in the *Republic*: he too is described as 'impious' (*anosios*), 'unjust' (*adikos*), and thoroughly wicked (580a4). But Socrates characterises him as miserable not because he is constantly surprised by unforeseen events or because his expectations are regularly confounded; rather, the tyrant is miserable because his soul is in thrall to his lawless appetites and, what is more, cannot properly satisfy even those desires it happens to have (577d–578a, 579d–e). In brief, the problem is not that the tyrant is simply unable to plan and predict adequately, but that his goals – what he is trying to plan and predict for – are too changeable and inconsistent for him ever to be successful.[19]

Interpretation 2 seems to me to be correct. But consideration of the example at 40a on its own will not be enough to show that it is. Looking just at the example at 40a it is certainly unclear why anyone would necessarily accept Socrates' attempt to attribute such mutability – and the false pleasures it tends to produce – to faults in an agent's ethical character. A full defence of this interpretation requires a much more expansive consideration of the dialogue up to this point and will explain why Protarchus agrees so readily to Socrates' suggestion.

The unity of a life

Three claims are made in the *Philebus* that count in favour of Interpretation 2: (i) a good human life is one which involves the retrospective and prospective consideration by an agent of his or her own life and character; (ii) a good human life is a temporally extended whole formed by reason into a good and harmonious unity; (iii) a harmonious and good life is a pious and virtuous life, while a life which fails to exhibit such harmony and unity is impious and wicked. All three claims also illuminate further Socrates' understanding of the relationship between pleasure and reason in a human life and the further relationship between human lives and divinity.

Before the examination of false pleasures, the dialogue has been building a picture of the nature of piety, justice, and goodness that lies behind Socrates' assertion and Protarchus' agreement that the impious and the unjust are the kinds of people likely to experience false anticipated pleasures. To assemble this picture, it is important to begin with some general

---

[19] A similar point might be made about the democratic man: 561d–e. Both he and the tyrant lack the focus and consistency found even in the oligarchic man. See Scott 2000.

considerations about the dialogue's conception of a human life most generally from which we can then proceed to consider more specifically the characteristic of a pious human life. It is not coincidental that this conception makes significant use of precisely the capacities of anticipation and memory that are evidently much to the fore in the example of false pleasure sketched at 40a.

Protarchus had conceded early in the discussion that their primary focus of attention should be on the 'mixed' life, a life combining the activities of reason and pleasure (22a). Further, he also accepted that a life without any rational activity at all would not be choiceworthy. This is the rejection of the 'life of a mollusc' at 21a–d. Most important for our purposes is Socrates' summing up of such a life at 21c1–8 since this will begin to fill in the picture of what must be involved in a human life from which we can go on to ask what must be involved in a good human life:

καὶ μὴν ὡσαύτως μνήμην μὴ κεκτημένον ἀνάγκη δήπου μηδ᾽ ὅτι ποτὲ ἔχαιρες μεμνῆσθαι, τῆς τ᾽ ἐν τῷ παραχρῆμα ἡδονῆς προσπιπτούσης μηδ᾽ ἡντινοῦν μνήμην ὑπομένειν· δόξαν δ᾽ αὖ μὴ κεκτημένον ἀληθῆ μὴ δοξάζειν χαίρειν χαίροντα, λογισμοῦ δὲ στερόμενον μηδ᾽ εἰς τὸν ἔπειτα χρόνον ὡς χαιρήσεις δυνατὸν εἶναι λογίζεσθαι, ζῆν δὲ οὐκ ἀνθρώπου βίον, ἀλλά τινος πλεύμονος ἢ τῶν ὅσα θαλάττια μετ᾽ ὀστρεΐνων ἔμψυχά ἐστι σωμάτων.
(*Phileb.* 21c1–8)

Indeed, without memory it is impossible to remember that you felt pleasure in the past, since as a pleasure falls away into the past not even the slightest memory of it remains. And without true opinion, then you would not think truly that you are experiencing pleasure when you do. And without reasoning, it is impossible to reason how you will experience pleasure in the future, living not a human life, but the life of a sea-slug or some other of the many shelled sea-creatures.

At the very beginning of the dialogue Socrates listed a number of things he considered better than pleasure for anything able to share in them. The list at 11b6–c2 included being wise (*phronein*), understanding (*noein*), remembering (*memnēsthai*), correct belief (*orthē doxa*), and true calculations (*alētheis logismoi*). Some of them return at 21c – memory (*mnēmē*), opinion (*doxa*), reasoning (*logismos*) – together with understanding (*nous*) in a list of the capacities missing from a life without *phronēsis* (cf. 21b6–9) and all are allowed to be present in the other candidate life: the life devoid of pleasure (21d9–e2). Together, as 21c1–8 makes clear, they allow an agent to consider and reflect upon pleasures that are being experienced, have been experienced, and will be experienced in various stages of his life. And at 39c–d, in preparation for his argument for the existence of false pleasures, Socrates will make a point of reminding Protarchus that pleasures and pains too can apply in all tenses. In the extreme case of the mollusc life, the total absence of rational capacities makes it impossible for a mollusc to form the thought 'I was pleased that P'. In the present, it prevents a mollusc conceiving 'I am pleased that P'. For the future, the most directly relevant case for our interest in false pleasures, the absence of rational capacities makes it impossible for the mollusc to form the thought 'I will be pleased that P'. Note that at this very early stage of his discussion with Protarchus, when trying to extract a commitment to the mixed life and the rejection of the mollusc life of pleasure, Socrates leaves entirely unexplored the question of whether these judgements about one's experience can themselves be sources of pleasure, although that is precisely the issue which he wants to explore later. He also leaves open the question of whether some of these capacities are present in some other non-human animals. Later he insists that memory, for example, does have a role in non-human animal desire as well as human desire.[20] For the moment, Protarchus simply recognises that a life without these capacities, however pleasant, is not a human life and not a life we would choose to live.[21]

The mollusc simply cannot conceive any thought in the form 'I will be pleased that P'. Perhaps molluscs have no shell-fish analogue for the scribe

---

[20] See 35c9–10 and 36b8–9. At 22b3–8 Socrates repeats that neither of the two lives contains the good by itself and neither is choiceworthy for a human (ἡμῶν 22b6). However, at 22b4–6 he adds that if either life were to contain the good then it would be sufficient, complete, or choiceworthy also for any animal or plant capable of always living a life of that kind (ἦν γὰρ ἂν ἱκανὸς καὶ τέλεος καὶ πᾶσι φυτοῖς καὶ ζῴοις αἱρετός, οἷσπερ δυνατὸν ἦν οὕτως ἀεὶ διὰ βίου ζῆν). This is sometimes thought to be an odd addition (see Gosling 1975, 89). The proviso: 'for those things capable of always living such a life' restates the qualification made twice by Socrates at the beginning of the dialogue when declaring his initial disagreement with Protarchus (11b6–c2). Cf. Frede 1997, 177 n. 111; Delcomminette 2006, 178–9.

[21] Compare Nussbaum 1995, 98–102. An alternative interpretation makes the absence of rational capacities prevent something like prudential reasoning and therefore diminish the pleasure of the life being considered. The diminished pleasure in turn leads Protarchus to see the necessity – if only in an instrumental sense – of reason for a good life, even if a good life is understood in hedonist terms. This view imagines that such a life is rejected because it cannot accommodate the possibility of forming plans about how to set about attaining some future pleasure. For μηδ᾿ εἰς τὸν ἔπειτα χρόνον ὡς χαιρήσεις δυνατὸν εἶναι λογίζεσθαι at 21c5–6 translators offer 'you couldn't even calculate that you would enjoy yourself later on' (Hackforth 1945); 'lacking the ability to predict you would be unable to predict your future pleasures' (Gosling 1975); 'being unable to calculate, you could not figure out any future pleasures for yourself' (Frede 1993). Unfortunately, the summary of this argument at the end of the dialogue (60d3–e5) refers only to the recognition of present and recollection of past pleasures. (See also Moore 1903, III §52, who interprets the message of the argument to be that it is the 'consciousness' of a pleasure that is valuable rather than the pleasure itself. His translation of 21c5–6 has: 'you cannot even have the power to reckon that you will be pleased in the future'.) See Evans 2007c, esp. 348–52, and Harte 2014b for excellent discussions of this passage. For the distinction between the 'reformable' Protarchus and the irredeemable Philebus see Frede 1996a.

and painter we are asked to imagine at work in a human soul. This means that a mollusc cannot engage in any of the activities of recollection or prediction which are integral to human desire and our human experience of pleasure. If so, the comparison with the mollusc helps only to a limited extent, namely with the observation that a mollusc cannot do such things either well or badly since it cannot do them at all; it will not of itself allow us to distinguish between better and worse agents who are capable of forming such thoughts. What the comparison with the mollusc does reveal, however, is that these capacities are taken by Socrates and Protarchus to be essential to a human life and that the good use of them will therefore presumably be part of a good human life.[22]

Having established at the outset that the ability to consider temporally remote experiences is a necessary characteristic of a choiceworthy human life, Socrates goes on to build a more detailed picture of human psychology which gives a central role to both memory and anticipation. The intense interest in the example of false anticipated pleasure has perhaps led to a relative neglect of the important role played by retrospection and memory in the *Philebus*' account of human psychology. It is clear, nevertheless, that a notable feature of the picture as it develops in the run-up to the discussion of false pleasures is the prominent role granted to memory even in the analysis of desire in general and humans' hopes for the future in particular. Socrates himself seems preoccupied with arguing for a division between the roles of the body and of the soul in desire, but he says that he thinks all desires and impulses which initiate a drive for the removal or replenishment involve some sort of memory (35c–d).[23]

ΣΩ. ἡ δ' ὁρμή γε ἐπὶ τοὐναντίον ἄγουσα ἢ τὰ παθήματα δηλοῖ που μνήμην οὖσαν τῶν τοῖς παθήμασιν ἐναντίων.

ΠΡΩ. πάνυ γε.

ΣΩ. τὴν ἄρα ἐπάγουσαν ἐπὶ τὰ ἐπιθυμούμενα ἀποδείξας μνήμην ὁ λόγος ψυχῆς σύμπασαν τήν τε ὁρμὴν καὶ ἐπιθυμίαν καὶ τὴν ἀρχὴν τοῦ ζῴου παντὸς ἀπέφηνεν. (*Phileb.* 35c12–d3)

---

[22] See Lang 2010, 155–9, who notes that pure pleasures will also require some kind of cognitive activity since they will require the perceiver to abstract pure whiteness, say, from other properties of a perceived object.

[23] Note that the general analysis of desire is intended to cover in general terms not only humans but also other animals which have the appropriate capacities for perception or memory. See e.g. *Phileb.* 35c9–10 and 36b8–9; this is emphasized by Lorenz 2006a, 102. (The mollusc of 21c which has no capacity for memory at all will presumably not be able to form a desire.)

SOC: The impulse that drives [the animal] to the opposite of its current experiences makes clear, I suppose, that there is a memory of the opposites of these experiences.

PROT.: Quite right.

SOC.: Then having shown that it is memory which drives the animal towards the objects of desire, the argument has revealed that every impulse and desire and the rule over every animal belong to the soul.

Specifically, the memory involved in desire is a memory of the state opposite to that in which the animal currently finds itself. The desire when a person is thirsty, for example, involves the memory of the state of not being thirsty. Presumably, the drive to find a drink to remove a thirst involves the conjuring from memory of some appropriate representation of the proper object of desire or perhaps of the proper state of that desire being fulfilled. Socrates then distinguishes two cases involving a person who is in pain but can remember the pleasant things he lacks. Socrates puts his point here in terms of a case concerning 'one of us' (*tis hēmōn*), which suggests that this is a phenomenon restricted to human animals, although he later seems to include other animals too (36b8–9). In any case, in the first example the person concerned has a 'clear hope' (*elpis phanera*, 36a8) of attaining what he lacks. In that case, the memory provides some pleasure while he is also experiencing pain (36a–b).[24] In the second, he is both in pain and also aware that there is no hope of replenishment. In that case his suffering is twofold (36b–c). Socrates and Protarchus go on to emphasise further the importance of such psychological capacities immediately prior to the discussion of false pleasures. At 40a3–4 Socrates asserts that 'every human (*pas anthrōpos*) is full of many hopes' and these hopes in 'us humans' (*hēmōn*, 40a6) are then quickly agreed to take the form of statements (*logoi*, 40a6) and 'painted images' (*phantasmata ezōgraphēmena*, 40a9). This specification and the

---

[24] What is the force of the qualification *phanera* at 36a8? There are two possibilities. First, it shows that to the hoper, as it were, the hope is clear and vivid. That clear and vivid character of the hope is what allows it to be a source of pleasure even though the hoper is also in pain. And the clear and vivid character of the hope is irrespective of whether in actual fact what is being hoped for is likely to be attained. It could be a very vivid and arresting sort of hope for something that is extremely unlikely to happen. Alternatively, the hope is *phanera* just when the object that is being hoped for is indeed likely to be obtained. (The same might be said of despair: I might have a 'clear' desperation both in cases where I merely think that what I need is unlikely to come my way although in fact it is not at all unlikely, and also in cases where I accurately recognise the unlikelihood of my getting what I need.) There is little in the text that points one way rather than the other for certain. And perhaps that is not a surprise. After all, it is in the next four pages or so that Socrates tries to persuade Protarchus that there is a very important distinction to be made between the pleasures to be had from hoping that are true and those that are false, although they may both seem pleasant enough to the hoper.

explicit connection with the earlier famous description of the scribe and painter within the soul show that Socrates has now moved from an account of desire that covers all animals to the discussion of a capacity present in humans alone and which is particularly relevant for understanding the kinds of pleasures proper for a good human life.

There is a lot more to be said about the complicated psychological picture which Socrates assembles, including its famous depiction of an internal scribe and an internal painter who have the jobs of composing and then depicting these *logoi* respectively.[25] But for now I want to take from it a relatively simple point. The picture of human psychology which emerges, both from the rejection of the 'mollusc life' and also from the extended analysis of the psychology of desire, gives a prominent place to the capacities of memory and hope. Importantly, Socrates is prepared to see memory and hope working in combination because he makes memory play an important role in future-directed attitudes such as hope and desire in general. In short, human psychology necessarily involves the use and combination of attitudes to both the past and the future since humans are animals who are aware of their living through time or, to put it most concisely, of living a human life. This temporal perspective has to be taken into account since the entire conversation is, after all, meant to determine which 'state or condition of the soul is able to provide all people with a happy life (*eudaimōn bios*)' (11d4–6). A good human life, evidently, is one in which the past and future of that life also must somehow be taken into account and is a life in which the person is able to take into account his own past and future in an appropriate way.[26]

Character and false pleasure

It might be thought at this point that Socrates has expended a great deal of time in developing what is on the face of it not a particularly surprising idea. However, the case of the false pleasures of anticipation is the first testing ground for the ramifications of this view of human psychology and of the nature of a human life. And whichever interpretation of the example at 40a is preferred, the error involved stems from some inconsistency between the

---

[25] For further discussion and comment see Russell 2005, 177–9; Evans 2007a, 86–90; Carpenter 2010; Moss 2012a, 265–7 and 2012b; Thein 2012; and Harte 2014a.

[26] Cf. Russell 2005, 198: 'The mistake that worries Plato about this way of valuing pleasure is a mistake about self-conception: what matters in life is the way in which one intelligently constructs a life, a future, and a self by one's actions and goals, in a way that will fulfil one's deepest needs as a human, and the view that pleasure makes one's life happy cannot make sense of that.'

present depiction of some future experience in the person's life and how that future experience turns out to be. There is, in short, some inconsistency between the agent's present and the agent's future or, more precisely, between the agent's present conception of his future and the agent's future conception of his present. Moreover, since we have now learned that the presence of a desire also involves the faculty of memory, in the full explanation of what goes wrong even in cases of false anticipated pleasure there must also be a part played by the agent's past. Since the depiction of the anticipated pleasure is conjured by the painter and scribe in the soul from the agent's store of memories, it must be derived to some extent from a past experience of pleasure. The inconsistency also involves, therefore, some relation between the agent now and his past.

It is no surprise that such an inconsistency should strike Socrates as a serious problem and might indeed be thought to be so significant as to cast doubt on the agent's moral character in general. After all, he is working with a conception of a human life as something temporally extended and therefore of a good human life as something to be evaluated not in terms of some episodic or moment-by-moment assessment of a person's state of wellbeing but rather in terms of its value as a temporally extended whole. A similar concern with the overall shape or structure of a life lies behind Solon's famous advice that we should 'call no man happy until he is dead' and Aristotle's more extended consideration of what sort of completeness we are right to demand from a good life. In the *Philebus* a similar concern can be detected, founded on a particular conception of human nature and, above all, the capacities for memory and anticipation that we all possess. But the *Philebus* also introduces two additional and sophisticated elements to this basic picture. First, Socrates adds the thought that human psychological powers allow us as agents considering the past and future to be aware of and concerned with the temporal extension of our lives. We can think about our lives from within, as it were, and indeed in cases when thinking or planning for the future are involved we are necessarily also involved in reaching back through memory to the past. Second, these capacities for memory and anticipation are themselves coupled with a more general conception of the role of reason in generating goodness in unities formed by systems and mixtures of various kinds, of which a human life and the cosmos as a whole are two prominent examples.

Before the consideration of the different kinds of pleasure and the argument for the possibility of false pleasure, the *Philebus* has seen Socrates and Protarchus spend considerable time and effort in drawing a link between divine and human reason and their respective products. Socrates' assertion, therefore, in the argument at 40b–c that good men are loved by the gods and as a result generally experience true pleasure, is neither mere rhetoric nor a nod to traditional theology. For example, early in the dialogue at 26b7–10 Socrates asserts that it is 'the goddess' who sees that there is no intrinsic limit to pleasures and sets an order and limit to them.[27] Moreover, she is said to do so with an eye to preventing hubris and every kind of wickedness and the resulting mixture of a limit applied to pleasures is listed along with good climate and 'all other things we have that are *kala*' (26b1–2), including health, beauty, strength, and fine characteristics of the soul (26b5–7).

That comment appears close to the beginning of the cosmological section of the dialogue where there is perhaps the most interesting evidence of Socrates' insistence on a moral and pious aspect to the business of living a life containing a properly and rationally determined set of pleasures. Pleasure is, of course, one of the necessary elements of the mixture that is characteristic of a good human life. But it is the task of reason to determine the kind and amount of pleasure to allow in. To illustrate this point, Socrates famously makes use of an analogy between a human life and the cosmos as a whole. An individual human body and soul should be thought of as parts of a greater cosmic body and soul and they ought to be ordered and arranged by our individual human reason as the cosmos as a whole has been well ordered and arranged by divine reason. In both the cosmos at large and also in a human life, one of the consequences of the proper activity of reason is the production of an ordered whole and this order is assumed to obtain not only at a moment but also to be an order over time.[28]

There is a clear temporal aspect to Socrates' two examples of good mixtures produced in this way: music and climate (26a–b).[29] The first of these involves the notion of a well-ordered unity across a temporal extension since Socrates makes explicit mention of the need to ensure the right combinations not only of high and low pitch but also of the fast and the slow (26a2). A good and unified piece of music must contain not only various correctly pitched notes but they must also be played in the correct order and each for the right amount of time. What determines the rightness

---

[27] There has been some discussion about the identity of the goddess. Frede 1993, 23 n. 1, insists it must be Aphrodite, despite Socrates' instructive caution about using a name which Philebus had hijacked to refer to pleasure (12b–c).

[28] For a good explanation of this relationship see Russell 2005, 145–9 and 171–4; for a wide-ranging discussion of the section see also McCabe 2000, 165–93.

[29] There is an excellent discussion of the notion of composition and unity in the *Philebus* in Harte 2002, 177–212.

of all these various variables is, of course, the desired final goal of a good and unified piece of music. Since a good piece of music has a unity that extends over time, that characteristic determines the proper arrangement of the various elements involved.

For the case of climate too, we might insist upon a necessary temporal dimension to proper unity, even though it is much less explicit in Socrates' presentation. Nevertheless, it is clear that the climate is moderated and harmonious not only because of a limit placed on the extent of the extremes of frosts and summers but also because of their being ordered in a particular way and being made to last the right amount of time so as to allow things to grow and flourish (26a6–b4). Socrates more than once insists that the order he sees being imposed upon otherwise indeterminate things is not only an ordered arrangement at some particular point in time but is also an ordered arrangement of things over time. For example, at 28e Protarchus takes as strong evidence against the possibility that the universe as a whole is governed merely by chance, not only the appearance (*opsis*, 28e3) of the sun, moon, and stars, but also their revolutions (*periphora*, 28e5). Together, these two characteristics are meant to demonstrate the fact that things are ordered by intelligence (*nous*). They point to both the beauty and order visible at any one time and also the rationality of the way in which their relative positions alter through various periods of time. The order of the universe and the ordered changes of the universe over years, seasons, and months are said at 30c2–7 to be the product of wisdom (*sophia*) and intelligence (*nous*).

From these analogies we are supposed to infer something about the characteristics of the mixture that is thought necessary for a good human life. Since a life is a temporally extended and ordered whole, that order will also require a proper relationship between its parts or stages. Perhaps the minimum requirement of order is consistency – the parts of an ordered whole must not be in conflict with one another – and so an ordered life will have to exhibit a consistency across its temporal extension. Furthermore, that order will be the product of a person's reason and intelligence operating on the various otherwise indeterminate elements (such as pleasures) that are components of a human life. In fact, Socrates famously claims that the relationship between a human and the cosmos when considered in this way is not merely analogical. Rather, he makes it clear that he considers humans to be microcosms of the greater whole (29a–30d). Both an individual human and the cosmos at large are to be thought of as ensouled bodies. And just as an individual human body is composed of and nourished by elements taken from the greater cosmic body, so too is the human soul derived from the soul of the cosmos.[30] Later we learn that the more familiar Olympian god, Zeus, possesses a supremely kingly intelligence and a supremely kingly soul (*basilikē psykhē* and *basilikos nous*, 30d1–4) in so far as he is the regulator of the whole cosmos. We can infer, in that case, that just as we should consider Zeus himself – or perhaps more specifically, Zeus's intelligence – to demonstrate his kingly virtue in the excellent governance of the cosmos, so too we should think that there is a relevantly similar, if inferior, virtue of kingship in the souls of those individual humans who are able to regulate and order their microcosmic selves to the best of their nature's capacities.[31] Socrates also makes it clear that we are craftsmen of our lives (*dēmiourgoi*, 59d10–e3) and encourages us to pray to whichever god is in charge of such mixtures when we try to create the correct blend of pleasure and intelligence, as though mixing water and wine to get the best drink (61b–c). The analogy of microcosm and macrocosm is invoked again at the end of the dialogue at 64b6–7 when Socrates declares that their current argument seems to have generated a kind of 'bodiless ordering (*kosmos tis asōmatos*) that rules well an ensouled body'. Since their topic throughout has been the kind of ordering required to produce the mixture that is necessary for a good and choiceworthy human life, it seems quite clear that here again we are asked to draw direct parallels between the good and rational ordering of the macrocosm – itself an ensouled body – and the similarly good and rational ordering of the microcosm of an individual human life.[32]

Reason, both human reason and divine reason, is the cause of good mixture. Divine reason is the cause of good mixture on a large scale, namely that of the cosmos itself. Human reason is the cause of good mixture on the smaller scale of a human life. The overall mixture produced by reason on either scale is supposed to be harmonious and the specification of such a mixture is supposed to be indicative of what is good both in the cosmos at large and in the life of humans. And a human who is able to order his life well will be acting as Zeus acts. It is reasonable to think of this as another example of the familiar Platonic notion that in living a good life a human will become in some sense like a god. Since it is an activity that allows us to imitate the divine, we may also think that this ability to regulate one's own self is the characteristic of someone who is pious. Certainly, the *Philebus*

---

[30] All the wise men agree that *nous* is the king (*basileus*) of heaven and earth (28c6–8). In fact, the wise men 'say in harmony' (συμφωνοῦσιν) that he is. Presumably, since this is the truth, the wise men will not only harmonise with each other but also, in so far as they are wise, they will also harmonise with Zeus's divine intelligence to the extent that this is possible for a human. For the claim that the *sophoi* here are intended to recall Anaxagoras' conception of *nous* see Pepe 2002, 113–28.

[31] Cf. Frede 1997, 220; Carone 2005, 96–100; Delcomminette 2006, 264.   [32] Cf. Frede 1997, 355.

regularly demonstrates a rather expansive notion of what might count as proper pious behaviour, including even the possession of a proper understanding of the fundamental structure of the cosmos itself. For example, at 28a4–6 Socrates remarks that they should all take care not to place reason, understanding, and intelligence in the incorrect category of things. To make a mistake in this way would be a kind of impiety (*asebeia*). And at 28e1–2 Protarchus agrees that it would not be pious (*hosion*) to think that the cosmos is ruled by irrationality and chance.

Throughout the dialogue, in fact, it is possible to find support for the close connection between piety and the enjoyment of true pleasures. In the final summing-up of the results of the dialogue, for example, it is made clear that certain pleasures are not at all to be admitted into the good human life. That is hardly surprising, but it is important to note the reason why they ought not to be admitted. The pleasures themselves see that they would be benefited by a proper blending with the activities of reason. This gives another reason why certain pleasures cannot be part of the best blend and, moreover, it is a reason that has the support of the pleasures themselves. Certain intense and violent pleasures cannot be part of a good life because they are incompatible with a harmonious blending with reason and intelligence. The same result is reached when Socrates imagines turning to reason and intelligence and asking how they would assess the pleasures with which they are happy to associate. The answer he imagines they would give – an answer that is also supposed to be given on behalf of memory and true opinion (64a4–5) – is telling.

ἀλλ' ἅς τε ἡδονὰς ἀληθεῖς καὶ καθαρὰς [ἃς] εἶπες, σχεδὸν οἰκείας ἡμῖν νόμιζε, καὶ πρὸς ταύταις τὰς μεθ' ὑγιείας καὶ τοῦ σωφρονεῖν, καὶ δὴ καὶ συμπάσης ἀρετῆς ὁπόσαι καθάπερ θεοῦ ὀπαδοὶ γιγνόμεναι αὐτῇ συνακολουθοῦσι πάντῃ, ταύτας μείγνυ· τὰς δ' ἀεὶ μετ' ἀφροσύνης καὶ τῆς ἄλλης κακίας ἑπομένας πολλή που ἀλογία τῷ νῷ μειγνύναι τὸν βουλόμενον ὅτι καλλίστην ἰδόντα καὶ ἀστασιαστοτάτην μεῖξιν καὶ κρᾶσιν, ἐν ταύτῃ μαθεῖν πειρᾶσθαι τί ποτε ἔν τ' ἀνθρώπῳ καὶ τῷ παντὶ πέφυκεν ἀγαθὸν καὶ τίνα ἰδέαν αὐτὴν εἶναί ποτε μαντευτέον. (*Phileb.* 63e3–64a3)

The true and pure pleasures you mentioned, consider them more or less appropriate for us and, in addition, the pleasures that come with health and temperance and all those belonging to every virtue which, like attendants of god, follow it around everywhere.[33] Mix these in. But those that always

---

[33] It is not clear who the θεός is. Many translators (e.g. Gosling 1975) read it as a reference to a goddess, given the feminine ἀρετή, but this is not obligatory. If a particular divinity is intended, the main contenders will be Aphrodite or Virtue or, if it is not a goddess, Zeus. (Compare the similar uncertainty about the identity of the goddess at 26b8.)

follow foolishness and other wickedness, it would be entirely irrational to mix them with intelligence if you want to see what the most beautiful and harmonious mixture and blend might be and to try to learn from it what is by nature good both in a human and in the universe and to divine its very form.

The harmony and beauty of a life can be produced only by reason mixing in the right kinds of pleasures. It is hardly surprising that the pleasures which are allowed in by reason and intelligence are those which derive from such things as health, temperance, and other kinds of virtue. Here at 63e5–6 reason says it is happy to welcome those pleasures which 'like attendants of god follow it around everywhere'; the point apparently being that virtue is always accompanied by pure and true pleasures.[34] Just as in 39e–40c, true and pure pleasures are associated with divinity and virtuous characters while mixed and false pleasures are associated with foolishness and wicked characters.[35]

The most pious human lives are most like the divine macrocosm of which each human is a microcosmic part. Pious human lives are the human lives that are best unified and made harmonious by the operation of reason, since this is the way in which they most closely approximate the excellent ordering of the cosmos by divine reason. And a pious life will not contain false pleasures of anticipation because the person concerned is in this way 'loved by the gods' (40b3). False pleasures of anticipation, in so far as they are generated by an insufficient mastery on the part of human reason over a person's life as a whole, are therefore plausibly taken by Socrates and Protarchus to be symptomatic of impious and non-virtuous human lives.[36]

Protagorean hedonism and consistency

We can now return to the question whether Protarchus thinks that all pleasures are true. Let us assume for the moment that Protarchus is a 'Protagorean hedonist' who accepts that all pleasures are true. If this is indeed Protarchus' position, then it is not a very promising stance for him to take. But a brief consideration of the problems that it is likely to generate will allow us to return to consider Socrates' picture of a good and pious human life with

---

[34] Frede 1993, 78 n. 1 (cf. Frede 1997, 354) also remarks that if Socrates is consistent in his notion that pleasures are always somehow remedial then these ought to be the pleasures involved only in the pursuit of virtue and not its possession and exercise. Cf. Delcomminette 2006, 555. The problem is analogous to one often detected for the pleasures of the philosopher in *Republic* book 9, on which see Chapter 2 above.

[35] A connection noted by Frede 1997, 354.

[36] Cf. Russell 2005, 145–8, on 'becoming like god' in the *Philebus*.

Protagorean hedonism from a new perspective since Socrates' pious life and a Protagorean hedonist life share the characteristic of being free from false pleasures of anticipation. A Protagorean hedonist faces a problem in accounting for pleasures such as those involved in the anticipation of future pleasures. To put the problem in the more familiar terms of beliefs: if all beliefs are true then all predictions – including an agent's predictions about his own later beliefs or experiences – must be infallible. This difficulty is familiar from Socrates' exploration of Protagorean accounts of the truth of beliefs in the *Theaetetus*, where a problem is raised at 178a–179b concerning the relationship between predictions and later beliefs with specific reference to the notion of expertise. We want to say that some people are more reliable predictors of what is going to happen than others: a farmer is a better guide than a lyre-player to whether this year's grape harvest will produce sweet wine (178c9–d2). Another of Socrates' examples in that dialogue involves predictions about pleasure. In the *Theaetetus* Socrates argues that a cook is a better predictor than a dinner guest of whether a meal will be pleasant:

οὐκοῦν καὶ τοῦ μέλλοντος ἑστιάσεσθαι μὴ μαγειρικοῦ ὄντος, σκευαζομένης θοίνης, ἀκυροτέρα ἡ κρίσις τῆς τοῦ ὀψοποιοῦ περὶ τῆς ἐσομένης ἡδονῆς. περὶ μὲν γὰρ τοῦ ἤδη ὄντος ἑκάστῳ ἡδέος ἢ γεγονότος μηδέν πω τῷ λόγῳ διαμαχώμεθα, ἀλλὰ περὶ τοῦ μέλλοντος ἑκάστῳ καὶ δόξειν καὶ ἔσεσθαι πότερον αὐτὸς αὑτῷ ἄριστος κριτὴς ἢ σύ, ὦ Πρωταγόρα, τό γε περὶ λόγους πιθανὸν ἑκάστῳ ἡμῶν ἐσόμενον εἰς δικαστήριον βέλτιον ἂν προδοξάσαις ἢ τῶν ἰδιωτῶν ὁστισοῦν; (*Theaet.* 178d8–e6)

And suppose a feast is being made ready. The person who is about to eat it, if he is not a cook, will have a less authoritative judgement than the chef's concerning the pleasure to come. (For let us not get into a fight over the discussion of the pleasure that each person has right now or that each person had in the past, but only over what is to come.) Will each person be the best judge for himself of what will seem and be in the future or would you, Protagoras, be better than some other private individual at predicting what speech will be persuasive for each of us in the law court?

We might find this argument peculiar since, after all, *de gustibus nil disputandum*. I am not inclined to think that if I dislike a meal at a restaurant I should defer to the chef's opinion that it is in fact delicious. But Socrates is less reticent in affirming that matters of gastronomic pleasure are analogous to matters of health, for example, in being the province of a kind of expertise. An uneducated palate might well not take pleasure in something it should. And in any case, Socrates is carefully restricting his discussion to what a guest will enjoy. Perhaps we are not so reticent to believe that, personal preferences notwithstanding, a chef is a better judge of which flavour combinations will produce a pleasant dish than a non-expert diner. Be that as it may, Socrates and Theaetetus are inclined to think that an individual is not necessarily the best judge of what will be pleasant to him. The diner might well look at the menu, see a dish, and form the belief that he will not enjoy it. But when the dish comes, the brave diner takes a bite and finds that he does enjoy it. Since therefore the diner is revealed to have been mistaken in his original prediction, this is a useful example of a false belief to add to the mounting case against Protagoras' assertion that 'man is the measure'.

Consider now the example of false anticipated pleasures at *Philebus* 40a. What this adds to the picture in the *Theaetetus* is simply that the guest's anticipation of the experience of eating the meal can itself be pleasant or painful. While the *Theaetetus* is interested in finding a false belief in the diner's pre-prandial predictions, the *Philebus* in interested in identifying a false pleasure in the diner's pre-prandial anticipation. (Think of someone who reads a menu, imagines that he will enjoy the starter and takes pleasure in this anticipation. However, when the starter arrives and he tastes it, it is much less pleasant that he had imagined.)

If Protarchus is committed to the idea that all pleasures are true, then when it comes to cases of evaluating his own pleasures, including anticipating future pleasures, he will face a problem similar to the problem about beliefs that is faced by Protagoras. If all pleasures are true, then all pleasant anticipations of future pleasures must be infallible.[37] But Protarchus accepts that, as a matter of fact, it does sometimes happen that we are mistaken about what will be pleasant and, moreover, take pleasure in anticipating something which is not pleasant later. He therefore ought not to be a Protagorean hedonist.

Note that if Protagorean hedonism is taken to hold not only that all pleasures are true but also that we are infallible about our own pleasures, it is not only impossible not to feel pleasure at an object one has earlier anticipated enjoying with pleasure;[38] it is also impossible to go on to feel pleasure at some object which one has anticipated not enjoying. (I distinguish here 'anticipating not enjoying' from 'not anticipating enjoying': I might not anticipate enjoying a surprise party, but that is because I

---

[37] Mooradian 1996 is inclined to attribute Protagorean hedonism to Protarchus: (110) 'Since Protarchus is claiming that x is pleasurable for P at t if P takes pleasure in x at t, he will have to admit that there may be a fact, namely, that P takes pleasure in x at t, and that, if it is predicted that this fact will obtain or fail to obtain, that prediction will be true or false.'

[38] Here I take Protagorean hedonism to claim about pleasures what a certain interpretation of Protagorean relativism claims about beliefs, namely 'P is true (for X) if f believes that P'.

have no inkling that it would take place; if I anticipate not enjoying a party, then the party is no surprise but I might take pleasure in it contrary to my expectation.) To illustrate: Socrates could equally have made a case against Protarchus not on the basis of false anticipated pleasure, but on the basis of something that was expected not to be pleasant. Sometimes I find myself thinking ahead to an event later in the day without any pleasure. However, it sometimes turns out that when the event occurs I do in fact – unexpectedly – enjoy myself. Such errors are also incompatible with Protagoreanism about pleasure.[39]

There may be cases in which it is in fact reasonable to think that the anticipation of enjoyment does indeed itself ensure that we take pleasure in some future event.[40] But even if there are such cases, there seem to be just as many cases in which the anticipation that something will be pleasant succeeds only in making the actual event something of a disappointment. Lastly, as a coda to this section we should note that Aristotle takes a characteristically sensible and subtle view of the matter when he discusses pleasure, anticipation, and memory in *Rhet.* 1.11 1370a27–b28. This is not an idle comparison, since it would be odd if Aristotle did not have the *Philebus* somewhere in his thoughts when composing this chapter: his example of feverish people who take pleasure in recollecting a drink even as they hope for something to slake their thirst (1370b15–22) is very like the example given by Socrates at *Phileb.* 33c. Aristotle assumes that for the most part the things we enjoy remembering are those which were pleasant when present; and for the most part the things we enjoy anticipating are those which will be pleasant when present. But he offers a minor correction of Plato's picture when he notes that there are cases in which we enjoy remembering something which was not pleasant when present. It can be pleasant to look back at previous suffering and take pleasure in its current absence (1370b2–10). We will return to discuss this example in more detail in Chapter 7.

Conclusions

It is not clear whether Protarchus starts the dialogue as a Protagorean hedonist. But there is a close cousin of Protagorean hedonism to which Socrates appears committed and this related position will allow us to return to the question of the pious and good person mentioned at 39e10–40a1 and

[39] Cf. Rowett 2013, 204–7.

[40] Burnyeat 1990, 40: 'There are occasions when my belief that I will enjoy a feast (an example from 178de) *brings it about that*, when the time comes, I do.'

40b2–c2. Socrates seems to think that the life of a pious and virtuous human will lack the false pleasures that many of us do experience. It seems that at least 'for the most part' (40b2–3) a good and pious man will live a life in which, if he takes pleasure in the thought that he will later enjoy something, then he will indeed, when the moment comes, take pleasure in it just as he had anticipated doing. (It is not a necessary condition of his enjoying something that the good man has anticipated doing so, clearly, but it is 'for the most part' a sufficient condition.) Crucially, Socrates uses the notion of a good and pious character to explain why there is this consistency and connection throughout such a person's life.[41] And this consistency and connection is generated by human psychological capacities for retrospection and anticipation which Socrates associates with the presence of *logismos*.

We should insist on an addition to this picture. The degree of consistency and connection needed between the different parts of a life should not be such as to require that a good and pious person cannot undergo changes during his life so that something that does not bring him pleasure at one point in time can bring him pleasure at another. It is perfectly possible, for example, for someone as a young man not to enjoy playing bowls and then as an older man to find it an extremely pleasant way to spend an afternoon. The objects of a person's pleasures may well vary across a life in such a way and it would be both harsh and implausible to say that such variation is a mark of wickedness. What matters is not that a person's character must be unchanged throughout his life but that the different parts of the life should be tied together and brought into a good and unified whole. The analogy with music is helpful once more: a good piece of music need not remain qualitatively the same throughout – indeed, we might say that a good piece of music must display some variety over its duration – but a good piece of music must not be disjointed and inconsistent; any variations must be appropriately integrated into the whole. And as for music, so with life: we will find it odd if a person's pleasures do not vary across the length of the life; it would be very peculiar indeed to remain attracted to the pleasures of childhood when an adult or when a child to take pleasure only in what adults enjoy.

For Socrates and Protarchus, by the time they come to consider the example of false pleasures of anticipation at *Phileb.* 40a, it is perfectly clear

---

[41] Compare, for example, Epicurus' characterisation of the sage. The sage can confidently take pleasure in his anticipation as he considers in thought future parts of his extended life. He is confident that his character is sufficiently stable that there will be no disjunction between what he now takes pleasure in anticipating and what he will later take pleasure in when it arrives. See Chapter 8 for further discussion.

that wicked and god-hated people are those with unstable and inharmonious characters and are therefore those who will for the most part experience false pleasures of anticipation. The creation of a life that qualifies as a good mixture, like the creation of a cosmos that is a good mixture, is the accomplishment of reason and intelligence displaying its kingly virtues. When a human manages all of that by means of his reason and intelligence then he is acting in a god-like and pious manner. A stable and harmonious character is quite capable of thinking about future pleasant occurrences and taking pleasure in that anticipation, confident that they will indeed be pleasant to him when they arrive. It is the mark of an unstable and inharmonious (and therefore impious) person, on the other hand, to be subject to the kind of misapprehension and inconsistency that leads to false pleasures of anticipation.

CHAPTER 7

Aristotle on the pleasures and pains
of memory

Aristotle has a lot to say about memory and a lot to say about the nature of pleasure. He also has something to say about the relationship between pleasure and memory and expectation. Sometimes it appears that Aristotle assumes a model like the one at work in Plato's *Philebus*. But at other times Aristotle seems to want to qualify or modify that picture in ways that we might find rather attractive. The richest passage for discussions of Aristotle's views is found in *Rhet.* 1.11. But there are some important passages in the *Nicomachean Ethics* that deserve our attention first.

Memory, character, and pleasure in the *Nicomachean Ethics*

We have already seen indications that Aristotle considers our enjoyment of memories and expectations to be indications of significant metaphysical truths about the nature of pleasure (e.g. *NE* 10.3 1173b13–20, Chapter 3 above). Such pleasures do not, he asserts, fit the model which thinks of pleasures as replenishments of a lack. But besides these important metaphysical observations and the related arguments about whether pleasure can be a good, Aristotle is also inclined to think that a subject's memories and expectations – again in the sense of 'autobiographical' or 'introversive' memory and expectation – reveal something important about that subject's moral character. What is more, he is inclined to think that people with depraved characters will be troubled by memories and expectations because they reveal the fractures and inconsistencies in their actions and preferences. For example, during his account of friendship, he suggests at *NE* 9.4 that there is a reflexive relationship of a subject to himself that is an analogue of the interpersonal relationships of friendship and enmity. In a discussion of people who are truly bad (*phauloi*) Aristotle comments that such people are sometimes driven to suicide or, failing that, try to 'escape themselves' in other ways. They are tormented, in moments of solitary reflection, by their memories and their expectations:

> ἀναμιμνήσκονται γὰρ πολλῶν καὶ δυσχερῶν, καὶ τοιαῦθ᾽ ἕτερα ἐλπίζουσι, καθ᾽ ἑαυτοὺς ὄντες, μεθ᾽ ἑτέρων δ᾽ ὄντες ἐπιλανθάνονται. (NE 9.4 1166b15–17)

> For when they are alone they recollect many terrible things and they expect more such besides; but when they are with others they forget them.

Such people are not pleasing to themselves and the constant internal discord in their character is evident in their being unable to enjoy their memories and hopes. When such a person looks back to his past experiences, these cause him distress; when he looks forward to what he expects to do in the future, this also causes him distress. The best respite for such a person is to be in the company of others, perhaps because then the tendency to look backwards and forwards at his own experiences is for the moment lessened and he can be distracted temporarily from such painful introspection by 'escaping himself' and instead concentrating on those around him. This miserable state contrasts with that of a good person who can truly be said to be a friend to himself and who will enjoy his own company. He wishes to spend time with himself and with his memories and expectations and he will take pleasure in such recollection and expectation:

> συνδιάγειν τε ὁ τοιοῦτος ἑαυτῷ βούλεται· ἡδέως γὰρ αὐτὸ ποιεῖ· τῶν τε γὰρ πεπραγμένων ἐπιτερπεῖς αἱ μνῆμαι, καὶ τῶν μελλόντων ἐλπίδες ἀγαθαί, αἱ τοιαῦται δ᾽ ἡδεῖαι. καὶ θεωρημάτων δ᾽ εὐπορεῖ τῇ διανοίᾳ. συναλγεῖ τε καὶ συνήδεται μάλισθ᾽ ἑαυτῷ πάντοτε γὰρ ἐστι τὸ αὐτὸ λυπηρόν τε καὶ ἡδύ, καὶ οὐκ ἄλλοτ᾽ ἄλλο· ἀμεταμέλητος γὰρ ὡς εἰπεῖν. (NE 9.4 1166a23–9)

> A person like this wants to spend time with himself, for he does this with pleasure. And the memories of what he has done are enjoyable and his anticipations of what is to come are good; and those sorts of memories and anticipations are pleasant. And, what is more, he has plenty of things to contemplate in his mind. And he shares his pleasures and his pains with himself in particular, for the same thing is consistently painful or pleasant and is not pleasant at one time but not another; for, in a word, he is without regret.

Significantly, the memories and expectations of such a person are pleasant because they harmonise with his present character and desires. And his character over the course of his life is such that he consistently takes pleasure in the same things and is pained by the same things. For a virtuous person, we should add, it will also be the case that he takes pleasure in what is genuinely good and pleasant and will be pained by what is genuinely bad and painful. Aristotle returns to make this point explicitly at 9.8 1170a8–11. This explains why Aristotle calls such a person 'without regret' since, unlike the unfortunate wayward characters with whom this person is contrasted, not only will he take pleasure in what is genuinely good and be pained by what is genuinely bad, he will also not look back and recall a past pleasure and think now that it was not something that should have been enjoyed.

Some precision is necessary here because it is not clear just how demanding is this requirement for being 'without regret'. The requirement is more demanding if Aristotle means that a person 'without regret' would even now make the very same choices as he made in the past and be pleased and pained by the same things as he remembers choosing and experiencing in the past. He looks back and approves of his past choices, pleasures, and pains, even from the standpoint of the present and with the benefit of hindsight and intervening experience. It is less demanding if Aristotle means that this person is simply content with the choices and pleasures and pains of his past; he is happy that those choices were the best he could make at the time and the pleasures and pains were reasonable ones for the person he was then to experience. This is less demanding because it does not require the agent also to agree that, if he were now faced with the same choice, he would make exactly the same decision again. Perhaps he has changed or has learned from his intervening experiences such that he would now choose differently, but nevertheless neither is he ashamed of nor does he regret his previous choice.

We can compare a comment made by Socrates at *Prot.* 356d4–e2. There Socrates remarks that the power of appearance will sometimes prevent us from making accurate assessments of value and, if it does, sometimes we will later come to regret (*metamelein*) our choices. The regret could be justified by the mere fact that the choice was incorrect: as a result of the particular choice, things turned out for the agent worse than they would have done had he chosen differently. The regret could also be justified by the additional thought that not only was the choice incorrect but that it would not have been made if only we had been able to make an accurate assessment of the true value of the different options available. We can regret making a wrong choice and we can also regret not having been able to see the true value of the options that were available at the time. In this context Socrates is contrasting what happens if we are subject to the power of appearance with what happens when we are armed with the art of measurement that will generate accurate measures of the values of the options available. Equipped with this art the agent will always choose the best option available and will always choose on the basis of a reliable method of assessment. The strong implication is that there is no room for regret once the art of measurement has been mastered.[1]

Given that 'being without regret' appears in *NE* 9.4 to be a trait of the very best characters, there is every reason to think that Aristotle is being very demanding in his account of what is required to be this kind of person. After all, he seems to say not only that the person 'without regret' will not feel distress at the recollection of past choices and experiences but that he will feel positive pleasure as he looks back to his own past. To be sure, a virtuous person will act and choose on the basis of the information available at the time. There might be occasions when the choice has bad consequences that could not have been foreseen, but in those cases too, the virtuous person will not look back and 'regret' or be pained by the choice. Aristotle may be relying on the thought that the past choices in question are themselves choices made by a virtuous agent: the virtuous person will certainly not look back at his past virtuous acts thinking that there is room for leniency on the basis simply of prior inexperience or imperfect character. His character was as good then as it is now; that is the principal reason why he has no reason ever to regret what he has done and will instead continue to take pleasure in recalling those actions and choices.[2] We should here recall the good and pious people of Plato's *Philebus* whose pleasures are true because they are consistent over time.[3] Aristotle does not put his point in terms of true and false pleasures, of course, but he evidently shares Socrates' assumption that vicious characters are subject to internal conflict in a way that is revealed by their memories and expectations. In particular, vicious characters will not take pleasure in their own memories. Regret (*metamaleia*) – distress at the thought of an action or choice in one's past – is therefore taken to be a sign of a disordered character.[4] We might think here that Aristotle ought also to

---

[1] As we saw in Chapter 5 above, the account in the *Protagoras* makes no reference either to brute unpredictable consequences that simply cannot be foreseen even by the best equipped planner nor to the possibility of unpredictable changes in the agent's own preferences and character.

[2] Pangle 2003, 144, comments: 'By setting up freedom from regrets as the standard of true virtue and inner harmony, Aristotle suggests how rare such virtue is, for even most very decent people have regrets. To escape them entirely, one would have to have a degree of self-understanding that is hard for most of us even to imagine ... If one might in retrospect have chosen otherwise in some instance, one would still have the peace of knowing that one chose the best course in light of everything one knew or could reasonably have been expected to know at the time.'

[3] See above, Chapter 6.

[4] Aristotle also discusses regret at *NE* 3.1 1110b18–24, where it is a sign of a 'counter-voluntary' (*akousion*) action. And at 7.7 1150a21–2 Aristotle remarks that the wanton (*akolastos*) person shows no regret and is therefore incurable; this contrasts with the akratic person who does regret his past choices (1150b29–31). (This implies that the *phaulos* discussed in 9.4 is not *akolastos*; cf. Pakaluk 1998, 177.) Compare Plat. *Rep.* 577d13–e2: a tyrannical soul will be full of turmoil and regret.

leave room for a sense of regret that can be felt by a person of good character looking back to actions and choices from a time in his past before he became the good person he now is. It seems right that there is a sense in which someone might, although no longer a vicious or disordered character, nevertheless look back and regret things in his past. True, even in this case the presence of regret marks a distinction between the current standpoint and his character in the past, but Aristotle ought perhaps to leave room nevertheless for a reformed or improved character to be able to look back and to regret – and even be pained at the thought of – a less virtuous past.

A little later, in 9.7, Aristotle offers some further remarks that make reference to the pleasures of memory and expectation. But here the argument is less clear and less successful. At 9.7 1168a9–19 Aristotle is wondering whether benefaction is good and pleasant more for the benefactor or for the recipient of the benefaction. The answer is complicated. In a way it is of course true that the recipient is benefited and enjoys the benefaction. However, Aristotle wants to maintain that the benefactor too will take pleasure in the action, perhaps more so in fact than will the recipient. This is because the benefactor, in a way, identifies himself with the action. He will love his work because he loves his own existence and will take pleasure in the fineness of the benefaction (its being *kalon*) in the recipient. Further, the recipient will take pleasure in the usefulness of the benefaction only in the present. The benefactor, on the other hand, will take pleasure in the memory of the fineness of the benefaction and the fineness will endure after the usefulness has faded. Here Aristotle notes that the opposite may be true of expectation: the expectation of receiving something useful is pleasant whereas the memory of having received something useful is less so (9.7 1168b18–19). It is not clear why this should be the case. It is not clear why it is not possible to take pleasure in the expectation of a fine action at least as much as in the expectation of a useful one. The benefactor can surely look ahead with pleasure to the fine action he is about to perform. Furthermore, Aristotle began with the plausible claim that the utility of a benefaction holds only while the benefaction is present while it is possible also to take pleasure in the fineness of a past benefaction that one recalls. He has now moved to the less plausible claim that not only the utility of the benefaction but also the pleasure at the thought of the benefaction is less when the benefaction is past. This too seems questionable. Once a benefaction is in the past, it is of course true that its recipient will no longer feel the benefit of the benefaction itself. But it seems that the recipient may nevertheless still take pleasure at recalling its utility at the time.

What begins as a contrast between the temporary goodness of what is merely useful and the persistent goodness of what is fine becomes complicated by concerns over whether and when it is appropriate to take pleasure in the recollection, present thought, or expectation of something useful and something fine respectively. Clearly, Aristotle wants the benefactor's appreciation of his own good deed as something fine to be superior to the recipient's appreciation of the benefaction as something useful. And he wants it to be superior on two accounts. First, in so far as the benefactor appreciates the deed as fine, this appreciation will not diminish over time since the fineness of the deed will not be as temporary as its utility. Second, it is apparently the case that a memory of a deed as fine will be pleasant in a way that the memory of a deed as useful will not. There is little justification offered for this claim even though it is evidently part of Aristotle's preparation for the claim in 9.8 that the virtuous person will be a 'self-lover' in a superlative and morally unobjectionable way since such a person will take pleasure in his own virtue and fineness.[5] Indeed, the pleasure taken by the virtuous person in what is fine is such that, were the choice necessary and he be forced into an act of noble self-sacrifice, he would prefer to live for only a brief time experiencing this intense pleasure than a longer time with milder enjoyment (9.7 1169a22–5).

Regardless of the local difficulties of the passage in 9.7, it should be clear from these two examples that Aristotle, like Plato before him, was interested in how memory and expectation are sources of pleasure and, more importantly, how memory and expectation differ in the pleasures and pains they offer to people of differing moral character and with different evaluative priorities. In both passages Aristotle is concerned to stress that someone of noble and virtuous character who takes pleasure in what is truly fine will also take pleasure in the recollection of fine deeds. Such a person will be able to take pleasure constantly and consistently in the thought of his past deeds and will be able to look forwards with confidence and pleasure to his continuing fine character. There is therefore a close connection between Aristotle's account of the pleasures to be had in perceiving and thinking of beautiful and well-ordered objects and the pleasure that a virtuous person will experience in looking forwards and backwards and recognising his own well-ordered life, littered with fine deeds that stem from a noble and consistent virtuous character. This is another example of the human capacity for enjoyment of the fineness of something as such.[6]

The virtuous person can, through memory and expectation, appreciate the fine nature of his life and deeds almost as an object of aesthetic enjoyment; the beauty and fineness (*kallos*) of his good and ordered life is something that will

---

[5] For similar dissatisfaction with this argument in 9.7 see Pakaluk 1998, 188–9.
[6] See above, Chapter 3.

be a cause of significant pleasure. In chapter 9.9 Aristotle develops the analogy between the fineness of the virtuous life and the aesthetic fineness of a piece of music even further (9.9 1169b30–1170a11). In fact, he says, a virtuous person will take pleasure in fine actions whether or not they are his own just as a musician is pleased by fine music, whether or not he is playing the music himself. This is one way in which Aristotle defends the claim that the virtuous and happy person will still need friends, although the virtuous person is as self-sufficient as any human can be. He does not have friends in order to experience pleasure in their company but, since he does share his activities and his life with others, he will take pleasure in their fine deeds and be pained by vicious deeds, just as he is pleased by his own fine actions.[7]

Memory and *phantasia*

Rhetoric 1.11 offers one of the most interesting discussions in the corpus of the relationship between pleasure and memory. The chapter begins with the assertion that pleasure is a certain motion or change of the soul – a claim it shares with *Phys.* 7.3 and which notoriously seems at odds with his considered view in the *Ethics* – and then relates pleasure to desire (1.11 1369b33–1370a27).[8] Aristotle next turns to address the connection between pleasure and perception. He first notes that experiencing pleasure depends on the perception of a certain kind of *pathos*. Next he adds the idea that imagination (*phantasia*), being a kind of weak perception of what is remembered or anticipated, always accompanies an act of remembering or anticipating since whenever we recall or anticipate something we must engage our capacity for imagination (1.11 1370a27–30). This allows Aristotle to note that all pleasures must come about either directly via perception itself (when the object is present) or via memory or anticipation (when the object is past or future respectively). In the latter case, therefore, they will come about via *phantasia*. This reference to the psychological faculty of imagination is

---

[7] For more on the role of the fine in the *Nicomachean Ethics* and elsewhere see Richardson Lear 2006, who emphasises the sense in which Aristotle thinks there is a particular delight and pleasure to be found by the virtuous agent in the enjoyment of the fine as such. Moss 2012a, 206–19, discusses the argument in *NE* 9.9 and emphasises how Aristotle describes the pleasures as pleasures of perception. In so far as this is sensory perception then, like human sensory enjoyment of beautiful objects, this is a perceptual pleasure available to us as rational perceivers. It is harder to understand the pleasures from memories and anticipations described at 9.4 1166a23–9 as strictly sensory in the same way. See also Coope 2012, 155–7, for an argument that this is a pleasure of the rational part of the soul.

[8] For discussion see Gosling and Taylor 1982, 194–9; Frede 1996b and 2009; Dow 2011, 61–71. For a discussion of the passage in *Phys.* 7.3 see Wardy 1990, 220–7.

worth further consideration before we press on with the remainder of the account in *Rhet.* I.II.

Much of the general model that emerges from Aristotle's account is relatively familiar from the Platonic texts we have considered previously, although we need to be cautious in determining the precise commitments of Aristotle's own theory. The *Philebus*, as we noted, explains the experience of pleasant anticipation in terms of a 'painter in the soul' generating images on the basis of statements written down by a 'scribe'; those images may include depictions of the anticipator at some time in the future taking pleasure at some imagined object. Aristotle himself in his psychological works insists on the close connection between both the faculty of imagination and that of perception (although these two are to be kept distinct) and also between the faculty of imagination and the human capacity for the deliberate recollection or deliberate anticipation of non-present events and experiences.[9] The overall picture seems to be something like the following. Aristotle agrees that we can experience pleasure or pain as a result of the form of weak perception that is involved when we engage our capacity to recall or anticipate our experiences. Furthermore, he is inclined to agree that for the most part – and we shall see that this qualification is important – things that are pleasant when present are also pleasant when anticipated or remembered (I.II 1370b9–10). This allows him to explain why it is that people who are suffering from a fever can take pleasure in remembering or looking forward to a cool drink and why people in love can take pleasure in talking or writing about their beloved since in engaging in this recollection of the beloved they think that they are in a way perceiving him (I.II 1370b15–22).[10]

Other passages point in a similar direction. For example, Aristotle comments at *De Mem.* 1 450a29–32 that memory is the retention of 'a sort of picture' (*zōgraphēma ti*), and that this imprint left by a perception is similar to those left by signet rings.[11] And in the *De Motu Animalium* he seems to

---

[9] However, in so far as Aristotle makes *phantasia* central to the workings of memory, he is happy to assign this capacity to some non-rational animals. In this sense, memory in general is not for Aristotle an exclusively rational capacity. For a recent account of the nature and scope of *phantasia* see Johansen 2012, 199–220. See also Schofield 1978 and Frede 1992a.

[10] Cf. Moss 2012a, 78–84.

[11] Cf. Sorabji 2004, 2–8. Lorenz 2006a, 161 n. 34, is right to detect allusions here to both the *Philebus* and the *Theaetetus* while noting that Aristotle adopts neither dialogue's account without qualification. Compare also *De Mem.* 1 449b22–3 for the claim that memory is 'a statement in the soul' and note the use of a 'wax block' analogy for memory at 450a25–b11. Scheiter 2012 develops an interpretation of Aristotle's account of *phantasia* in *De An.* 3.3 that emphasises this Platonic background (cf. Moss 2012a, 85–7). At *In Phileb.* §175 Damascius compares the scribe and painter in Plato's *Philebus* with Aristotle's characterisation of the soul as a blank writing-slate at *De An.* 3.4 429b31–430a2.

entertain the view that when we conceive of, remember, or anticipate some experience then we also on occasion come to feel as we would were the imagined scenario genuinely happening in the present. For example, he writes:

> αἱ μὲν γὰρ αἰσθήσεις εὐθὺς ὑπάρχουσιν ἀλλοιώσεις τινὲς οὖσαι, ἡ δὲ φαντασία καὶ ἡ νόησις τὴν τῶν πραγμάτων ἔχουσι δύναμιν· τρόπον γάρ τινα τὸ εἶδος τὸ νοούμενον τὸ τοῦ θερμοῦ ἢ ψυχροῦ ἢ ἡδέος ἢ φοβεροῦ τοιοῦτον τυγχάνει ὂν οἷόν περ καὶ τῶν πραγμάτων ἕκαστον, διὸ καὶ φρίττουσι καὶ φοβοῦνται νοήσαντες μόνον. (*MA* 7 701b17–22; cf. 8 702a5–7 and 11 703b18–20)

> For perceptions are immediately alterations of a kind, but imagination and thinking have the power of the things themselves; for in a way the form of what is hot or cold or pleasant or frightening that is being thought of is in fact just like each of the things themselves. And that is why people shiver and are afraid just from thinking of something.

Aristotle is sometimes prepared to explain or illustrate the workings of memory and anticipation in terms that involve the internal viewing of representations of some object experience. Certainly, memory involves the use of *phantasmata* (see *De Mem.* 1 450a19–25) and Aristotle sometimes seems to describe the role of *phantasmata* in terms of images of some kind in the soul.[12] Nevertheless, it is not certain at all that these *phantasmata* should be understood in fact to be internal images. Perhaps it would be better to say that Aristotle often borrows Plato's means of explaining the workings of *phantasia* without being committed to the literal truth of a kind of internal theatre of the mind.[13] All the same, these *phantasmata* that are involved in memory can sometimes produce the same kind of effects – and produce the same pleasures and pains – as simple direct perception of the external world, although Aristotle allows that the intensity of these effects may not be quite the same.

There are two texts which offer important further perspectives on this familiar picture. First, in his discussion of *phantasia* in *De An.* 3.3, Aristotle

---

[12] On *De Mem.* 1 450a19–25, see also Caston 1998, 257–9 and esp. n. 21. At 450a29–30 Aristotle also compares memory to the possession of a picture (*zōgraphēma*) in the soul.

[13] There has been considerable discussion and disagreement over the nature of Aristotelian *phantasia* and whether *phantasmata* are thought by him to be like a viewed picture. For a brief summary of recent debates see Sorabji 2004, xi–xx and King 2009, 40–62, who comments: (58): 'Aristotle nowhere says that representations are images but in several places he *compares* them with pictures or images.' For examples of such comparisons: *De An.* 3.3 427b21–4 (see below), 3.8 432a7–14 and *De Mem.* 1 450a1–451a8. See also Nussbaum 1978, 222–31; Wedin 1988, 90–9; Caston 1998, 281–4; Caston 2009, 323–6, which has a concise introduction to recent discussions; and Johansen 2012, 199. See Warnock 1987, 15–36, for a critical survey of the theme of memory images in modern philosophy.

distinguishes *phantasia* from other psychic capacities such as perception (*aisthēsis*), thinking (*dianoia*), and supposing (*hypolēpsis*).[14] He offers two reasons for distinguishing *phantasia* from belief that deserve our attention (427b17–24). His first reason points towards the connection between *phantasia* and memory; he observes that *phantasia* is 'up to us' (*eph' hēmin*) in a way that belief is not since we can call up this experience (*pathos*) at will. Here Aristotle notes that it is possible to use *phantasia* to bring things 'before our eyes' (*pro ommatōn*), as is shown by the practice of those who use mnemonic techniques that involve the generation of images.[15] His second reason is worth more detailed consideration.

> ἔτι δὲ ὅταν μὲν δοξάσωμεν δεινόν τι ἢ φοβερόν, εὐθὺς συμπάσχομεν, ὁμοίως δὲ κἂν θαρραλέον· κατὰ δὲ τὴν φαντασίαν ὡσαύτως ἔχομεν ὥσπερ ἂν εἰ θεώμενοι ἐν γραφῇ τὰ δεινὰ ἢ θαρραλέα. (*De An.* 3.3 427b21–4)

> Whenever we have a belief that something is terrible or frightening, we immediately feel the accompanying *pathos*, and similarly for something encouraging; but in the case of *phantasia* we are like people looking at something terrible or alarming in a picture.[16]

This comment is evidently concerned with the connection between *phantasia* and *pathē* and therefore should shed some light on the relationship between memory and pleasure and pain.[17] Aristotle seems to say that, while believing that something is terrible will immediately generate the feeling of fear and perhaps an associated pain, choosing to call up a *phantasma* of something terrible may well not generate a similar affective response.[18] If this applies also to the kinds of images generated by recalling past experiences – that is, to the deliberate use of the capacity of memory to call up such *phantasmata* – then it will follow that there is no reason to assume that if some past experience was, for example, frightening and painful, then the deliberate recollection of that experience will once again generate the same *pathos*. Certainly, it will sometimes be the case that a *phantasma* will generate an immediate physiological effect but this is not

---

[14] On this passage see Caston 1996, 43–6. Cf. 431b7: 'as if seeing' (ὥσπερ ὁρῶν) and *De Mem.* 1 450a5.
[15] On these techniques see Sorabji 2004, 22–34, and Small 1997, 81–137. On this passage in *De An.* 3.3 cf. Wedin 1988: 74–5. Cic. *Fin.* 2.104–5 offers reasons to think that our powers of memory are not entirely 'up to us': see below, p. 198.
[16] Cf. *De An.* 3.9 432b29–433a1 and 1.1 403a23–4: it is possible to be frightened when nothing frightening is present.
[17] See also Dow 2009, 164–5.
[18] Compare *De An.* 3.9 432b29–433a1: when someone contemplates (θεωρῇ) something there is not necessarily any call to pursuit or avoidance; even when someone thinks (διανοεῖται) about something fearful it is not necessary that the person experience fear. Cf. Caston 1996, 46–52.

always the case, and perhaps most notably this often fails to happen when the *phantasma* is conjured up deliberately.[19] Note also that, presumably in part to explain the difference between the affective reactions to beliefs and recollections, Aristotle compares the latter with what we experience when we are looking at something in a picture. He is often tempted to explain the working of memory as a kind of deliberate contemplation of a representation of a past experience. By observing that when we call things to mind with *phantasia* then we stand to those contents as we do when viewing a picture – presumably, seeing what we call to mind in some way as a depiction – he can allow the possibility of such a state of mind's having a different effect from the direct perception of whatever it is that is depicted in this way. No doubt, there are pleasures and pains involved in viewing depictions of things. (And we can even identify pleasures and pains involved in viewing depictions of ourselves experiencing past experiences; think of the feelings conjured up by looking at pictures of yourself in a photograph album.) But these should be distinguished from the pleasures and pains involved in the direct experience of the kind of thing being depicted.

When we choose to cast our minds back to some past experience and thereby conjure up a *phantasma*, there is no necessary connection between any affective response that the *phantasma* might generate in us and how we would normally – perhaps necessarily – feel were we directly faced with experiencing in the present what the *phantasma* represents. So, while I will feel terror, break out into a cold sweat, find my heart racing, and so on, if I am confronted by a tiger or – perhaps more precisely – believe that I am confronted by a tiger, there is no sufficient reason to think that I will always experience those same responses when later on I choose to recall that incident. And even if I choose to recall my past experience of being terrified when I saw the tiger, there is again no sufficient reason to expect that that act of recollection will itself generate the same affective responses as were involved in the original object experience. For these reasons, it should be clear that there is no necessary connection between, for example, a past experience that was painful and a particular affective response that a person will feel when he or she chooses to recall that past experience.[20]

---

[19] *MA* 7 701b17–22, cited above, stresses how *phantasia* and belief sometimes have the same effect as a perception. My imagining that there is a dangerous animal hiding in the bushes is likely to cause various physiological effects. See also Schofield 2011, 131–2.

[20] Hamlyn 1968, 131 ad loc. comments briefly and approvingly: 'What Aristotle says in the latter half of the passage seems quite correct.'

The memories of Eumaeus

The second qualification to the simple picture can be found in *Rhet.* 1.11, this time with more explicit reference to the pleasures and pains of memory in particular. Aristotle observes that while it is usually the case that we take pleasure in remembering things that were pleasant when originally experienced and we are pained by remembering things that were painful when originally experienced, this is not always the case. Sometimes we recall with pleasure a past pain. There are therefore circumstances in which the affective response to something recollected may be different from the response that the recollected events originally provoked. For example, there is no simple and direct connection between what it is pleasant to experience now in the present and what it might be pleasant to remember having experienced:

> τὰ μὲν οὖν μνημονευτὰ ἡδέα ἐστὶν οὐ μόνον ὅσα ἐν τῷ παρόντι, ὅτε παρῆν, ἡδέα ἦν, ἀλλ' ἔνια καὶ οὐχ ἡδέα, ἂν ᾖ ὕστερον καλὸν καὶ ἀγαθὸν τὸ μετὰ τοῦτο. (*Rhet.* 1.11 1370a35–b3)

> But things that are pleasant when remembered are not only those that were pleasant when they were present. But sometimes also things that were not pleasant [*sc.* when present are pleasant when remembered], provided that what comes after this was fine and good.

The thought is characteristically compressed and provokes a number of immediate questions which turn on the proper understanding of the important qualification '. . . provided that what comes after this (*to meta touto*) was fine and good'. For example, does Aristotle mean that we can recall with pleasure some painful experiences provided that they are merely followed by something fine and good? Alternatively, does Aristotle mean just that we can recall with pleasure some painful experiences provided that their consequences were pleasant? In that case, is he claiming that we can recall the prior pain with pleasure because in doing so we also bring to mind, as it were, the causal connection between that prior pleasure and our current positive state? Such an interpretation of the qualification 'provided that what comes after this was fine and good' makes the originally painful experience somehow instrumentally pleasant: had we not undergone those toils we would not have experienced the consequent pleasure. But this seems odd. It is not, after all, the consequences we are said to remember with pleasure but the originally painful experience itself. Nor does it seem that Aristotle means that what was originally thought painful is now revealed as pleasant in comparison with the present state of affairs, as is claimed by the opponents whom Socrates dismisses in *Republic* book 9.[21]

We need to determine the precise relationship between the memory and pleasure. Why is it that what was originally a painful experience can sometimes be pleasant when recalled later? There are various options:

(a) It is now pleasant to recall the event because we recall the pleasant excitement and intensity of the experience rather than the pain and struggle.

(b) It is now pleasant to recall the event because, although painful at the time, it is now over. When we recall the event our attention is drawn to its past-ness and that is a pleasant thought.

(c) It is now pleasant to recall the event because, although it was painful at the time, when we recall the event our attention is drawn to our comparatively positive state now and that is a pleasant thought.

(d) It is now pleasant to recall the event because, although painful at the time, it had beneficial consequences which are pleasant.

(e) It is now pleasant to recall the event because, although it was painful at the time, in retrospect we see the event itself – not just its consequences – as something positive and beneficial.

Some of these possibilities can be ruled out rather swiftly. Option (a) is inspired by a remark by Sidgwick. He writes:

> To this case it seems due that past hardships, toils, and anxieties often appear pleasurable when we look back upon them, after some interval; for the excitement, the heightened sense of life that accompanies the painful struggle, would have been pleasurable if taken by itself; and it is that that we recall rather than the pain.[22]

This seems to be a rather implausible claim in itself but it reveals nevertheless how Sidgwick is evidently tempted to look for some pleasant aspect in the original experience itself which is now being recalled with pleasure in the present. His intuition seems to be that, if it is pleasant to recall some past experience, then there must originally have been some pleasant aspect of that experience which is responsible now for the pleasure of the recollection. This is not, I think, what Aristotle has in mind. Rather, he is envisaging a case in which we recall with pleasure an experience which, when it was originally present, was in no way pleasant.

Option (b) might put us in mind of A. N. Prior's claim that the fact that we can reasonably say 'Thank goodness, that's over!' about some past event

---

[21] See Warren 2011b.   [22] Sidgwick 1907, 144.

suggests that there is indeed some genuine property of past-ness to which we are now referring and which can be the cause of relief or even positive pleasure. Prior goes on to claim, notoriously, that we cannot give a complete tenseless equivalent for such statements and that this in turn suggests that time does indeed flow.[23] The metaphysics of time that this kind of locution may or may not imply can be left aside on this occasion, provided that we notice only that we do indeed seem to be able to take pleasure in an event's past-ness, however we choose to analyse what 'past-ness' amounts to. In other words, what we take pleasure in or express relief at is not so much the content of the past experience as the fact of its being a past experience.[24] However, I think it is not likely that this is what is on Aristotle's mind either.

The examples that follow Aristotle's comments in *Rhet.* 1.11, drawn from epic poetry and tragedy, shed some more light on what he means. It seems to me that they might fit options (c), (d), and (e) above, although Aristotle does not make their precise sense explicit.[25] For his first example, Aristotle simply cites a line from Euripides' *Andromeda* (fr. 133 Nauck[2]): 'Pleasant it is when rescued to remember toils (*ponoi*)' (ἀλλ' ἡδύ τοι σωθέντα μεμνῆσθαι πόνων). It is a succinct example of an interesting exception to the general rule that things that are pleasant when remembered were pleasant when first experienced. Sometimes, as a result of some intervening event, we might remember with pleasure something – here, the toil – that was painful when present.[26]

The other example comes from Homer, *Od.* 15.400–1: Eumaeus the swineherd is addressing the disguised Odysseus and is about to tell the story of how he was taken from his birthplace as a young boy by some Phoenicians and later bought as a slave by Laërtes, Odysseus' father. He says to Odysseus, 'Let us cheer one another by both recalling our sad cares', and

---

[23] See Prior 1959. Cf. Mellor 1981, which provoked various other pieces helpfully collected in Oaklander and Smith 1994, Part III.

[24] Seneca, for example, seems to be pointing to this possibility at *Ep. Mor.* 78.14: 'Eventually, what was bitter to undergo is pleasant to have undergone: it is natural to take pleasure at the ending of one's harm' (*deinde quod acerbum fuit ferre, tulisse iucundum est: naturale est mali sui fine gaudere*).

[25] Option (c) seems to be the likely force of some of the Epicureans' comments collected by Plutarch at *Non Posse* 1091A–B (Usener 423 and Metrodorus fr. 28 Körte). Indeed, to Plutarch's annoyance, the Epicureans appear to claim that this is the greatest pleasure possible. But Plutarch does report the Epicureans' insistence that it is not sufficient merely to have suffered and to be suffering no longer. It is also important to recall the past suffering, recognise it, and feel gratitude at its absence. See further below, Chapter 8.

[26] The plot of the lost *Andromeda* is not certain, but it is possible that the line was spoken by Perseus, perhaps recounting his relief at having escaped his encounter with the Gorgon. See Webster 1967, 192–9, esp. 195, and Wright 2005, 121–33.

then in the lines which Aristotle cites Eumaeus explains the apparent paradox of this recommendation.

κήδεσιν ἀλλήλων τερπώμεθα λευγαλέοισι,
μνωομένω· μετὰ γάρ τε καὶ ἄλγεσι τέρπεται ἀνήρ,
ὅς τις δὴ μάλα πολλὰ πάθῃ καὶ πόλλ᾽ ἐπαληθῇ. (*Od.* 15.399–401)[27]

Let us two cheer one another with recollections of our wretched sorrows. For a man who has undergone many sufferings and has wandered far is cheered even by his pains.

A closer look at the *Odyssey* will help to explain why Aristotle may have thought that this an interesting illustration of his point since the situation to which Aristotle alludes by citing these lines is complicated not only by the narrative of disguise, sincerity, and concealment that is at work at this point of the epic but also by the characters themselves drawing attention to that very complexity. The broader context of Eumaeus' claim suggests an interest on the part of the epic poet in the effects that stories of past sufferings – both truthful and deceitful – may have on the audience and on the speaker. Remember that Eumaeus not only asserts that it can be pleasant to recall what were painful experiences but also that he imagines this taking place within a context of mutual exchange: 'Let us cheer one another by sharing our sad tales.'[28] But the exchange is not quite the fair and sincere one that Eumaeus expects.

In telling his story, Eumaeus is answering the Cretan story concocted by the disguised Odysseus and recounted in the previous book (beginning at 14.192): a false story that nevertheless managed to generate an emotional response in Eumaeus who says that his 'heart was stirred' by the tale (14.361–2). We might wonder whether, given that this was a deliberately false story, it can have had the same sort of cheering effect on Odysseus himself as he told it. When Eumaeus' turn comes to tell a story in return, the old man hopes that recounting his own story will have such an effect on both Odysseus and himself; he hopes that the mutual sharing of stories will

---

[27] It is also possible to use this idea as a means of consolation during periods of suffering by offering the thought that in the future perhaps the recollection of even these present sufferings may bring pleasure: cf. Sen. *Ep. Mor.* 78.15, where he cites Virgil, *Aeneid* 1.203: 'perhaps there will be a time when it will be pleasant to recall even this' (*forsan et haec olim meminisse iuvabit*). Plotinus, *Enneads* 4.3.28 offers as an indication that the memory of having a desire is not retained in the desiring part of the soul the fact that something which was originally pleasant when experienced is not always pleasant to recall. See King 2009, 167–8.

[28] Aristotle also comments at *Rhet.* 2.13 1390a6–11 that the elderly are more likely to spend time engaged in – and enjoying – such reminiscences. The young are more inclined to dwell on the future and for the most part live 'in anticipation' (ζῶσι τὰ πλεῖστα ἐλπίδι) (2.12 1389a20–4).

be positive for both speaker and audience. But this is where the effects of two speeches diverge since Eumaeus' sincere recollection and Odysseus' artifice, although perhaps indistinguishable to their respective audiences, will presumably differ in the effects each has on its own speaker. Eumaeus begins his account with the lines cited by Aristotle, setting out his hope of some positive emotional benefit as a frame for his tale. But when he concludes his tale at 15.484 with his first arrival on Ithaca, he makes no further comment on whether he has in fact experienced any present emotional impact in recalling those events, so we are left perhaps simply to remember his opening statement and infer that this has indeed been a positive experience. Odysseus, on the other hand, replies by noting that Eumaeus' story has moved him, more or less repeating the pair of lines with which Eumaeus had responded to Odysseus' first – and deceitful – tale (15.486–7, cf. 14.361–2). Odysseus also comments that although Eumaeus' story – like his own – included many sufferings, it ended well with Eumaeus' arrival at the home of a good master and a long and happy life (15.488–92).

The situation in the epic is perfect for Aristotle to use as an example for a very specific point and a very specific qualification of his general thesis. Aristotle does not appear to cast any doubt on the truth of the memory involved in the recollection of one's past experiences. By the 'truth of the memory' I mean only that the situation recalled did happen in just the way in which it is remembered. In Eumaeus' case this will amount to the claim that Eumaeus remembers truly the events of his being taken and enslaved and brought to Ithaca. Furthermore, Aristotle presumably will also allow that Eumaeus' memory might be authentic in the sense that in addition the old man recalls correctly that he was afraid and distressed at the time by those events.[29] Nevertheless, something about Eumaeus' affective response to recalling these events and these attitudes is distinctive and that is why his situation interests Aristotle. For Eumaeus reports that he remembers being enslaved, remembers how it felt at the time but nevertheless now is pleased when he thinks back to those events. There must be some important characteristic of this situation that will make sense of this unusual aspect.

It is likely that Eumaeus' original claim that such reminiscences can bring pleasure is licensed not simply by the fact that the sufferings in question have ended but rather by the fact that they have ended well. Indeed, this is likely to be what Aristotle has in mind when he insists that the phenomenon in question is dependent on some subsequent or consequent good coming

---

[29] See Bernecker 2010, 215–17.

from the painful past experience (ἂν ᾖ ὕστερον καλὸν καὶ ἀγαθὸν τὸ μετὰ τοῦτο). For Eumaeus, we might say that it is pleasant to recall his prior sufferings because they resulted in his arrival in Ithaca and the good life he was able to live there. What is important for Aristotle is that this allows Eumaeus to recall the prior sufferings themselves and not the later positive consequences of those sufferings and to take pleasure in that recollection. Eumaeus can, with hindsight, now see those sufferings as leading to a later good whereas obviously this was not possible at the time when he was originally experiencing the toils. And it is because he now recalls the toils as leading to a later good that he can now take pleasure in recalling them and not just in recalling their later good results. Eumaeus therefore provides an example of option (e) above and perhaps also of option (d): the painful events led to good consequences and therefore can themselves now be considered in hindsight to be good. It is therefore pleasant now to remember them.

In the case of the line from Euripides' *Andromeda* we are hampered by a lack of the original context. Perhaps here too the character in question is expressing an appreciation for the positive results that came from prior perils. But the emphasis seems different: it is the simple fact of now being safe that matters rather than some additional positive result. To be sure, in some way or other it is necessary to be in peril in order later to be rescued and in this way the rescue and the pleasure of being rescued may well be thought of as resulting from being first imperilled. Just as it was necessary for Eumaeus to be snatched from his home for him to arrive in Ithaca so too it was necessary for Perseus, let us say, to undergo various perils before he could be rescued from them. And in this sense we can say that the good of being saved is a consequence of the prior dangers. We might even go so far as to identify a particular pleasure in being saved from danger at the very last moment: a euphoric feeling of unexpected salvation. But it would be a little perverse to imagine that prior peril is a necessary precondition of enjoying being safe and sound. Rather, Perseus can look back and recall the various toils which he has undergone and which are now in his past. As a result, he is able to take special pleasure in his current safety since he realises that things might not have turned out as they did. Perseus therefore might be an example of option (c) above.

In both cases, Aristotle shows that he is not prepared to be shackled by a simple account according to which *phantasia* always brings along with it the affective response occasioned by the original experience upon which it is based. And he is right to do so. He can also offer a reasonable account of how this can happen in terms of his own moral psychology since it is likely that he considered human perceptions and our consequent ability to 'envisage' both prospects and also our own pasts to be conceptually rich. It is therefore correct to say that now Eumaeus 'sees' the events in his past differently from the way in which he originally saw them (or, they 'appear to him' differently) and hence he now experiences pleasures as he re-envisages them whereas he originally experienced pains. He now sees and understands those events as being beneficial and good – hence pleasant – whereas he originally saw them as harmful and painful.

CHAPTER 8

Epicureans and Cyrenaics on anticipating and recollecting pleasures

Just as the Hellenistic philosophers and their later Roman commentators were interested in the pleasures of learning and knowing, so too were they interested in prudential planning and in the pleasures of memory and anticipation. In particular, the Hellenistic hedonist schools of Epicureans and Cyrenaics were interested in the power and limits of our ability to look ahead and look back in order to maintain a life of pleasure. They agree that the best human life is the most pleasant life and also that we should arrange our desires and choices so as to experience as much pleasure and as little pain as possible. However, they disagree about the possibility of maximising pleasure over time by means of a prudential calculus of the kind we have already seen examined in Plato's *Protagoras* (Chapter 5). They also disagree about the efficacy of our powers of memory and anticipation in establishing and maintaining a life of pleasure. This second disagreement continues the interest in the relationship between pleasure, anticipation, memory, and character that we saw in Plato (Chapter 6) and Aristotle (Chapter 7).

Epicurean prudential reasoning

The principal evidence for the Epicurean version of the hedonistic prudential calculus comes from Epicurus' *Letter to Menoeceus*. Here Epicurus describes how his theory allows the hedonist to be sensitive to and strive to attain long-term goals of maximising pleasure, by forgoing more proximate but lesser or potentially damaging pleasures. In brief outline, this is a recipe for temporally sensitive hedonistic choice-making.[1] I have divided the passage into four parts for ease of reference.

---

[1] Critics who have looked previously at this passage tend to find it unsatisfying. Mitsis 1988, 28, finds it 'disappointingly vague', while Annas 1993, 190, allows that '[a]s often, Epicurus uses misleadingly crude language for a position which is in fact not crude'. I argue below that the language used is not, in fact, crude.

[1] ταύτην [sc. ἡδονήν] γὰρ ἀγαθὸν πρῶτον καὶ συγγενικὸν ἔγνωμεν, καὶ ἀπὸ ταύτης καταρχόμεθα πάσης αἱρέσεως καὶ φυγῆς, καὶ ἐπὶ ταύτην καταντῶμεν ὡς κανόνι τῷ πάθει πᾶν ἀγαθὸν κρίνοντες. [2a] καὶ ἐπεὶ πρῶτον ἀγαθὸν τοῦτο καὶ σύμφυτον, διὰ τοῦτο καὶ οὐ πᾶσαν ἡδονὴν αἱρούμεθα, [2b] ἀλλ᾽ ἔστιν ὅτε πολλὰς ἡδονὰς ὑπερβαίνομεν, ὅταν πλεῖον ἡμῖν τὸ δυσχερὲς ἐκ τούτων ἕπηται· [2c] καὶ πολλὰς ἀλγηδόνας ἡδονῶν κρείττους νομίζομεν, ἐπειδὰν μείζων ἡμῖν ἡδονὴ παρακολουθῇ πολὺν χρόνον ὑπομείνασι τὰς ἀλγηδόνας. [3] πᾶσα οὖν ἡδονὴ διὰ τὸ φύσιν ἔχειν οἰκείαν ἀγαθόν, οὐ πᾶσα μέντοι αἱρετή· καθάπερ καὶ ἀλγηδὼν πᾶσα κακόν, οὐ πᾶσα δὲ ἀεὶ φευκτὴ πεφυκυῖα. [4] τῇ μέντοι συμμετρήσει καὶ συμφερόντων καὶ ἀσυμφόρων βλέψει ταῦτα πάντα κρίνειν καθήκει. χρώμεθα γὰρ τῷ μὲν ἀγαθῷ κατά τινας χρόνους ὡς κακῷ, τῷ δὲ κακῷ τοὖμπαλιν ὡς ἀγαθῷ. (*Ep. Men.* 129–30)

[1] For we have recognised this [pleasure] as the first and natural good, and we begin every choice and avoidance from this starting point and we return to it when we judge every good by feeling, like a yardstick. [2a] And since this is the first and connate good, for this reason we also do not choose every pleasure, [2b] but on occasion we pass over many pleasures when the discomfort to us which follows from them is greater, [2c] and we consider many pains to be better than pleasures, when a greater pleasure over a long period comes to us after undergoing those pains. [3] So every pleasure is a good because it has an appropriate nature, but not every pleasure is choice-worthy. Just so, every pain is also a bad, but not every pain is always by nature to be avoided. [4] However, it is right to judge all of them by comparative measurement and by the recognition of both advantages and disadvantages. For we sometimes treat the good as a bad, and conversely the bad as a good.

This argument follows Epicurus' identification of pleasure as the single natural good and his insistence that it should be treated as the criterion by which we measure the goodness of an action. Section [1] introduces the metaphor of a yardstick, a measurement against which we can compare various possible courses of action and the pleasure or pain likely to result from them.[2] The text then proceeds to offer an elaboration of this claim, perhaps aware that as it stands the imperative to pursue pleasure might raise strong objections. Epicurus explains that we should take a long-term view of pleasure-seeking. Sometimes we should knowingly forgo pleasure and sometimes we should undergo pain, but this does not jeopardise the overall hedonistic structure of choice-making since this is always done with a view

---

[2] There are analogies with Epicurean epistemology, which uses three sources of information as 'criteria' of truth – standards on which we must base all beliefs. Indeed, the *pathē* are criteria of truth: DL 10.31. Cf. Gosling and Taylor 1982, 397–9.

to maximising pleasure and reducing pain in the longer term. Section [2] gives the substance of this claim, and it is generalised in section [3] where Epicurus also restates that it is consistent with his claim that pleasure is the only good. Section [4] promises to offer some help in understanding how this calculus is to be achieved.

It is unclear whether the first-person verbs throughout this section refer to people in general or to the Epicureans in particular. If the former, then Epicurus is here advocating psychological hedonism: all agents do act in this way in order to maximise pleasure. It is certainly true that the Epicureans claim elsewhere that infants and non-rational animals instinctively seek after pleasure (the so-called 'Cradle Argument'), and it may also be true that the argument is intended to endorse the feeling which remains even in the case of adults that pleasure is something to be pursued.[3] However, although Epicurus asserts that sometimes even non-Epicureans act in order to secure pleasure, it is not so clear whether he thinks that non-Epicurean adults also always seek after pleasure – but are mistaken about how to obtain and maximise that pleasure, and so aim for money, power, and the like – or that they occasionally replace a drive for pleasure with a drive for these other goods *per se*, without thinking that money, power, and the like are routes to securing pleasure.[4]

In the preceding paragraph of the *Letter* (§128), Epicurus first asserts that 'we' do everything 'for the sake of being neither in pain nor in terror'. This sounds like a special Epicurean doctrine. Further on in that same section Epicurus asserts that 'we say' (*legomen*) that pleasure is the beginning (*arkhē*) and goal (*telos*) of life. This too is not an assertion made by everyone, even if there are non-Epicureans such as Eudoxus who may endorse some version of it. However, the picture is confused a little by the tense of '*egnōmen*' ('we have recognised') in [1]. This may indeed be a reference to a prior stage in life, namely infancy, in which everyone does act in order to secure pleasure and which the Epicureans take to be prime evidence for their hedonistic thesis. But again, this contrast in tense with the verbs used to describe the present employment of correct prudential reasoning may suggest that although we (in this case perhaps we all, but the Epicureans are therefore included too) once recognised the connate good, we certainly do not all do so now. In any case, whether or not in

---

[3] On these cradle arguments see: DL 10.137, Sext. Emp. *PH* 3.194, and Brunschwig 1986, 113–44. Cf. Sedley 1996, 313–39, at 321 n. 15. Compare Eudoxus' argument at Arist. *NE* 10.2 1172b9–15 and cf. Warren 2009, 252–65.

[4] For an argument against ascribing psychological hedonism to Epicurus, see Cooper 1999b, 486–90. Woolf 2004 replies in favour of a psychological hedonist interpretation.

adulthood everyone, in their various ways, aims for pleasure is not the primary concern of this passage, and Epicurus does not make clear his position on this question. Instead, Epicurus is interested in telling his reader – a budding Epicurean – how to go about maximising true katastematic pleasure. Likewise, the fact that a depressingly large number of people may use similar prudential reasoning in order mistakenly to maximise fame, power, and so on, is also of no concern at this stage.[5]

Epicurus' treatment includes two characteristics we have already noted in Socrates' version of the hedonic calculus discussed in Chapter 5. First, Epicurus assumes a situation in which it is possible to know all the relevant information concerning the pleasure and pain provided by different situations, even those in the future. Second, Epicurus' argument refuses to offer anything other than the most general and imprecise characterisation of the various quantities of pleasure, pain, and time involved. Epicurus speaks only of 'greater' pain or pleasure or 'long' periods of time.

In [2c] he argues that on occasion we should undergo a pain in order to secure a greater pleasure over a longer period. In general terms a good may be preferred either because it is greater (a more intense pleasure, perhaps) or longer lasting (a pleasure lasting several hours is preferable to an equally intense pleasure which lasts only minutes). Consequently, a more intense and longer-lasting pleasure is preferable on two counts. In Epicurean terms, however, this scheme may be complicated by the Epicureans' controversial view that once a state of painlessness has been reached, the value of that state is not increased by mere prolongation.[6] *KD* 19 offers the claim that a finite and an infinite amount of time contain the same amount of pleasure, if you measure it correctly. This might make it appear that Epicurus should not, as he does here in *Ep. Men.* 129, be recommending that we prefer longer-lasting to brief pleasures. Nevertheless he can

---

[5] Compare Cic. *Fin.* 1.32–3. This passage asserts that no one rejects pleasure *per se* and that the pursuit of pleasure has been criticised because of the painful results which arise from imprudent choices. This falls short of asserting that everyone does in fact always pursue pleasure. Torquatus' remarks at *Fin.* 1.47–8 similarly suggest that people can be overcome by the enticements of present pleasure but, again, this falls short of asserting that everyone always acts in pursuit of pleasure. Perhaps the closest suggestion of something like psychological hedonism can be found in one of the later Epicurean defences of the assertion that pleasure is the *telos* at *Fin.* 1.31: 'So they say that there is as it were a natural and ingrained idea in our souls such that we feel that pleasure is to be pursued and pain is to be avoided' (*itaque aiunt hanc quasi naturalem atque insitam in animis nostris inesse notionem, ut alterum [sc. voluptatem] esse appetendum, alterum [sc. dolorem] esse aspernandum sentiamus*).

[6] See Epic. *Ep. Men.* 131, *KD* 3, and *KD* 18; Cic. *Fin.* 1.37–8.

argue that it is better to maximise as far as possible the ratio of pleasure to pain within a life. The less time within a life spent feeling pain the better.[7] There remains the problem of evaluating a lesser but longer-lasting pleasure over a greater but briefer pleasure (or a lesser but longer-lasting pain over a greater but briefer pain). The brief treatment of the 'hedonic calculus' in the *Letter to Menoeceus* does not delve into such questions, and perhaps understandably so. As we have noted before, there lingers over such accounts of hedonist calculation the concern that the pleasures and pains being evaluated vary in incommensurable ways. If this suspicion is true, then perhaps there is no way in which two goods which differ in both of these characteristics might be comparatively ranked. Further, even on the assumption that the pleasures and pains are commensurable, for practical purposes in most cases the *comparanda* will in all likelihood differ both in pleasantness and in duration. We might well think we are owed some more extensive remarks by Epicurus, perhaps just some sketchy rules of thumb, for the sort of comparisons which an agent is likely to have to make. Of course, the *Letter to Menoeceus* is something of a protreptic epitome of Epicurean ethics, and an omission here is not necessarily a sign of an omission in Epicurus' theory as a whole. Nevertheless a theory of this sort of reasoning cannot ignore such difficulties and this must be regarded as an important and potentially damaging lacuna in the overall theory. (Epicurus cannot, of course, take the escape route available to Socrates and Plato of saying that this hedonist calculus is nothing more than a dialectical device aimed at 'the many'; he is a self-confessed hedonist and is offering this account *in propria persona*.) Notably, Epicurus does not take the route advocated by Aristotle of explicitly denying that there is much sense to this sort of legislation, given that practical reasoning will be employed in circumstances for which the relevant factors to be taken into account are so many and variable that any rule offered would be subject to innumerable exceptions and qualifications.[8] Either Epicurus did not see this problem or

---

[7] Compare Gosling and Taylor 1982, 350, who ascribe to Epicurus the implausible claim that there is nothing to choose between a year of pleasure followed by one month of pain, and two years of pleasure followed by one month of pain. The important question here is: what will happen in the year following the period of the first *comparandum*? There will follow either a year of pleasure (in which case the two are alike), or a year which contains some pain (in which case the first is obviously preferable), or death (and the question of what this would mean for the choice between the two is a more difficult question. See e.g. Warren 2000, 242; 2004, 110–15.

[8] See *NE* 2.2 1104a3–10 and 5.10 1137b27–32: 'The rule for what is indefinite is itself indefinite, like the lead rule used for Lesbian masonry' (τοῦ γὰρ ἀορίστου ἀόριστος καὶ ὁ κανών, ὥσπερ καὶ τῆς Λεσβίας οἰκοδομίας ὁ μολίβδινος κανών). Lesbian polygonal masonry is formed by interlocking irregularly shaped blocks. A flexible *kanōn* is required which can be moulded to the shape of the previous block and then used as a template for shaping the next block to fit exactly. Cf. Wiggins 1987, 229.

he felt that this was sufficiently obvious to require no mention. In any case, he offers only a highly generalised account of the sort of reasoning involved.[9]

Certainly, Epicurus' version of hedonism recommends the occasional avoidance of a pleasure. Section [4] expands on this theme. Sometimes a hedonist avoids a pleasure as though it were a bad (although pleasures are good *per se*) and sometimes suffers pain as though it were a good (although pains are bad *per se*).[10] Epicurus claims that I should not always act to promote what *at that particular time* will produce the most pleasure. Rather, I should act in order to produce the most pleasure *over time*. Epicurus endorses a form of temporal neutrality about value; closer pleasures are not to be preferred merely because they are closer. In Cicero's *De Finibus* the Epicurean Torquatus notes how people fall for the 'enticements of present pleasures' (*Fin.* 1.33), suggesting that the Epicureans also thought that the temporal proximity of a pleasure or pain was irrelevant to its value. Although Torquatus describes such people as 'blinded by desire' (*occaecati cupiditate*), which sounds rather like the explanation of this behaviour offered by those whom Socrates is criticising through his intellectualist account in the *Protagoras*, the Epicurean account of desire firmly links it to beliefs and more specifically to beliefs concerning value. Epicurean therapy is aimed at the removal of 'false beliefs' and the re-education of desires, which is an intellectual process. I therefore suspect that the Epicurean diagnosis of a bias towards nearer pleasures would be just as intellectualist as that offered by Socrates.

---

[9] It may be that further advice on specific matters was contained in Epicurus' work *On Lives*. Diogenes Laertius 10.117–21 provides a collection of specific pieces of advice (such as: 'a wise man will not marry') which come from a number of sources (Diogenes' *Epitome of Epicurus' Ethical Thoughts*: 10.118 and *Epilekta* 10.119; Epicurus' *Puzzles* (*Diaporiai*), *On Nature*, *Symposium*, and *On Lives*: 10.119).

[10] Aristocles *ap.* Euseb. *PE* 14.21.1–4 mistakenly argues that there is an inconsistency in Epicurus' system between (1) pleasure is the criterion for choice and avoidance and (2) not all pleasures are to be pursued. Aristocles concludes that, for Epicurus, reason (λόγος) – as opposed to the *pathē* – judges what to pursue and what to avoid. This confusion is all the more surprising give that Aristocles himself provides statements by Epicurus which make clear the hedonist motivation for this doctrine: 'It is better to withstand these pains in order for us to enjoy greater pleasures' (ἄμεινόν ἐστιν ὑπομεῖναι τούσδε τινὰς τοὺς πόνους ὅπως ἡσθείημεν ἡδονὰς μείζους) and 'It is advantageous to forgo these pleasures so that we do not suffer more distressing pains' (συμφέρει τῶνδέ τινων ἀπέχεσθαι τῶν ἡδονῶν, ἵνα μὴ ἀλγῶμεν ἀλγηδόνας χαλεπωτέρας). Aristocles seems caught between trying to attack the consistency of Epicurus' hedonism, and trying to argue that Epicurus too relies on reason (*sc.* rather than feelings) in matters of choice and avoidance. Even this latter criticism is ill-aimed. Reason is the instrument by which an Epicurean can weigh up alternative courses of action, but they are always evaluated in terms of resulting pleasure and pain.

At *Fin.* 1.48 Torquatus draws a further consequence from this explanation of hedonistic prudential reasoning:

> ex quo intellegitur nec intemperantiam propter se esse fugiendam, temperantiamque expetendam non quia voluptates fugiat sed quia maiores consequatur.

> It is understood from this that intemperance is not to be avoided for its own sake, and temperance is to be pursued not because it avoids pleasures but because it pursues greater ones.

A critic of hedonism could otherwise have pointed to the Epicureans' approval of this sort of reasoning to argue that they are in fact, and contrary to their hedonist principles, praising the avoidance of pleasures for its own sake. After all, they do agree that sometimes it is right to forgo pleasures. Torquatus here makes it clear that although the Epicureans do indeed recommend temperance, they do so not because there is anything intrinsically valuable in forgoing pleasures. Rather, the temperance they promote is an instrument towards the promotion of greater pleasure overall.

[2b] and [2c] also make clear another facet of Epicurus' theory. Sometimes an agent will forgo a pleasure because of the pains which follow from it. Sometimes he will suffer discomforts in order to secure the pleasures which follow from those discomforts.[11] Importantly, Epicurus is interested in the causal connections between pleasures and pains: pleasures which produce pains, and pains which produce pleasures. He is concerned with the consequences of choices of action, and especially the long-term effects of choices which at first glance appear either to be consistent with hedonism but are indirectly opposed to the maximisation of pleasure, or which appear to be inconsistent with hedonism but indirectly produce the maximisation of pleasure.

It emerges that in order to perform the correct 'calculation' the ideal Epicurean agent will have to have a clear and comprehensive understanding of the various causal relationships between objects of pursuit and avoidance and subsequent effects. In order to assess correctly a particular course of action he will need to be able to foresee the likely consequences of each

---

[11] Cf. Cic. *Fin.* 1.32: 'For no one rejects or hates or avoids pleasure itself because it is pleasant, but because there follow from it great pains ... Nor is there indeed anyone who loves, pursues or wishes to obtain pain itself, because it is a pain, but only because sometimes circumstances are such that he might pursue some great pleasure through toil and pain' (*nemo enim ipsam voluptatem, quia voluptas sit, aspernatur aut odit aut fugit, sed quia consequuntur magni dolores ... neque porro quisquam est, qui dolorem ipsum quia dolor sit, amet, consectetur, adipisci velit, sed quia non numquam eius modi tempora incidunt, ut labore et dolore magnam aliquam quaeret voluptatem*).

choice. How far into the future such foresight must reach is not clear and presumably will depend upon the sort of choice under consideration. When deciding what to eat for lunch I need not look very far ahead, but when choosing a particular career I may need to take into account the whole of my lifetime. Any wrong decisions about such choices can therefore have one or both of the following causes. First, it may be that the agent incorrectly assesses the amount or duration of pleasure and pain brought about by the object of pursuit or avoidance or of any consequent pleasure or pain. Second, it is possible that the agent is mistaken in his assessment of the likely consequences of any choice. Glancing ahead to section [4] once again, there may be a distinction between the two instruments by which the Epicurean is said to regulate his choice-making: *symmetrēsis* and *blepsis*. The first of these is the faculty by which the agent compares and evaluates various outcomes. And *blepsis* is the faculty by which he considers and foresees the various chains of consequence which follow on from the individual choices, recognising the possible advantages and disadvantages which follow from each. Only if both of these faculties are employed correctly will the correct decision knowingly be made.

Epicurus does not stress the second possible source of error (the lack of foresight of the consequences of a particular choice), but it is a clear implication of his brief presentation that an awareness of such 'rules of consequence' is an important part of the pattern of practical decision making. It is also noteworthy that in its predecessor – Plato, *Prot.* 354e– 357e – the concern is entirely with the relative assessment of individual potential objects of pursuit, and the distortion which temporal distance creates. This new emphasis on the consequences of particular choices is an important addition to Epicurus' version of the theory.[12]

There are signs also in this brief passage that Epicurus has thought about other possible objections. We noted in discussing the *Protagoras* that it might be thought that such systems require an impossible form of quantitative precision in the assessment of the value of the pleasures and pains under consideration.[13] No quantitative precision is required by Epicurus'

---

[12] Cf. Cic. *Fin.* 1.47: Torquatus describes those who mistakenly opt for present blandishments as 'conquered and overcome by the apparent hope of pleasure' (*victi et debilitati obiecta specie voluptatis*). Their mistake is compounded by a lack of foresight (*nec ... provident*) concerning the consequences of their actions. Compare 1.48, which similarly notes those who are minded to pursue pleasures that do not produce subsequent pains, retain their judgement and are not overcome by pleasures. These people often obtain the greatest pleasure by forgoing pleasures (*qui autem ita frui voluptatibus, ut nulli propter eas consequantur dolores, et qui suum iudicium retinent, ne voluptate victi faciant id, quod sentiant non esse faciendum, ii voluptatem maximam adipiscuntur praetermittenda voluptate*).

[13] See e.g. Taylor 1991, 197.

model in the sense that the task does not involve assessing various courses of action by assigning to each of them some unit of pleasure-production. Rather, the question is one of preference between different courses of action. Plato termed the particular skill involved in assessing courses of action a *tekhnē metrētikē*. Epicurus, however, in section [4] uses a more specific term: *symmetrēsis*. The prefix (*sym-*) makes clear that the process envisaged is not the measurement of one choice and then the measurement of another, but rather a *comparative* sizing up of two or more possibilities against one another. There is no need, for example, to assign a quantity of 'hedons' to each of the various possibilities before making a comparative assessment of which is the more pleasant. Instead, they are to be compared immediately against one another for their chances of producing the desired result. Epicurus' use of the word *symmetrēsis* is a clear signal that he wishes to stress the thoroughly comparative nature of the procedure.[14]

Indeed, the metaphor introduced in section [1] of a yardstick (*kanōn*), which also is put to use in Epicurean epistemological theory, confirms this approach. It should not be understood to imply any quantitative assessment (and if the translation 'yardstick' encourages such an understanding then it is misleading) since a *kanōn* seems originally to have been something like a straight-edge. A *kanōn* is a standard against which things are compared and evaluated accordingly.[15] At *NE* 3.4 1113a31–3 Aristotle uses the term in a metaphorical way similar to that found in Epicurus:[16]

καθ᾽ ἑκάστην γὰρ ἕξιν ἴδιά ἐστι καλὰ καὶ ἡδέα, καὶ διαφέρει πλεῖστον ἴσως ὁ σπουδαῖος τῷ τἀληθὲς ἐν ἑκάστοις ὁρᾶν, ὥσπερ κανὼν καὶ μέτρον αὐτῶν ὤν.

For according to each disposition there are particular goods and pleasures, and perhaps the good man is especially good at seeing the truth in each, being like a standard and measure of them.

Clearly, the idea here is not that the good man is able to quantify these goods, nor that he must serve in some sense as a unit of measure for such things. Rather, in each case what the good man determines to be good and pleasant is in fact good and pleasant. He and his conception of value should serve as a correct standard for any other evaluation. By comparing our conceptions against those of the good man and aligning them with his, we can be sure of being right. This model of the *kanōn* as a standard or

---

[14] It is not clear that the *Protagoras* requires or implies quantitative precision either, of course, but Epicurus has certainly been explicit in casting the procedure he envisages in simple comparative terms. Annas 1993, 334–5 and n. 3, agrees that Epicurus does not intend to offer a quantitative calculus but seems to think that in this passage (and this passage alone) he writes as if he does.

[15] See Striker 1996b, 31–3.   [16] And compare *NE* 5.10 1137b29–31.

touchstone is also at work in Epicurean epistemology. By remaining consistent with the content of sense perceptions, *pathē*, and *prolēpseis*, we can ensure that any beliefs we infer are reliable (*Ep. Hdt.* 38, 63). Again there is no notion of absolute quantification, only of the use of an agreed standard of relative assessment.

Of course, there remains the problem that two pleasures may not be directly comparable. If the two pleasures under consideration differ both in intensity and in duration (i.e. the choice is between a shorter but greater pleasure and a longer but lesser pleasure), then how can a choice be made between them? Nothing in the brief passage from the *Letter to Menoeceus* even alludes to this possibility, nor is there any extant discussion of the problem in other surviving Epicurean sources. On that basis, not only are we in no position to conclude that Epicurus did in fact consider and discuss the issue, we are also – and for the same reasons – in no position to declare that he did not, or could not.

Apart from Epicurus' own writings, other sources expand on the demands and methods required by such prudential reasoning and also outline various ways in which people might fail to maximise pleasure in this way. In Cicero's *Fin.* 1.33, for example, the Epicurean Torquatus offers a criticism of people who make mistakes in such choices.

> at vero eos et accusamus et iusto odio dignissimos ducimus qui blanditiis praesentium voluptatum deleniti atque corrupti quos dolores et quas molestias excepturi sint occaecati cupiditate non provident, similique sunt in culpa qui officia deserunt mollitia animi, id est laborum et dolorum fuga.

> On the other hand, we denounce and think worthy of the greatest opprobrium those who through the enticements of present pleasures are led astray and corrupted. Blinded by desire they fail to see the pains and discomforts which they are going to face. Similarly blameworthy are those who desert their duties and chores through mental weakness, i.e. in flight from toils and pains.

Torquatus does mention the attraction of present pleasures, but the emphasis here is on a lack of foresight and a lack of awareness of the consequences of certain choices.[17] The Epicureans endorse the general assumption that Socrates is keen to press in the *Protagoras* that the damaging desire for present pleasures ought to be understood as a cognitive failure; the people being criticised here are mistaken in pursuing a lesser but apparently greater pleasure over what is genuinely preferable. We might nevertheless contrast the way in which present pleasures are here said to 'blind' the agent to later but greater pleasures that he

---

[17] Cf. Cic. *Fin.* 1.47.

might otherwise attain with the metaphor from the *Protagoras* of the 'power of appearance' leading people astray. While for Socrates the danger is that people, as it were, are overly impressed by the sight of pleasures, for Torquatus – as we might expect from an Epicurean committed to the truth of all sense impressions – the metaphor has a different force: we would act rightly if only we could see clearly the various pleasures available.

A work sometimes attributed to Philodemus, perhaps entitled *On Choices and Avoidances* (*PHerc.* 1251), includes one passage which indicates that there was something of a disagreement on this matter between different members of the Epicurean school.

[ὃ | διὰ] τὰ π[ε]ρὶ τῶ[ν] τεττάρω[ν εἰ]ρ]ημένα λέγεται, το[ῦ] τὴ[ν περί]ληψιν τὴν περὶ τῶν κυρι[ωτ]ά[[τ]ων καὶ τὴν μνήμην τ̯[ολ]]λὰ συμβάλλεσθαι πρὸς τὰς | οὔσας αἱρέσεις καὶ φύγας οὐ|κ ἴσου τιθεμένου, καθάπερ | ἐξεδέξαντό τινες ἀγροί|κως, τῶι τινας ἀναφέρεσ|θαι τῶν αἱρέσεων καὶ φυγῶν | ἐπὶ τὰς περὶ τούτων ἀτα|ραξίας, ἀλλὰ τῶι κ[α]τορθοῦσ|θαι μὲν αὐτὰς τοῖς τέλεσι | τοῖς τῆς φύσεως παραμε|τ[ρ]ούντων ... (XI.5–20)

This is said because of what has been stated about the four cardinal principles; for the thesis that the understanding and the memorisation of the cardinal tenets contribute greatly to actual choices and avoidances is not equal to claiming that some choices and avoidances are traced back to the states of tranquillity concerning them [*sc.* the cardinal tenets] – as some have clumsily stated – but to claiming that they [*sc.* the choices and avoidances] are accomplished successfully when we measure them by the ends laid down by nature ... (trans. Indelli and Tsouna-McKirahan).

Here the author agrees with some unnamed but unsophisticated opponents that a memorisation of the four cardinal doctrines, the *tetrapharmakos*, is an essential and powerful tool for producing happiness. However, he does not agree that the cardinal doctrines are directly relevant merely for the production of tranquillity about the subjects which they specifically address. Presumably he means the view that they are useful merely in that they remove fear of the gods or death or for the chance of avoiding pain. Instead, he claims that they also can be used in constructing choices concerning what to pursue and what to avoid – choices always taken with a view to the connate goal of life.[18] The author unfortunately does not, at least in the surviving text, elaborate on how he envisages this practical application.

There is one further piece of evidence for the Epicurean conception of this sort of reasoning. Part of Diogenes of Oinoanda's enormous Epicurean inscription describes how most people are not convinced by the Epicurean

---

[18] See Indelli and Tsouna-McKirahan 1995, 48–51, 160–6.

claim that the pleasures of the soul are greater and more valuable than those of the body.

ἀλλ’ ὅταν μὲν ἐν ταῖς | σωματικαῖς ἀλγηδόσι | τυνχάνῃ τις, φησὶ ταύ|τας τῶν ψυχικῶν εἶναι | μείζονας, ὅταν δ’ ἐν | [ταῖς ψυχικαῖς, ἐκείνων] | μ[ε]ἰ[ζονας εἶναί φησι] | ταύτας. τ[ῶν γὰρ ἀπόν]|των αἰεὶ τὰ [παρόντα πι]|θανώτερα κα[ὶ ἐπίδοξος] | ἕκαστός ἐστιν ἢ δ[ι’ ἀνάν]|κην ἢ διὰ ἡδονὴν τῷ | κατέχοντι αὐτὸν πά|θει τὴν ὑπεροχὴν ἀπ[ο]|δεδωκέναι. σοφὸς | δὲ ἀνὴρ τὸ δυσεπιλό|γιστον τοῦτο τοῖς πολ|λοῖς ἐξ ἄλλων τε ἀν[α]|λογίζεται πολλῶν . . . (fr. 44.II.10–III.14)

Instead, when someone encounters bodily pains, he says that these are greater than those of the soul; and when [he encounters those of the soul he says that] they [are greater than the others. For] what [is present is] invariably more convincing [than what is absent], and each person is [likely], either through [necessity] or through pleasure, to confer pre-eminence on the feeling which has hold of him. However, this matter, which is difficult for ordinary people to gauge, a wise man calculates on the basis of many factors . . . (trans. M. F. Smith).

Unfortunately the text breaks off before Diogenes can tell us just how the Epicurean wise man manages to perform this difficult task and fr. 45 – which Smith suggests follows on directly – is extremely badly preserved. Nevertheless Diogenes offers some clues. First, he offers a version of the observation that pleasures which are at hand seem to be more valuable than those which are more distant. In this case, he uses the principle to characterise the unreflective majority as inconstant in their assessment of the relative merits of bodily and psychic pleasures. At any given moment, the pleasure they are currently experiencing appears to be the most valuable, simply as a result of its proximity. Second, Diogenes is the first Epicurean source to note that the task of the wise man in counteracting and mitigating this tendency is a difficult one. Furthermore, the adjective he uses to describe the task, *dysepilogiston* – coupled with the related verb *analogizetai* – suggests that the procedure to be followed – although difficult – is one of rational calculation and comparative evaluation.[19]

The limits of prudential reasoning

The brief account of prudential reasoning in the *Letter to Menoeceus* offers a boldly optimistic account of how, through clear foresight and understanding

[19] See Schofield 1996, esp. 229. Schofield surveys appearances of *epilogismos* and its cognates in Epicurean texts and concludes that the primary significance is that of 'comparative appraisal'.

coupled with an ability to evaluate different options comparatively, we might be able to arrange our choices to maximise pleasure over time. The procedure being recommended involves the imaginative consideration and comparison of different possible future experiences and therefore – as we have noticed before – involves considerations of our future preferences and desires. This might be problematic, particularly for accounts which advocate general neutrality with regard to future pleasures and pains such that the different temporal location of these experiences is irrelevant to their respective values.[20]

There is no explicit reference in the text of the *Letter to Menoeceus* to any specific time range across which this sort of comparison of goods is to be exercised. I assume, therefore, that Epicurus' account is intended to be flexible. In some contexts the relevant decision will concern different options and their consequences in only the next few minutes or hours. But sometimes it will concern years, even a whole lifetime. *Kyria Doxa* 16 certainly claims that *logismos*, which in this context is apparently a reasoning capacity able to direct and guide the most important facets of a life, is a faculty which operates throughout one's life.[21] Epicurus bases much of his discussion of the reasons for prudential action on the thought that there always should be an overarching desire to promote one's natural good. The pursuit of *ataraxia* is constant and should underpin any other desires an agent may conceive. The desire for *ataraxia* is more akin to a general principle of prudential reasoning: that one should always act in one's best interests. The pursuit of *ataraxia* is the Epicurean specification of what is in fact in one's best interests.

An Epicurean must always ensure that any beliefs he does conceive are consistent with this natural and necessary drive for mental painlessness. Certainly, an Epicurean may conceive new desires – he may decide to travel to Lampsacus or write a new poem – but these are all geared towards the fulfilment of this overarching desire and are therefore in this sense inter-changeable. If they do come into conflict, therefore, the conflict is not a serious one. They will certainly never be in conflict with the Epicurean's one major concern. This final goal is so dominant, in fact, that it may be seen as the only project to which the Epicurean is intensely dedicated; all

---

[20] The Epicureans hold, in broad terms, a common-sense view of personal identity, although this is to some extent complicated by consequences of their atomist cosmology – consequences which I have discussed elsewhere. See Warren 2001c.

[21] *KD* 16: 'Chance hinders the wise man only to a small degree, but reason has arranged the greatest and most important matters and does and will manage them throughout his whole life' (βραχέα σοφῷ τύχη παρεμπίπτει, τὰ δὲ μέγιστα καὶ κυριώτατα ὁ λογισμὸς διῴκηκε καὶ κατὰ τὸν συνεχῆ χρόνον τοῦ βίου διοικεῖ καὶ διοικήσει).

other desires and projects are instrumental and subordinate to that goal. The upshot of all this is that, once someone has become a committed Epicurean and has arranged his desires as Epicurus recommends, there is no reason at all for any of those goals and desires to alter as the Epicurean ages. We might object by insisting that the projects of a young man are quite unlike those of an elderly person and, moreover, that this is how things ought to be. This stance is often captured by talking about the 'shape' of a life, a conception which not only embraces this idea that certain projects are appropriate for certain stages in a life but also includes the notion that the overall goodness of a life is not provided merely by the sum of momentary states of wellbeing. An important additional factor is the supervening structure and narrative shape of a person's life.[22] Epicurus, however, claims that so far as the desires appropriate for attaining *eudaimonia* are concerned, there is no difference at all between stages in a life. Young and old alike may attain happiness by removing pain and discarding unnatural and unnecessary desires. In that respect, an Epicurean life does not necessarily have a narrative shape. A good life for an Epicurean is a life without pain. And the beliefs which best promote that particular end are the same no matter how old one is. An Epicurean, for the whole of his or her life, will have the same overarching desire and any contrary beliefs and desires which were held before becoming an Epicurean are discarded as false or groundless.

> οὐ νέος μακαριστὸς ἀλλὰ γέρων βεβιωκὼς καλῶς· ὁ γὰρ νέος ἀκμῇ πολὺς ὑπὸ τῆς τύχης ἑτεροφρονῶν πλάζεται· ὁ δὲ γέρων καθάπερ ἐν λιμένι τῷ γήρᾳ καθώρμικεν, τὰ πρότερον δυσελπιστούμενα τῶν ἀγαθῶν ἀσφαλεῖ κατακλείσας χάριτι. (*SV* 17)

> We should think blessed not the youth but the old man who has lived well. For a young man in his prime is manipulated and caused to wander by chance. But the old man has docked in old age as if in a port and has secured those goods formerly despaired of with a sure joy.

The only relevant criterion for the comparative assessment of the lives of the young and the old is that the former have a greater period of life ahead of them and therefore there is a greater opportunity for chance to take a hand and upset matters. The young person is also liable to have his head turned

---

[22] See Bigelow, Campbell, and Pargetter 1990; Velleman 1991; Feldman 2004, 124–41, and – with reference to Epicureanism – Striker 1988 and Warren 2004, 115–53. Compare also Rawls 1971, 420–1 and Slote 1983, 24 on whether we might prefer goods to be in the future rather than the past because we take more pleasure in anticipating than recollecting goods. The Epicureans, I suggest, see no such asymmetry; indeed, they might prefer the pleasures to be had from the security of goods being in the past to the uncertainty of possible goods in the future.

and lose sight of what is valuable. What the young man may despair of achieving in the future, the old man has already achieved.[23] To a degree, therefore, Epicurus agrees with the intuition behind the old maxim 'Call no man happy until he is dead.' The young person, however well he is doing, might nevertheless be anxious about his future and be pained by worrying that he will fail to achieve what he hopes for. And there is always the danger that even when one is an old and successful man, chance will take a hand and overturn the original assessment of the good of one's life.[24] But Epicurus is not committed to the thought that a young man cannot yet be happy simply because he is young and has not yet lived a full and mature life. Indeed, the Epicureans sometimes cite the example of one especially prodigious student, Pythocles, who was thought to have attained happiness at a very young age.[25]

Here we should contrast the view of the competing Hellenistic hedonists: the Cyrenaics. The state of the surviving evidence for the Cyrenaics is not good. Above all, we are without any accounts written by the Cyrenaics themselves of their view of a good life. It is also often difficult to disentangle two probably distinct phases of Cyrenaicism: that propounded by Aristippus 'the Elder' and that propounded by his grandson, who was also – infuriatingly – named Aristippus. It is sometimes claimed that Cyrenaicism did not become a full-blown hedonistic theory until the time of the younger Aristippus. It is also not always clear to which Aristippus our sources are referring, and even discussions of the elder Aristippus may be contaminated with the philosophy of the later Cyrenaics. (This may be the case for DL 2.66.)[26]

---

[23] Here τὰ δυσελπιστούμενα τῶν ἀγαθῶν must mean 'the goods that the young man expects not to achieve' (but which the old man did achieve). The young man is anxious because he expects not to get them; the old man takes pleasure in recalling that he did achieve them. Contrast ἀπελπίζωμεν in *Ep. Men.* 127 (cited below) and cf. Damascius, *In Phileb.* §147, which categorises δυσελπιστία as the positive expectation that some harm will be incurred.

[24] This is the thought lying behind the famous discussion between Solon and Croesus related by Arist. *NE* 1.9 1100a24–1.10 1101a21. Aristotle insists that happiness requires not only complete virtue but also a complete life (although he too resists the idea that this latter commits one to saying that only at or after death can someone rightly be called happy).

[25] See Philodemus, *De Morte* XII.36–XIII.1 and Plut. *Adv. Col.* 1124c. This view also helps Epicurus to claim that death cannot be premature, provided one has attained the Epicurean *telos*. See Warren 2000 and 2004, 109–59. Diogenes of Oinoanda seems to have composed a treatise *On Old Age* (frs. 137–77 Smith) but the remains are extremely fragmentary and what does survive indicates that Diogenes was keen to insist that old age was no different from other stages of life, certainly as regards the chances of becoming sick, decrepit, or handicapped.

[26] See Giannantoni 1958, 55–73; Annas 1993, 229; Tsouna-McKirahan 1994, 377–82; Long 1999, 632–9; Zilioli 2012, 17–46; Warren 2014.

A common conception of the ethical theory of the Cyrenaic school holds that a Cyrenaic lives only for present pleasure and does not take into account any view of his life as a whole.[27] Diogenes Laertius suggests that this is just what Aristippus the Elder did:

ἀπέλαυε μὲν γὰρ ἡδονῆς τῶν παρόντων, οὐκ ἐθήρα δὲ πόνῳ τὴν ἀπόλαυσιν τῶν οὐ παρόντων. (DL 2.66)

For, he revelled in the pleasure of the present and did not toil in seeking out the enjoyment of what was not present.

Epicurus might have agreed with this in part. *Vatican Saying* 14 also tells us not to lose present pleasure in chasing more remote goals. Further, Epicurus would advise us to take into account the amount of toil involved in seeking out other pleasures: if the amount of work involved is not sufficiently offset by the rewards, then do not bother. Aristippus here emphasises the pain and toil involved (πόνῳ θηρᾶν): a characterisation no doubt designed to dissuade anyone from such a clearly arduous, difficult, and quite possibly fruitless search. If the process of pursuing non-present pleasures is described in this way, it is easy to see why a hedonist might be attracted to Aristippus' view.

Cyrenaics appear to recommend that we concentrate on enjoying the present rather than toiling in the promise of some future benefit or being overly concerned with what is in the past. But their reasons for such a recommendation are less clear. I think that the Cyrenaic concentration on the present is the result of their generally pessimistic view of the chances of being able to employ prudential reasoning effectively; their position is therefore primarily a pragmatic one. Even from the little evidence we have, it is clear that the Cyrenaics who followed the younger Aristippus – and who would have been best known to Epicurus – were not entirely dismissive of practical reasoning. The Cyrenaics themselves, we are told, praised *phronēsis* as an instrument of providing pleasure, just as the Epicureans did.[28] All the same, they did not place a great deal of confidence in the chances of such practical reasoning guaranteeing a happy life. And they were aware of the consequences of their position, particularly for the possibility of their hedonism's providing a route to *eudaimonia*.

---

[27] See Annas 1993, 229–36; O'Keefe 2002.

[28] DL 2.91: 'They say that wisdom is not good *per se*, nor is it choiceworthy *per se*, but only for its consequences' (τὴν φρόνησιν ἀγαθὸν μὲν εἶναι λέγουσιν, οὐ δι' ἑαυτὴν δὲ αἱρετήν, ἀλλὰ διὰ τὰ ἐξ αὐτῆς περιγιγνόμενα).

διὸ καὶ καθ' αὑτὴν αἱρετῆς οὔσης τῆς ἡδονῆς τὰ ποιητικὰ ἐνίων ἡδονῶν ὀχληρὰ πολλάκις ἐναντιοῦσθαι. ὡς δυσκολώτατον αὐτοῖς φαίνεσθαι τὸν ἀθροισμὸν τῶν ἡδονῶν εὐδαιμονίαν ποιουσῶν. (DL 2.90)

Hence, while pleasure is *per se* choiceworthy, objects which produce some pleasures often result in opposing pains. Thus it appears to them that the collection of pleasures which produce happiness is a most difficult thing.

While the Epicureans counsel us to avoid or eliminate those pleasures that lead to later greater pains and always keep an eye on the long term and on *eudaimonia*, the Cyrenaics simply conclude that such pleasures show that *eudaimonia* is a difficult (and perhaps even impossible) state to attain.[29] They may even have allowed, in disagreement with all the other Hellenistic schools, that the wise man does not necessarily live in a permanently pleasant state; he lives pleasantly only 'for the most part' (DL 2.91). The collection (*athroismos*) of pleasures is further explained at DL 2.88. Since the Cyrenaics recognise only episodic pleasure (*merikē hēdonē*) and hold only these to be the good, *eudaimonia* – a happy life – is choiceworthy only in so far as it is a life which contains such pleasures. The episodic pleasures themselves are the Cyrenaics' primary object of pursuit. A good life is merely a collection (*athroismos*) of such pleasures.[30]

Some recent accounts of time-relative theories of self-interest rely upon a conception of personal identity which erodes the 'common sense' view of an agent persisting throughout a life and therefore rejects the assumption that the temporal stages in the same agent's life must all be taken into account in every rational choice. One explanation of the Cyrenaics' emphasis on the pleasures of the present argues that this view was based upon a reductive view of personal identity.[31] But there is no evidence for any such conception of the self in the extant sources for Cyrenaicism, and what the sources do present is incompatible with such an account. The Cyrenaics present no doubts at all about the fact that an agent should conceive of himself as a

---

[29] Hegesias may have taken the extremely pessimistic stance that since happiness is unattainable and pain inevitable, a hedonist would do best by committing suicide. His lectures were banned by Ptolemy (Cic. *Tusc.* 1.83). See Matson 1998. Compare Sidgwick 1907, 130 n.: '[T]he conclusion that life is always on the whole painful would not prove it to be unreasonable for a man to aim ultimately at minimising pain, if this is still admitted to be possible; though it would, no doubt, render immediate suicide, by some painless process, the only reasonable course for a perfect egoist – unless he looked forward to another life.'

[30] This is the subject of some disagreement. See, for example, Laks 1993, 30–6, for the view that the Cyrenaics are not eudaimonists *stricto sensu* (cf. Striker 1993, 17). Tsouna 1998, 134–5, is less inclined to see a Cyrenaic rejection of eudaimonism. She argues this at greater length in Tsouna 2002.

[31] Irwin 1991. He does recognise (69) that the extant texts do not ascribe this position to the Cyrenaics explicitly. Zilioli 2012, 113–20 and 161–3, offers a similar interpretation; compare Warren 2014, 416–21.

single, temporally extended, and persistent individual.[32] There is one particularly important and interesting text worth considering in detail.

καὶ ἥ γε Κυρηναικὴ καλουμένη ἀπ᾽ ᾽Αριστίππου τοῦ Σωκρατικοῦ τὴν ἀρχὴν λαβοῦσα, ὃς ἀποδεξάμενος τὴν ἡδυπάθειαν ταύτην τέλος εἶναι ἔφη καὶ ἐν αὐτῇ τὴν εὐδαιμονίαν βεβλῆσθαι· καὶ μονόχρονον αὐτὴν εἶναι, παραπλησίως τοῖς ἀσώτοις οὔτε τὴν μνήμην τῶν γεγονυιῶν ἀπολαύσεων πρὸς αὐτὸν ἡγούμενος οὔτε τὴν ἐλπίδα τῶν ἐσομένων, ἀλλ᾽ ἑνὶ μόνῳ τὸ ἀγαθὸν κρίνων τῷ παρόντι, τὸ δὲ ἀπολελαυκέναι καὶ ἀπολαύσειν οὐδὲν νομίζων πρὸς αὐτόν, τὸ μὲν ὡς οὐκέτ᾽ ὄν, τὸ δὲ οὔπω καὶ ἄδηλον. (Athenaeus, *Deipnosophistai* 12, 544a–b)

And the so-called Cyrenaic sect which took its cue from the Socratic Aristippus [also takes this view]. He accepted that this feeling of pleasure was the goal of life and said that happiness was to be found in it. He also said this feeling was unitemporal, and just like luxury-seekers he thought that the memory of past pleasures and the hope of those to come are of no concern to him, but he judged the good solely in the present. He thought that 'having enjoyed' or 'enjoying in the future' were nothing to him since the first is no longer, the second not yet and unclear.

Since, according to this report, Aristippus clearly did consider that he had experienced past pleasures and would experience future ones there is no doubt in his mind that there is a persistent individual across these times. It is also clear that Aristippus the Elder thought that past and future pleasures were 'nothing to him' and the passage offers a number of possible reasons for that claim. First, Aristippus offers what looks like a metaphysical analysis of past and future pleasures – the former are no longer and the future are not yet. This is probably intended to cast aspersions on the reality – at present or from the present perspective – of those past and future pleasures. Their existence is compromised by their temporal location and they are therefore not possible sources of value. Third, in addition to making future pleasures 'not yet' he claims that enjoyment of future pleasures is 'unclear'. This can plausibly be interpreted as the familiar claim that by being in the future these pleasures are not certain to occur, and therefore no clear prospect of them can be formed and used as a factor in present decision making. (Past pleasures are not 'unclear'; they most certainly did happen but their being in the past is nevertheless sufficient to rule them out as present sources of pleasure.) The possible reasons for rejecting temporal neutrality are therefore complex and several, but they certainly make no reference to questions of personal identity.

---

[32] Tsouna 1998, 132–3, collects the relevant evidence. She argues further against Irwin's interpretation in Tsouna 2002. Cf. O'Keefe 2002, 398–401.

Second, Aristippus characterises pleasures as unitemporal (*monochronos*). This means that pleasures can be enjoyed only in the present – simultaneously with the occurrence of the object of the pleasure.[33] When Diogenes Laertius describes the difference of opinion between the Epicureans and the Cyrenaics on this matter (2.89–90), he offers an additional piece of information which explains why Aristippus should characterise pleasure in this way. According to Diogenes, the Cyrenaics confine pleasure to the present since 'the motion of the soul is dispersed by the passage of time' (ἐκλύεσθαι γὰρ τῷ χρόνῳ τὸ τῆς ψυχῆς κίνημα). The motion of the soul in question is precisely the 'pleasant feeling' (ἡδυπάθεια) which Aristippus thinks is the *telos*. The Cyrenaics, of course, recognise only what Epicurus dubbed 'kinetic' pleasures and these – so we are told – are not enduring. The conception of pleasure as 'unitemporal' will not, however, sufficiently explain the Cyrenaics' stance on the limits of prudential reasoning. A more optimistic assessment of our chances of reliably planning for the future might also accept the Cyrenaics' conception of pleasure (it is, after all, a conception which is certainly more intuitively appealing than the Epicurean version) and simply argue that it is in an agent's interests to plan in order to enjoy as many of such pleasures as possible.

In that case, let us look elsewhere for the Cyrenaics' reasons for advocating a concentration on the present. In particular, Aristippus' assertion that future enjoyment is 'not yet and unclear' deserves greater attention. Again, a comparison with the Epicureans is helpful. In the account of prudential reasoning at *Ep. Men.* 129–30, Epicurus overlooked or chose not to dwell upon an additional important factor in the comparison of goods in the near and more distant future, namely the obvious fact that the more distant future is less certain than the nearer future. (I mean here 'certain' primarily in an epistemological sense: we can at present be less sure what will occur in the further than the nearer future since there is a greater intervening period between that time and the present in which various unforeseen things might happen.)[34] However, there is plenty of evidence to show that Epicurus was well aware of the vagaries of chance and indeed offered some advice for how the recognition of this fact should affect one's decision making.

---

[33] Tsouna 1998, 16: '[I]t is one and the same pleasure that occupies the time unit of its occurrence (unity requirement) and … this pleasure that we are experiencing is unrelated to other times present or future (singularity requirement); it has no prospective or retrospective value, and can only be enjoyed while it is actually occurring.'

[34] Epicurus denies the bivalence of certain future-tensed propositions as part of his avoidance of (logical) determinism. In that case, the further future (which state of affairs depends upon various factors which are at present not yet true or false) is indeed metaphysically as well as epistemologically less certain than the nearer future.

Some of Epicurus' pithy ethical maxims may give the impression that he too advocated a *carpe diem* attitude. The future is indeed uncertain, so it is best to gather as much pleasure as possible while it is available. For example:

γεγόναμεν ἅπαξ, δὶς δὲ οὐκ ἔστι γενέσθαι· δεῖ δὲ τὸν αἰῶνα μηκέτι εἶναι· σὺ δὲ οὐκ ὢν τῆς αὔριον κύριος ἀναβάλλῃ τὸ χαῖρον· ὁ δὲ βίος μελλησμῷ παραπόλλυται καὶ εἷς ἕκαστος ἡμῶν ἀσχολούμενος ἀποθνῄσκει. (*SV* 14)

We have come to be once, and it is not possible to be born twice. For ever after, it is necessary that we will be no more. But you, not being the master of tomorrow, throw away what is pleasant. Life is destroyed by procrastination, and each single one of us dies deprived of leisure.

This brief saying combines the assertion that 'you only live once' with the claim that the future is – at least to some extent – beyond anyone's control (οὐκ ὢν τῆς αὔριον κύριος). In that case, the reasonable conclusion is that procrastination (*mellēsmos*) is a foolish policy.[35] Nevertheless, Epicurus does not claim that the future is entirely out of our control. He insists that although the contingencies of life must be taken into account there is a degree to which future-directed planning can affect and determine future happiness. While the future may not be wholly ours to control, it is not entirely beyond our abilities to predict and direct what will occur.

μνημονευτέον δὲ ὡς τὸ μέλλον <οὔτε πάντως ἡμέτερον> οὔτε πάντως οὐχ ἡμέτερον, ἵνα μήτε πάντως προσμένωμεν ὡς ἐσόμενον μήτε ἀπελπίζωμεν ὡς πάντως οὐκ ἐσόμενον. (*Ep. Men.* 127)

Remember that the future is neither entirely ours, nor entirely not ours, so let us neither be altogether confident that it will be nor despair that it will altogether not be.

The far future may be less predictable than the near future. He asserts that although the future is indeed uncertain we need not despair as a result and would presumably also claim that although the further future is less certain than the near – and to that extent should not be relied upon with the same degree of certainty – again this is not a reason for total despair. In his discussion of the appropriate attitude to take to the future most generally, Epicurus takes a moderate line – reminding us that it cannot be relied on entirely but should not be considered entirely unreliable – and this outlook

---

[35] For further discussion of this passage see Warren 2000, 237 n. 17 and 2001c. Compare *SV* 35 'We should not ruin what we have by desiring what we do not have, but we should bear in mind that even what we have is a gift of fortune' (οὐ δεῖ λυμαίνεσθαι τὰ παρόντα τῶν ἀπόντων ἐπιθυμίᾳ, ἀλλ' ἐπιλογίζεσθαι ὅτι καὶ ταῦτα τῶν εὐκταίων ἦν). This line of thought has a good Democritean heritage. See Democritus DK 68 B202, 224, 286.

can be applied also to decisions concerning competing goods in the more and less remote future. Epicurus can justify this moderate confidence by maintaining that an Epicurean should arrange his desires in such a way that fortune has the least possible chance of frustrating them. In brief, he must retain only natural and necessary desires, and these are sufficiently general that they can be satisfied easily. So an Epicurean desires 'food', not any particular kind of food.[36]

The Cyrenaics, on the other hand, have no interest in asking us to reduce or examine our desires. Fortune, therefore, has a much greater chance of frustrating ambitions and removing potential sources of pleasure. This is combined with the Cyrenaics' generally pessimistic assessment of our chances of accurately predicting or controlling the future. In contrast with Epicurus' guarded optimism, Aristippus (probably Aristippus the Elder)[37] is decidedly negative.

πάνυ σφόδρα ἐρρωμένως ἐῴκει λέγειν ὁ Ἀρίστιππος, παρεγγυῶν τοῖς ἀνθρώποις μήτε τοῖς παρελθοῦσιν ἐπικάμνειν μήτε τῶν ἐπιόντων προκάμνειν· εὐθυμίας γὰρ δεῖγμα τὸ τοιοῦτο καὶ ἵλεω διανοίας ἀπόδειξις. προσέταττε δὲ ἐφ᾽ ἡμέρᾳ τὴν γνώμην ἔχειν καὶ αὖ πάλιν τῆς ἡμέρας ἐπ᾽ ἐκείνῳ τῷ μέρει, καθ᾽ ὃ ἕκαστος ἢ πράττει τι ἢ ἐννοεῖ. μόνον γὰρ ἔφασκεν ἡμέτερον εἶναι τὸ παρόν, μήτε δὲ τὸ φθάνον μήτε τὸ προσδοκώμενον· τὸ μὲν γὰρ ἀπολωλέναι, τὸ δὲ ἄδηλον εἶναι εἴπερ ἔσται.[38] (Aelian, *Varia Historia* 14.6)

Aristippus seems to speak with particular conviction when he encourages people neither to bother themselves in retrospect over what has passed, nor to toil in prospect of things to come. For this kind of behaviour is the mark of happiness and proof of a gracious frame of mind. He told them to pay attention to each day as it comes and similarly to pay attention to that part of the day in which the individual's action or thought takes place. For he said that only the present is ours: not what has gone, nor what is anticipated. For, the former has perished and it is unclear if the latter will be.

With the clear injunction to 'take each day as it comes' this is perhaps the best indication we have of time-relativity being embraced and promoted by a Cyrenaic. But once again the reason given for this attitude has nothing to do with any particular conception of pleasure, nor any particular view of personal identity, and everything to do with their assessment that the future is 'uncertain'. Aristippus is simply not able to state definitively, or indeed with the degree of certainty which would be required for some system of

---

[36] See *KD* 16 and the discussion in Annas 1993, 191–200.
[37] See Mannebach 1961. He takes Epic. *Ep. Men.* 127 to be a reply to this Cyrenaic position.
[38] Note the two forms: ἐπικάμνειν and προκάμνειν. The former seems to have been coined for this context (LSJ s.v.) in order to balance the latter.

prudential future-planning, whether things will be one way or another. In that case the best we can do is focus on the moment and make sure that we make the best of it we can.

Epicureans and their critics on memory, anticipation, and pleasure

Concerns for the future – fears – and painful memories of the past – regrets – are two forms of psychic pain and distress. In this sense, memory and anticipations might seem to be obstacles to the Epicurean goal of living a life of *ataraxia*. However, it is also clear that these fears and regrets usually stem from false beliefs about what is good and bad. People are often pained by the fear of death, for example, even though in fact death is 'nothing to us'. A proper understanding of what is truly good and bad can therefore neutralise any potentially damaging effects of memory and anticipation. What is more, the Epicureans then make a case for the positive contribution to our wellbeing made by our capacities for recollecting and anticipating non-present experiences. In their account of a good and pleasant life the Epicureans made significant use of our ability to recall past pleasures since they asserted that we can, by recalling past pleasures and anticipating future pleasures, offset any present physical pains and guarantee a state of pain-lessness. They adopt what we identified earlier as a simple account of the affective aspect of memory and anticipation – namely, that we enjoy recalling past pleasures and are pained by recalling past pains, and so on – and set this capacity to work in ensuring a present pain-free state. The Cyrenaics, in contrast, take a stand against the dominant way of understanding the affective aspect of introversive memory and anticipation and, furthermore, find implausible the Epicureans' optimism about the therapeutic value of memories and expectations. The Epicureans, in other words, offer a picture very much like that we found in the *Philebus* while the Cyrenaics, for reasons based on their particular account of the *pathē* in general, reject that picture.

The most extreme example of the Epicurean faith in the power of the pleasures of memory comes from the biographical accounts of Epicurus himself. He is supposed to have said on his very last day that despite serious physical distress, he nevertheless was living without any mental pain and therefore in a state of the highest mental pleasure – *ataraxia* – because he was able to recall pleasant philosophical conversations he had previously had with his friends.[39] Epicurus manages not merely to distract himself from his

---

[39] See DL 10.22 for Epicurus' *Letter to Idomeneus* and compare the Latin version at Cic. *Fin.* 2.96.

current sickness; rather, he claims to be able to summon up genuine psychic pleasure (DL 10.22; Cic. *Fin.* 2.96) which counterbalances the physical distress. Recalling previous pleasant experiences is therefore a way of generating present pleasure, presumably simply because the Epicureans think that by recalling the experiences they are reliving those past experiences in some way, including the past pleasures.[40] Since we are able to some degree to direct what we recall and what we do not, we can deliberately call up particular pleasant experiences as the situation demands and use the pleasures that are generated to counteract any present pains.

Another context in which the Epicureans made reference to the power of memory is in the treatment of grief. Consistent with their general stance on the nature and value of death, they insist that it would be wrong to think that the deceased, by being dead, is harmed in any way. However, they do recognise that someone might nevertheless feel grief not, presumably, because of any concern for the now deceased but because the loss of a friend might be painful (DL 10.119). The advice they offer is distilled in another pithy saying quoted by Plutarch at *Non Posse* 1105E:

ἡδὺ πανταχόθεν ἡ φίλου μνήμη τεθνηκότος.

The recollection of a dead friend is pleasant in every way.[41]

Is it appropriate to grieve for a dead friend? The answer appears to be that grief of a kind is indeed appropriate and, moreover, beneficial: the recollection of a deceased friend is guaranteed to bring pleasure. Most likely, Epicurus means that whenever we deliberately recall a friend who is now dead, the recollection will be of some pleasant experience shared with that friend or, perhaps more generally, the recollection will be of the friendship itself. Just as we saw Epicurus maintain that the recollection of a past pleasant experience will generate pleasure in the present, so too we are assured that, since the experiences while the friend was alive were pleasant, it will be pleasant to recollect that friend and that friendship although the friend is now dead. Any painful grief at the loss of the friend is then supposed to be alleviated.

Such optimism is perhaps laudable. But it is difficult to share. After all, we might instead draw a lesson from Aristotle's account of Eumaeus'

---

[40] For a recent discussion see Giovacchini 2007.
[41] Compare Sen. *Ep. Mor.* 99.25 and Epic. *SV* 66: 'Let us grieve for our friends not with laments but by thinking of them' (συμπαθῶμεν τοῖς φίλοις οὐ θρηνοῦντες ἀλλὰ φροντίζοντες). For some more discussion of Epicurean accounts of grief see Warren 2004, 39–41; LaBarge 2012, esp. 328, and Konstan 2013.

memories and insist that the recollection of a dead friend, at the very least, cannot be relied upon always to be pleasant. It is likely that recalling a past pleasant experience from that friendship will always be accompanied by the reminder that this friend is no longer alive. At worst, we might worry that the recollection will be painful since it will bring to one's mind once again how much this friendship did bring pleasure and how it is now conclusively over – a thought that might well be painful if the friendship itself was ever previously thought to be valuable. Of course, it is open to Epicurus to claim that such a bitter-sweet recollection is not necessary; a good Epicurean wise man will be able to look back and recall the friendship with pleasure and without any painful grief that it is now over. But this might raise our suspicions about the worth of the friendship in the first place and, in any event, is little more than a confident assertion. Furthermore, the Epicureans either neglected the importance of the present context of the recollection itself which seems to have been recognised by Aristotle or they were simply of the opinion that a clear-minded Epicurean sage would be sufficiently adept at homing in on the pleasant aspects of any memories that he would never be subject to unwanted distress.

In large part, the Epicurean emphasis on the power of memory and anticipation appears to have been a response to the charge that, in identifying pleasure as the good, they will have to admit that any goods we experience are merely temporary: pleasure simply 'flows away' once it has been enjoyed. If that were true, then it would jeopardise the Epicurean claim that a sage can guarantee stable and lasting happiness given that physical pain is to some extent an unavoidable fact of human life.[42] Recollection, however, is for the Epicureans the capacity that allows us to recall and relive past pleasures, suggesting that these pleasures are never entirely lost and, moreover, can be used to counteract any physical pain we encounter.

This Epicurean stance has never been found particularly plausible.[43] Cicero launches an attack on it at *Fin.* 2.104–6 arguing, first of all, that memory is not in our power to the extent that the Epicureans claim; some things we would like to forget but cannot and some things we wish we could remember but cannot. Next, he argues that there are some pains that we ought not to forget, either because they were the result of virtuous deeds or

---

[42] See also Cic. *Tusc.* 5.95; Augustine, *Sermones* 348.3.

[43] There is an obvious plausibility to the thought that recollecting a past good that is now lost can be a source of pain. See e.g. Aquinas, *Summa Theologica* 2.2.36.1; Boethius, *Consolatio Philosophiae* 2.4.; Dante, *Inferno* 5.121–3: 'nessun maggior dolore | che ricordarsi del tempo felice | ne la miseria'. (I owe these references to Oliver Thomas.)

because it might even be pleasant to remember past sufferings. Here, Cicero offers his Latin version of a verse from Euripides' *Andromeda* that we have already seen used also by Aristotle in his account of memory, pleasure, and pain in *Rhet.* 1.11: 'pleasant is the memory of past sufferings'.[44] Presumably the phrase is sufficiently proverbial that we need not think of any direct connection between the Ciceronian and Aristotelian texts but it is possible that Cicero has taken the fragment from a critical discussion of the Epicurean view in an Academic source.[45]

Another critic – Plutarch – puts his dissatisfaction with the Epicurean view in terms that point to a more serious disagreement. We have already looked at this passage when thinking about his general dissatisfaction with the kinds of pleasures which he thinks the Epicureans enjoy. But it also shows his distaste for the role the Epicureans assign in particular to memories of past pleasant experiences.

εἰ δ' ἀκούεις αὐτῶν μαρτυρομένων καὶ βοώντων, ὡς ἐπ' οὐδενὶ ψυχὴ τῶν ὄντων πέφυκε χαίρειν καὶ γαληνίζειν πλὴν ἐπὶ σώματος ἡδοναῖς παρούσαις ἢ προσδοκωμέναις, καὶ τοῦτ' αὐτῆς τὸ ἀγαθόν ἐστιν, ἆρ' οὐ δοκοῦσί σοι διεράματι τοῦ σώματος χρῆσθαι τῇ ψυχῇ, <καὶ> καθάπερ οἶνον ἐκ πονηροῦ καὶ μὴ στέγοντος ἀγγείου τὴν ἡδονὴν διαχέοντες ἐνταῦθα καὶ παλαιοῦντες οἴεσθαι σεμνότερόν τι ποιεῖν καὶ τιμιώτερον; καίτοι γ' οἶνον μὲν χρόνος διαχυθέντα τηρεῖ καὶ συνηδύνει, τῆς δ' ἡδονῆς ἡ ψυχὴ παραλαβοῦσα τὴν μνήμην ὥσπερ ὀσμὴν ἄλλο δ' οὐδὲν φυλάσσει· ζέσασα γὰρ ἐπὶ σαρκὶ κατασβέννυται, καὶ τὸ μνημονευόμενον αὐτῆς ἀμαυρόν ἐστι καὶ κνισῶδες, ὥσπερ ἑώλων ὧν τις ἔπιεν ἢ ἔφαγεν ἀποτιθεμένου καὶ ταμιεύοντος ἐπινοίας ἐν ἑαυτῷ καὶ χρωμένου δηλονότι ταύταις προσφάτων μὴ παρόντων.

(*Non Posse* 1088E–1089A)

But when you hear their loud protest that the soul is so constituted as to find joy and tranquillity in nothing in the world but pleasures of the body either present or anticipated, and that this is its good, do they not appear to you to be using the soul as a decanter of the body, and to imagine that by decanting pleasure, like wine, from a worthless and leaky vessel and leaving it to age in its new container, they are turning it into something more respectable and precious? Yet there is a difference: the new vessel preserves the wine that has settled in the course of time and improves its flavour, whereas in the case of pleasure the soul takes over and preserves the memory of it, as it were the bouquet, and nothing else; for the pleasure effervesces in the flesh and then

---

[44] *suavis laborum est praeteritorum memoria* (= Eur. fr. 133 Nauck²). Cicero comments that 'you all know the line in Greek' (*nostis omnes*). *Pace* Madvig 1879 ad loc., this might mean: 'All you *Epicureans* know the line, since then Cicero can make a subtle jibe against the Epicureans: they remember this *bon mot* about memory but fail to recognise it as a counter-example to their theory.

[45] The same fragment is cited at Plut. *Quaest. Conv.* 630E.

goes flat, and what is left of it in recollection is faint and greasy, as though a
man were to lay away and store up in himself the thoughts of yesterday's food
and drink, resorting to these, we must suppose, when nothing fresh is at
hand (trans. Einarson and De Lacy).

Note the insistence that although a good storage jar can preserve and
even enhance the substance and flavour of a wine, memory is able to
preserve only the mere bouquet of the past pleasure. The soul cannot
repeat the full original bodily pleasure.[46] The bouquet of a wine is, of
course, related to the full taste of the wine; sniffing a decanter or a
recently pulled cork will produce an experience that, despite lacking
the depth and richness of the full range of sensations involved, may
capture part of the experience of drinking the wine itself. But even so this
will fall far short of the full experience of drinking the wine. Plutarch's
criticism is well aimed and it is easy to think of other similar examples.
Consider the pleasure of sitting outside on a lawn on a warm day. Later
in the year, perhaps on a cold November afternoon, I might think back
and recall that past experience. It might be pleasant to recall it; perhaps
the thought might lift my autumnal gloom a little. Then again, perhaps
it will make me feel worse if I also reflect upon how long ago that was and
how long it will be before I feel that warmth again. But it certainly will
not generate on that cold November afternoon the pleasure of a sunny
summer's afternoon even if I have a 'clear expectation' that I might feel
such a pleasure soon enough.[47]

   A little later, at 1091A–B, Plutarch returns to his general complaint that the
Epicureans mistakenly think that the absence of pain – particularly the
absence of bodily pain – is the greatest pleasure. (We discussed this in
Chapter 4 above.) He cites two texts to show that this is the Epicureans'
view: a passage from Metrodorus' *Against the Sophists* (fr. 48 Körte) and a
sentence from an unnamed work by Epicurus himself (Usener 423).

---

[46] See also Cic. *Fin.* 2.106. Here Cicero refers to Aristotle's contempt for the epitaph of Sardanapalus.
The Syrian king, on an inscription on his tomb, boasted of taking with him all his past bodily
pleasures. Aristotle apparently retorted that it was a nonsense that a dead man could retain any
experiences at all, let alone those pleasures which, even when Sardanapalus was alive, lasted only as
long as the experiences that caused them. For Sardanapalus as the standard-bearer for a brutish kind
of hedonism see Arist. *NE* 1.5 1095b19–22. The criticism Cicero reports does not appear in any of our
extant Aristotelian texts.

[47] Cf. Cic. *Tusc.* 5.73–4 for a similar point made by someone more used to suffering hot Italian
summers. Cicero cannot see how it would help someone to cool down just to remember being
surrounded by cool streams (*ut si quis aestuans, cum vim caloris non facile patiatur, recordari velit sese
aliquando in Arpinati nostro gelidis fluminibus circumfusum fuisse; non enim video quo modo sedare
possint mala praesentia praeteritatae voluptates*).

In between these two citations, however, Plutarch himself adds a comment that adds something important to the Epicureans' view. Plutarch observes that Epicurus is claiming that the nature of the good arises from the mere escape from evil and from the recollection (*mnēmē*), recognition (*epilogisis*), and gratitude (*kharis*) that this has happened.[48] It is likely that Plutarch is paraphrasing Epicurus here – certainly, Epicurus refers to *kharis* in a similar fashion at *Ep. Men.* 122 and in *SV* 17 and *epilogisis* is probably a piece of Epicurean terminology[49] – and together the trio of recollection, recognition, and gratitude show how the Epicureans are interested in sometimes deliberate consideration of one's current state of painlessness as itself a possible source of pleasure. Pleasure can therefore be generated through looking back and comparing one's current painless state with some past suffering no less than by looking backwards or forwards when in a present state of suffering and recalling or anticipating a later or earlier state of painlessness.

Cyrenaic recommendations

The spirit of Plutarch's criticism would be warmly endorsed by the Cyrenaics and we are now in a position to understand their recommendation that we should enjoy each pleasure 'as it comes' (DL 2.91). This is a claim which is taken in the sources to be a criticism of the Epicurean confidence in the power of anticipating some future pleasant event or recalling some previous pleasant event. (DL 2.89 makes an explicit contrast with the Epicureans.) The Cyrenaics counter by insisting that pleasure is 'unitemporal' (*monochronos*: Athenaeus 12, 544a–b; cf. Aelian, *Varia Historia* 14.6). The best interpretation of this claim recalls the foundational assertions of Cyrenaic epistemology. Pleasure and pain are *pathē* and therefore are constituted by a particular interaction between a perceiver and a given object. A particular pleasure is both private and tied to a specific such interaction: in the absence of either the perceiver in this particular state or the object in this particular state that particular pleasure cannot be experienced. *Pathē* are also unrepeatable. For example, if I take pleasure at the thought of enjoying opening my birthday gifts later this year, I am not

---

[48] Plut. *Non Posse* 1091B: ὅμοια δὲ καὶ τὰ Ἐπικούρου λέγοντος τὴν τοῦ ἀγαθοῦ φύσιν ἐξ αὐτῆς τῆς φυγῆς τοῦ κακοῦ καὶ τῆς μνήμης καὶ ἐπιλογίσεως καὶ χάριτος, ὅτι τοῦτο συμβέβηκεν αὐτῷ, γεννᾶσθαι.

[49] ἐπιλόγισις is not a common word but it does occur also at Epic. *Nat.* 28 (*PHerc.* 179/1417) 13.VII.18, VIII.13 Sedley. For its meaning see Sedley 1973, 32–3, where he argues that *epilogisis* is the faculty of which *epilogismos* is the activity (although Sedley suspects that Plutarch may have misunderstood this distinction).

taking an advance instalment of the pleasure I will experience on that day since my pleasure when I do open the gift will be a *pathos* constituted by an interaction at that time between me and the various objects I perceive. Any pleasure I take in the anticipation of that event, on the other hand, will be a distinct *pathos*, constituted by a different interaction. It is not clear just what the two participants in that interaction are that constitute the *pathos* of pleasure as I anticipate a future pleasant experience.[50] Perhaps we are invited to think once again in terms of the *Philebus'* analysis of some kind of representation of a past experience, together with its original affective aspect. When someone anticipates or remembers feeling pleased, this is an internal viewing of a depiction of the event in question and that the event will include a depiction of the person's affective response at the time of the anticipated event. In that case the new *pathos* will be generated internally as a result of the consideration of that internal depiction. The event that I view in anticipating the birthday present is 'my enjoying opening my present' and I experience a *pathos* in considering that depiction of the event.

However it is generated, the Cyrenaics think that the *pathos* of pleasure when a person anticipates or recollects occurs only at the time of the anticipation or recollection and its identity is dependent solely on the condition of its occurrence at that time. To enjoy anticipating a pleasure is not to receive an advance instalment of some *pathos* yet to come and, similarly, to enjoy the recollection of a pleasure is not to receive some recovered instalment of a past pleasure.[51] (As reported at DL 2.89, the motion of the soul 'dissipates' over time.) Rather, if anticipation or recollection is accompanied by pleasure then this is a new *pathos* to be identified with some presently obtaining psychic motion: pleasure and pain must always be present *pathē* generated by something present.

The Epicureans insist on the efficacy of recalling past pleasures as a means of mitigating present pains. The Cyrenaics doubt that this is likely to be effective even if a 'recollected pleasure' is not a revived past *pathos* but is rather a brand new present *pathos*. However, there is an important role for anticipation in

---

[50] The Cyrenaic sources are not very helpful on this point although there is reasonably strong evidence that they took all pleasures to involve a cognitive element. See DL 2.90 and Plut. *Quaest. Conv.* 674A–B (*SSR* IV A 206). They argue that we can enjoy listening to someone merely performing a song of mourning. But we do not take pleasure in listening to someone who is genuinely in mourning singing the same song. And two phenomenologically identical experiences (e.g. hearing (i) a crow and (ii) someone imitating the call of a crow) may reasonably cause different hedonic responses because of a person's understanding of the situation. We can enjoy the latter but be irritated by the former. For more discussion see Warren 2013b.

[51] Note that what allows us to be sure that this is a memory at all is an appropriate connection between the internal representation and a past experience. See the remarks in Bernecker 2010, 235–9.

Cyrenaic psychology and ethics which might at first glance appear to be in tension with their criticism of the Epicureans. The Cyrenaics think that it is possible to ready oneself against likely future pains by a form of 'pre-rehearsal' of suffering (*praemeditatio mali*): by focussing attention on a future pain we might lessen the harm when that pain eventually comes.[52] In his account Cicero ascribes to the Cyrenaics the implausible claim that only unexpected pains are painful (*Tusc.* 3.28). More likely, and more in keeping with the remainder of their discussion, by thinking in advance of the supposed pain the Cyrenaic will lessen the pain of the event when it eventually occurs. It cannot be that the future *pathos* is being experienced in advance and its intensity eased by its thereby being spread more extensively through time since this would violate the Cyrenaics' insistence that pain must be unitemporal: any pain experienced in advance must be a distinct *pathos* from the future and expected *pathos* of pain. And even if the effect of pre-rehearsal were that the single pain is spread out over a longer time ('suffering in instalments') this would be unlikely to amount to a diminution of pain overall. The best explanation is that by thinking in advance of possible harms the Cyrenaic's soul becomes arranged and prepared such that, should the imagined harm occur, it will generate a less intense *pathos* of pain. For example, if the Cyrenaic has been constantly thinking that his children are mortal and fragile it will apparently be less painful for him should one of them be injured or die. The Cyrenaic does not conjure up for himself the painful grief in advance. (Aelian, *Varia Historia* 14.6 reports that Aristippus advised against both 'toiling in retrospect over things past' and 'toiling in prospect (*prokamnein*) over things to come'.) Rather, the Cyrenaic constantly reminds himself that a certain painful event is possible, ensuring that it will not be a shock should he ever experience it in the future. The pre-rehearsal is either not itself painful at all or, if it is painful to some extent, the combination of the pre-rehearsal and the eventual lessened pain is not as bad as an unexpected and intense pain.

Epicurus denies that this mitigation occurs and claims that, on the contrary, anticipating misfortune merely makes future evils felt in the present. He proposes instead that evils can be lessened or avoided by his controversial tactic of recalling past pleasures or anticipating future ones. Cicero's spokesman, for his part, finds neither Epicurean claim plausible (*Tusc.* 3.34–8).[53]

---

[52] See Cic. *Tusc.* 3.28–35. Cf. Graver 2002a, 96–101 and 195–201; 2002b; O'Keefe 2002.

[53] Irwin 1991, 73–5, connects this disagreement with his picture of the Cyrenaics as sceptics about personal identity, but to do so he has to make the Cyrenaic *praemediatatio mali* 'impersonal anticipation'. He admits that the Cyrenaics might allow anticipation to take a 'first-person' form (and that it would be more effective if it did). Epicurean anticipation is always first-personal. Cf. Sorabji 2000, 233–9.

The pleasures of confident expectation

Epicurus' recipe for happiness includes the notion that we can guarantee the secure hope of its continuance and look back and enjoy past pleasures whenever we choose. The Cyrenaics, however, are much less confident and prefer to err on the side of caution: assume and expect that pain will come; enjoy the present while you can. We are at last in a position to pinpoint the major difference between the Epicurean and the Cyrenaic positions. Epicurus thinks that we can, through powers of planning, expectation, and recollection, make positive use of past and future pleasures to maintain or increase our present hedonic state. The Cyrenaics do not.

In brief, the Epicureans hold that the temporal location of any particular object of pleasure is irrelevant; an Epicurean can at will recollect past objects of pleasure and anticipate future ones, and he can in effect transform any past or future pleasure into present pleasure.[54] In this way the assurance of a future pleasure is not merely relevant for future wellbeing by legitimising the use of prudential reasoning, but it can be made to do double duty by bolstering an agent's present pleasure through the sure expectation that the future contains no threats of pain.

For example, SV 33 asserts that someone who has and expects to have in the future all the goods required to live without pain rivals Zeus in happiness:[55]

> σαρκὸς φωνὴ τὸ μὴ πεινῆν, τὸ μὴ διψῆν, τὸ μὴ ῥιγοῦν. ταῦτα γὰρ ἔχων τις καὶ ἐλπίζων ἕξειν κἂν <Διι> ὑπὲρ εὐδαιμονίας μαχέσαιτο.

> The cry of the flesh is to feel no hunger, no thirst, and no cold. For someone having and expecting to have these would rival even Zeus in happiness.

An important characteristic of this god-like happiness is the combination of present wellbeing with the assurance of its continuation. The certainty of future painlessness fortifies the pleasure of the present.[56]

---

[54] See in particular Torquatus' account at Cic. *Fin.* 1.57 and compare *Tusc.* 5.95–6. Seneca takes up the theme of the availability of past pleasures (and their being invulnerable to fortune) at *De Brevitate Vitae* 10.2–6, *Ep. Mor.* 99.5.

[55] Cf. Warren 2000, esp. 246–7. Compare Cic. *Tusc.* 3.38: [Zeno of Sidon] 'would argue and maintain in a loud voice that the happy man is he who enjoys present pleasures and is confident that he will enjoy them in the future either for the whole of his life or for the most part of it . . .' (*contendere et magna voce dicere solebat, eum esse beatum, qui praesentibus voluptatibus frueretur confideretque se fruiturum aut in omni aut in magna parte vitae . . .*).

[56] Similarly, the Epicureans also assert that if it is known that an event in the future will not be painful, no distress can be felt at present at its prospect: *Ep. Men.* 125. On the role played by this principle in their arguments against the fear of death see Warren 2001b, 2001d, and 2004.

At Plutarch, *Non Posse* 1089D–1090D, Plutarch's spokesman Theon notes that not only do the Epicureans consider the good to be a 'stable condition' (εὐσταθὲς κατάστημα) of the flesh, they also include as a characteristic of this ideal state the presence of a 'secure anticipation' (πιστὸν ἔλπισμα) of its continuation. (Theon is citing Epicurus' own words, again from the *Peri Telous* or *On the Goal of Life*.)[57] Theon himself considers this last point to be implausible – such sure expectation is impossible – and echoes the reports of Aristippus by Athenaeus and Aelian in basing this disagreement on the idea that 'the future is unclear' (1090A: τὸ γὰρ μέλλον ἄδηλον). Since, he claims, it is impossible to legislate for all manner of possible future harms, including those diseases which Epicurus and his followers suffered, the Epicureans cannot possibly have such confident expectation of a continuing stable state. In reply, the Epicureans might rely again on the idea that the harms Plutarch mentions are mere bodily pains which can be counteracted – as Epicurus himself showed – by recalling past pleasures. But since Plutarch has no time for that idea either, it is hard to think that he would be persuaded to revise his harsh assessment. Furthermore, he thinks that since the pleasures that are being expected are mere bodily pleasures, this is an impoverished kind of experience for the soul and is yet another example of the Epicureans' failure to give proper weight to the pleasures for which the soul is naturally fitted (1096D).

Indeed, in a passage cited by Philodemus and perhaps also from Epicurus' *Peri Telous*, there are signs of what amounts to a hedonist counterpart of the argument of Plato's *Phileb.* 21a–c, which concluded that the faculties of memory and anticipation are necessary parts of a choiceworthy life. Here, they are necessary parts of a good and pleasant life because they allow a person to recall and anticipate pleasures, thereby contributing to the present state of the soul.

ὡς γὰρ | ἐλπίδος ὁ καιρὸ[ς ἐ]ψιλώθη | καὶ τῆς κ[ατὰ σάρκα ἡδονῆς | καὶ
ἐπιμ[ονως] ἀ[π]ελείφθη | τῆ[ς τῶν γεγονότ]ων χάρι|τος, ἆρ᾽ [ἂν ἔτι
τη]ρήσαιμι, ᾧ | Μητ[ρόδωρε, τοιοῦτ]ον κατάστη|μα ψυ[χῆς; ...
(Philodemus, *On Epicurus* (*PHerc.* 1232) XVIII.10–17 Tepedino Guerra)[58]

---

[57] The phrase: τὸ εὐσταθὲς σαρκὸς κατάστημα καὶ τὸ περὶ ταύτης πιστὸν ἔλπισμα cited by Plutarch also appears in other sources (Origen, *Contra Celsum* 3.80, Aulus Gellius 9.5, Cleomedes 166.1–7) and can plausibly be attributed to Epicurus' work *On the Goal of Life* (Usener 68). Demetrius Laco (*PHerc.* 1012 Puglia) notes variation in some Epicurean copies of the text in which ἔλπισμα has become ἐγκατέλπισμα. See Puglia 1988, 231–2 and cf. Purinton 1993, 286 n. 8.

[58] For discussion see Tepedino Guerra 1987 and 1994 and Purinton 1993, 298–9.

For when the (present) moment has been stripped of expectation and of bodily pleasure and has permanently been deprived of the pleasure of past [experiences], could I still, Metrodorus, maintain such a state of the soul?

Let us assume that this is a rhetorical question expecting a negative answer. In that case, it proposes that the ability to look ahead and to look backwards, to anticipate and to remember pleasures, is essential for the maintenance of a good and pleasant state of the soul. So anticipation and pleasure are necessary for a choiceworthy human life precisely because they are means of contributing to and maintaining a current good and pleasant state. In particular, it seems that a settled state of the soul will require the ability to look backwards and forwards to recall and anticipate a settled state of the flesh. If I am unwell, for example, I might calm the mental anxiety it causes by recalling or anticipating a state of health just as I might recall or anticipate various psychic pleasures. On the assumption that Epicurus is the speaker, there is an added poignancy to this question since we have already seen the famous case of Epicurus using his memories of past pleasures in just the fashion envisaged here to maintain a pleasant state of the soul in the face of the physical pains that afflicted him when he was close to death.

Finally, there is one more interesting piece of evidence that offers another perspective on the Epicureans' account of pleasure and expectation. Consider this Epicurean argument against divination, found in a scholion to Aeschylus, *Prometheus Bound* 624 (Usener 395):

> Ἐπικούρειον ἐστι δόγμα ἀναιροῦν τὴν μαντικήν. "εἱμαρμένης γὰρ", φησί, "πάντων κρατούσης πρὸ καιροῦ λελύπηκας †εἰπὼν τὴν συμφορὰν ἢ χρηστόν† τι εἰπὼν τὴν ἡδονὴν ἐξέλυσας". λέγουσι δὲ καὶ τὸ "ἃ δεῖ γενέσθαι, ταῦτα καὶ γενήσεται".

> There is an Epicurean doctrine that denies divination. Epicurus says: 'If fate controls everything then, when you foretell a misfortune, then you have been pained before the right moment. Alternatively, if you foretell something positive, then you have ruined the pleasure.' These people also say: 'What has to be will be.'[59]

It is not a very good argument against divination. At best, it is a pragmatic argument that divination is something you ought not to do. If it is not reliable then it is useless; if it is reliable then it is of no benefit. You go to a fortune teller and ask about your future. If the fortune teller tells you that something bad will happen then this will increase your overall distress.

---

[59] The line in Aeschylus' *Prometheus Bound* is spoken by Prometheus: τὸ μὴ μαθεῖν σοι κρεῖσσον ἢ μαθεῖν τάδε. Also compare the evidence of Epicurus' attitude to prophecy in the citation from the *Short Epitome* at DL 10.135.

Given that the event is fated and therefore inevitable you have simply added the dread of expectation to the eventual pain to come. But if the fortune teller tells you that something good will happen then this ruins the pleasure to come.

The first arm of the dilemma accords well with the now familiar claim that prescience or anticipation of a pain merely makes a pain present. It is the mirror image of the claim found also in Epicurean texts that the memory of a pain will make a pain present or the memory of a pleasure will make a pleasure present. The second arm of the dilemma, however, seems to run counter to the Epicurean claim that knowledge and expectation of a future pleasure can produce confidence and pleasure in the present. And unless the fortune teller reveals that your friend has organised a surprise party for you tomorrow and the pleasure of that party should come mostly from the fact that it is a surprise then it seems to me not true that knowing some pleasure will come about will diminish the pleasure. Perhaps it does not diminish the pleasure of the event itself but it might diminish any extra pleasure that might come from its being unexpected. Even so, that seems to me to be outweighed by the pleasure produced by the confident expectation of the happy event. Imagine, for example, you are told that you will win big on the lottery next year. (And imagine also that this is a reliable prediction.) Will this make the win any less pleasant? It might make it less of a surprise, for sure, but the surprise is surely not what is pleasant about winning the lottery. And just imagine the pleasure you will experience in knowing the windfall is on its way.

Conclusions

Not only do the Epicureans maintain that it is necessary always to aim for the greatest overall pleasure, by careful planning and foresight and sometimes by forgoing nearer lesser pleasures, but they also argue that through deliberate acts of recollection and anticipation a trained Epicurean can bridge any temporal gap between himself and an object of pleasure to transform that pleasure into a present experience. To be sure, we humans are sometimes pained by regrets for the past and sometimes we are pained by anxieties for the future. But the same capacities that can usher in such pains can also, when combined with a proper understanding of what is really good and what is really bad, equip us to maximise our mental pleasure by recalling and anticipating positive experiences. The Epicureans display a clear and laudable understanding of the role that faith in the future plays in the happiness of the present. Confident anticipation of future wellbeing is a powerful force for ensuring not only pleasure in the future, but also pleasure in the present.

These two claims about the function of confidence in future goods might appear to be in tension. On the one hand, the Epicureans are counselling us to look always to the greatest future pleasure and take care to have a long-term view in matters of decision making. On the other hand, the techniques of recollection and anticipation seem to make it irrelevant just when these past and future objects of pleasure are located; the temporal dimension can easily be bridged by thought. The question is why an Epicurean would need to perform the complex and difficult task of practical decision making as outlined in *Ep. Men.* 129–30, if he is easily capable of reaching out and bringing future pleasures to life in the present through anticipation.

There are two answers to this. First, there is the simple matter of physical necessity. It may be possible to cheer oneself up in a time of crisis by anticipating a nice meal next week, but this is not going to have much effect in actually filling one's stomach. Practical decision making is a necessity caused in part by human physiology and it is an inescapable fact of being human that we do indeed live temporally extended lives.[60] Second, it is not the case that the 'proxy enjoyment' of temporally distant objects through recollection and anticipation is entirely independent of the actual experience of those same objects when they were/will be present. It is certainly true, for instance, that I cannot truly be said to enjoy remembering some pleasant event unless at some time in the past I did in fact enjoy that event. The later enjoyment of a pleasant memory is dependent upon some previous actual experience.[61]

This notion is built into the conception we have of 'memory'. It is difficult to conceive of someone remembering a pleasure which they did not in fact experience in the first place; at least, there would be something strange in calling such a thing a memory. The analogous claim would be that anticipation of pleasures can occur only in cases in which the pleasure being anticipated will indeed (or at the very least is most likely to) occur in the future. Here we need to tread more carefully. It would be strange to say of someone that he is 'anticipating' some pleasurable future event if that event is known not to be going to happen. But, as the *Philebus* reminds us, it is certainly possible mistakenly to anticipate some future pleasure and to

---

[60] See Warren 2000, 244–7.

[61] For example, when Epicurus says that on his deathbed his suffering is alleviated by the memory of past philosophical questions (DL 10.22), this depends on Epicurus actually having had such pleasant conversations in the past.

take pleasure in anticipating a future experience that does not in fact provide the pleasure as expected. There are, of course, pleasures of day-dreaming, of contemplating fantastic states of affairs which are known to be impossible or unlikely, but these are different from the pleasures of, for example, awaiting the morning post for a parcel one knows has been sent.[62]

And yet in order to secure the possibility of anticipating and recollecting pleasures, the wise man must still go out and plan to experience those pleasures when they are presently available. Anticipation and recollection do not absolve the Epicurean from needing to plan ahead in order to secure present pleasures. On the contrary, only if he successfully arranges his life in order to experience pleasures as and when they are in fact available will be able to recollect them later and anticipate them before they occur. And since the Epicurean wise man has such a simple set of desires then we can presume that his anticipated pleasures will be simple and reliable too. His desires and preferences will not alter over time since, in order to attain his wise state, he has pared down his desires only to those that are necessary and natural. He desires only the general objects that will rid him of hunger, thirst, cold, and the like. In that case, it is as unlikely as it can be that an Epicurean wise man will take pleasure in anticipating a future experience that, when it arrives, he does not in fact enjoy.

The Epicureans and the Cyrenaics agree that ideally the wise man should be able to plan for future episodes of pleasure, future kinetic pleasures. But they differ in their assessment of our chances of being able to attain that ideal. That difference is partly the product of their differing view on the number and sort of desires which one should seek to fulfil. The Epicurean's restricted set of easily fulfilled general desires allows him to be much more confident in planning to satisfy them in the future. The confidence that he will experience these pleasures makes the Epicurean experience a lack of anxiety in the present. Just as the Epicurean's acceptance of various doctrines concerning the far future – namely that death is annihilation and there is no post-mortem judgement and punishment – is supposed to bring about present peace of mind, so does the very promise that he will experience the pleasurable episodes for which he plans contribute to a present feeling of pleasant security. Since the Cyrenaics do not allow that such absence of anxiety is itself a pleasure, this further positive role of future pleasures is unavailable to them.

---

[62] This last consideration is relevant to the question of whether Epicurus ought to have written a will. According to *KD* 2 and the basis it offers for agreeing that 'death is nothing to us', post-mortem events cannot affect an agent's wellbeing. So the contemplation of those events (seeing one's great-grandchildren well looked-after) can only be of the 'day-dreaming' type of anticipation, not an anticipation of a pleasure which the agent will experience later.

CHAPTER 9

Epilogue

There are many pleasures to be had from learning, knowing, remembering, and anticipating. And all the ancient philosophers we have met in these chapters agree that those pleasures are part of what it is to live a human life. However, it might also appear from these chapters that our human capacities for reasoning and the associated affective aspects of engaging those capacities provide, at best, a mixture of benefits and harms in our lives. Consider, for example, this passage at the end of Lucretius' set of arguments for the conclusion that the human soul is mortal and disperses when the person dies.

> praeter enim quam quod morbis cum corporis aegret,
> advenit id quod eam de rebus saepe futuris
> macerat inque metu male habet curisque fatigat,
> praeteritisque male admissis peccata remordent.
> adde furorem animi proprium atque oblivia rerum,
> adde quod in nigras lethargi mergitur undas. (*DRN* 3.824–9)

For, what is more, the soul sickens along with diseases of the body, and often something comes along which tortures it with concerns for things to come and it is held in fear and worn down by cares. And errors gnaw away at it in memories of past mistakes. Add to these the madness that belongs just to the mind and add in forgetfulness; add in the fact that it is drowned in the black waves of coma.

This passage is immediately followed by Lucretius' famous statement that 'death is nothing to us' and there is doubtless some sense of gradual transition from the closing image of the loss of mental powers, then of consciousness, and finally the oblivion of eventual annihilation. But before the supposedly uplifting message that death really is the end of all sensation, Lucretius leaves behind the impression that our rational powers are as much a source of fear, anxiety, remorse, regret, and other pains as they are a source of pleasures and delights. Perhaps, we wonder whether, in their enthusiasm for the joys of learning and knowing, of planning and recalling, our philosophers have failed to give due attention to the negative counterparts of these pleasures of reason. A lion may be unable to feel the pleasure of acquiring the knowledge of a mathematical theorem, may be unable to enjoy recognising a statue as a representation of Apollo, and may be unable to cheer himself up by recalling a warm afternoon of feasting on a freshly killed deer. But that same lion will not be disturbed by the realisation that he does not know how to solve a complex equation, or be pained at the thought of the coming winter and the possibility of starvation. Perhaps in various ways the lion is better placed than we are since it is free from any of these pains of reasoning.[1]

We can generalise this concern so that it threatens not just the hedonist Epicureans but Plato and Aristotle too. In fact, there are two general concerns that they will need to address. First of all, it is certainly true that fears and regrets and their associated pains can enter into human lives because we are animals able to reminisce and to anticipate. We sometimes form beliefs about our past or future that are painful. Second, it is also true that as creatures capable of forming beliefs and thinking about our own futures and pasts we might find ourselves holding false beliefs about such things or making incorrect estimations of various outcomes. These false appearances and false beliefs might also generate in us various pains. They might even generate in us various pleasures that we might feel are best avoided or at least should not be indulged, precisely because they are generated by false beliefs and misunderstandings. As we have seen, Plato was particularly interested in the ways in which our capacity for reasoning and imagining various past or future experiences might be fallible. In short, our ability to think can bring pains into our lives and our propensity to make mistakes can bring both pleasures and pains into our lives that we might prefer to do without. And conversely, the pleasures and pains we experience, particularly as we think about the past and future, can encourage the adoption of false beliefs and make us susceptible to various kinds of error.

And yet, Plato and Aristotle will agree with the Epicureans that these are all problems which can be rectified or avoided. Provided that we come to see what really should be feared and what really should be regretted then we can live without any unnecessary distress of that kind. First of all, these ancient philosophers tend to the view that we should strive to become the kind of person for whom there really is nothing very much that ought to cause anxiety or regret. A good person is such that his past will cause him no regret

---

[1] See Warren 2002a, 129–42.

and his future will contain nothing to dread. So there are very few true beliefs about his past or future that should cause a good person any pain. Good people will also, we are assured, live a life free from the misapprehensions and other errors that might provoke the sorts of pleasures and pains we would prefer to do without. A good person will be entirely or to the greatest degree possible free from any false beliefs about his past or future and therefore free from pains of that sort too. But most of all, according to these philosophers there is also – as I hope the previous chapters have made clear – a range of overwhelmingly positive benefits to the presence in our lives of these abilities to think, to learn, to recollect, and to anticipate. Whatever their various disagreements over the details of just what constitutes a good human life and just what pleasures and pains really are, these ancient philosophers share a commitment to two important views. A good human life is a life lived by a thinking rational animal. And a good human life will be a pleasant life.

References

Adam, H. (1974) *Plutarchs Schrift non posse suaviter vivi secundum Epicurum*, Amsterdam: Gruner Publishing

Adam, J. (1902) *The Republic of Plato (Edited with Critical Notes, Commentary and Appendices)*, 2 vols., Cambridge University Press

Albini, F. (1993) *Plutarco: Non posse suaviter vivi secundum Epicurum. Introduzione, traduzione, commento*, Genoa: D. AR. FI. CL. ET. "F. Della Corte"

Annas, J. (1981) *An Introduction to Plato's Republic*, Oxford University Press
  (1992) 'Aristotle on memory and the self', in M. C. Nussbaum and A. O. Rorty (eds.), *Essays on Aristotle's De Anima*, Oxford University Press: 297–311
  (1993) *The Morality of Happiness*, Oxford University Press
  (1999) *Platonic Ethics, Old and New*, Ithaca: Cornell University Press

Asmis, E. (1995) 'Epicurean poetics', in D. Obbink (ed.), *Philodemus and Poetry*, Oxford University Press: 15–34

Aufderheide, J. (2013) 'Processes as pleasures in *EN* vii 11–14: a new approach', *Ancient Philosophy* 33: 135–57

Bernecker, S. (2010) *Memory: a Philosophical Study*, Oxford University Press

Bailey, C. (1926) *Epicurus: the Extant Remains*, Oxford University Press

Bigelow, J., Campbell, J., and Pargetter, R. (1990) 'Death and well-being', *Pacific Philosophical Quarterly* 71: 119–40

Blank, D. (2009) '*Philosophia* and *technē*: Epicureans on the arts', in J. Warren (ed.), *The Cambridge Companion to Epicureanism*, Cambridge University Press: 216–33

Bobonich, C. (2002) *Plato's Utopia Recast*, Oxford University Press

Bostock, D. (1988) 'Pleasure and activity in Aristotle's *Ethics*', *Phronesis* 33: 251–72

Boys-Stones, G. (1997) 'Thyrsus-bearer of the Academy or enthusiast for Plato? Plutarch's *de Stoicorum repugnatiis*', in J. Mossman (ed.), *Plutarch and his Intellectual World*, London: Duckworth: 41–58

Brink, D. O. (1992) 'Sidgwick and the rationale for rational egoism', in B. Schultz (ed.), *Essays on Henry Sidgwick*, Cambridge University Press: 199–240

Broadie, S. (1991) *Ethics with Aristotle*, Oxford University Press
  (2012) 'A science of first principles (*Metaphysics* A 2)', in C. Steel (ed.), *Aristotle's Metaphysics Alpha*, Oxford University Press: 43–67

Brunschwig, J. (1986) 'The cradle argument in Epicureanism and Stoicism', in M. Schofield and G. Striker (eds.), *The Norms of Nature*, Cambridge University Press: 113–44

Burnyeat, M. F. (1990) *The Theaetetus of Plato*, Indianapolis: Hackett

(2002) '*De anima* II 5', *Phronesis* 47: 28–90

(2008) '*Kinesis* vs. *Energeia*: a much-read passage in (but not of) Aristotle's *Metaphysics*', *Oxford Studies in Ancient Philosophy* 34, 219–92

(2011) 'Episteme', in B. Morison and K. Ierodiakonou (eds.), *Episteme, etc. Essays in Honour of Jonathan Barnes*, Oxford University Press: 3–29

Cambiano, G. (2012) 'The desire to know (*Metaphysics* A 1)', in C. Steel (ed.), *Aristotle's Metaphysics Alpha*, Oxford University Press: 1–42

Carone, G. R. (2000) 'Hedonism and the pleasureless life in Plato's *Philebus*', *Phronesis* 45: 257–83

(2005) *Plato's Cosmology and its Ethical Dimensions*, Cambridge University Press

Carpenter, A. (2003) 'Phileban gods', *Ancient Philosphy* 23: 93–112

(2006) 'Hedonistic persons: the good man argument in Plato's *Philebus*', *British Journal for the History of Philosophy* 14: 5–26

(2010) 'What is peculiar to Plato's and Aristotle's psychologies? What is common to them both?', in V. Harte, M. M. McCabe, R. W. Sharples, and A. Sheppard (eds.), *Aristotle and the Stoics Reading Plato* (Bulletin of the Institute of Classical Studies Supplement 107), London: Institute of Classical Studies: 21–44

(2011) 'Pleasure as genesis in Plato's *Philebus*', *Ancient Philosophy* 31: 73–94

Caston, V. (1996) 'Why Aristotle needs imagination', *Phronesis* 41: 20–55

(1998) 'Aristotle and the problem of intentionality', *Philosophy and Phenomenological Research* 58: 249–98

(2009) '*Phantasia* and thought', in G. Anagnotopoulos (ed.), *A Companion to Aristotle*, Oxford: Blackwell: 322–34

Cherniss, H. (1976) *Plutarch's Moralia: Volume XIII Part 1* (Loeb Classical Libary), Cambridge, Mass.: Harvard University Press

Cockburn, D. (1997) *Other Times: Philosophical Perspectives on Past, Present, and Future*, Cambridge University Press

Cole, E. B. (1992) 'Theophrastus and Aristotle on animal intelligence', in W. W. Fortenbaugh and D. Gutas (eds.), *Theophrastus: His Psychological, Doxographical and Scientific Writings* (Rutgers University Studies in Classical Humanities 5), New Brunswick: Transaction Publishers: 44–62

Coles, A. (1997) 'Animal and childhood cognition in Aristotle's biology and the *scala naturae*' in W. Kullmann and K. Abel (eds.), *Aristotelische Biologie: Intentionen, Methoden, Ergebnisse*, Stuttgart: Franz Steiner Verlag: 287–323

Coope, U. (2012) 'Why does Aristotle think that ethical virtue is required for practical wisdom?', *Phronesis* 57: 142–63

Cooper, J. (1996) 'An Aristotelian theory of emotions', in A. O. Rorty (ed.), *Essays on Aristotle's Rhetoric*, Berkeley: University of California Press: 238–57

(1999a) 'Plato's theory of human good in the *Philebus*', in his *Reason and Emotion: Essays on Ancient Moral Psychology and Ethical Theory*, Princeton University Press: 151–64

(1999b) 'Pleasure and desire in Epicurus', in his *Reason and Emotion: Essays on Ancient Moral Psychology and Ethical Theory*, Princeton University Press: 485–514

Corcilius, K. (2011) 'Aristotle's definition of non-rational pleasure and pain and desire', in J. Miller (ed.), *Aristotle's Nicomachean Ethics. A Critical Guide*, Cambridge University Press: 117–43

Delcomminette, S. (2003) 'False pleasures, appearance and imagination in the Philebus', *Phronesis* 48: 215–37

(2006) *Le Philèbe de Platon: introduction à l'agathologie platonicienne*, Leiden: E. J. Brill

Denyer, N. (2008) *Plato: Protagoras*, Cambridge University Press

Destrée, P. (2012) 'Le plaisir "propre" de la tragédie est-il intellectuel?', *Methexis* 25: 93–108

(2014) 'Aristotle on the paradox of tragic pleasure', in J. Levinson (ed.), *Suffering Art Gladly: the Paradox of Negative Emotion in Art*, Basingstoke: Palgrave Macmillan: 3–27

Dow, J. (2009) 'Feeling fantastic? Emotions and appearances in Aristotle', *Oxford Studies in Ancient Philosophy* 37: 143–75

(2011) 'Aristotle's theory of the emotions: emotions as pleasures and pains', in M. Pakaluk and G. Pearson (eds.), *Moral Psychology and Human Action in Aristotle*, Oxford University Press: 47–74

Einarson, B. and De Lacy, P. H. (1967) *Plutarch's Moralia: Volume XIV* (Loeb Classical Library), Cambridge Mass.: Harvard University Press

Erginel, M. M. (2004) 'Pleasures in *Republic* IX', PhD dissertation, University of Texas at Austin

(2011) 'Inconsistency and ambiguity in *Republic* IX', *Classical Quarterly* 61: 493–502

Erler, M. (2012) '*Aplanēs theoria*. Einige Aspekte der Epikureischen Vorstellung vom *Bios theōrētikos*', in T. Bénatouïl and M. Bonazzi (eds.), *Theoria, Praxis and the Contemplative Life after Plato and Aristotle*, Leiden: E. J. Brill: 41–55

Evans, M. (2007a) 'Plato and the meaning of pain', *Apeiron* 40: 71–93

(2007b) 'Plato's anti-hedonism' (with commentary by V. Harte), *Proceedings of the Boston Area Colloquium in Ancient Philosophy* 23: 121–52

(2007c) 'Plato's rejection of thoughtless and pleasureless lives', *Phronesis* 52: 337–63

(2008) 'Plato on the possibility of hedonic mistakes', *Oxford Studies in Ancient Philosophy* 35: 89–124

(2010) 'A partisan's guide to Socratic intellectualism', in S. Tenenbaum (ed.), *Desire, Practical Reason, and the Good*, Oxford University Press: 6–33

Feldman, F. (2004) *Pleasure and the Good Life: Concerning the Nature, Varieties and Plausibility of Hedonism*, Oxford University Press

Ferrari, G. R. F. (2002) 'Plato *Republic* 9.585c–d', *Classical Quarterly* 52: 383–8

(2003) *City and Soul in Plato's Republic*, Sankt Augustin: Akademia Verlag

Frede, D. (1985) 'Rumpelstiltskins's pleasures: true and false pleasures in the Philebus', *Phronesis* 30: 151–80

(1992a) 'The cognitive role of *phantasia* in Aristotle', in M. Nussbaum and A. O. Rorty (eds.), *Essays on Aristotle's De Anima*, Oxford University Press: 279–95

(1992b) 'Disintegration and restoration: pleasure and pain in the *Philebus*', in R. Kraut (ed.), *The Cambridge Companion to Plato*, Cambridge University Press: 425–63

(1993) *Plato: Philebus*, Indianapolis: Hackett

(1996a) 'The hedonist's conversion: the role of Socrates in the *Philebus*', in C. Gill and M. M. McCabe (eds.), *Form and Argument in Late Plato*, Oxford University Press: 213–48

(1996b) 'Mixed feelings in Aristotle's *Rhetoric*', in A. O. Rorty (ed.), *Essays on Aristotle's Rhetoric*, Berkeley: University of California Press: 258–85

(1997) *Platon: Philebos. Übersetzung und Kommentar*, Göttingen: Vandenhoeck & Ruprecht

(2009) '*NE* VII.11–12: Pleasure', in C. Natali (ed.), *Aristotle: Nicomachean Ethics VII*, Oxford University Press: 183–208

Giannantoni, G. (1958) *I Cirenaici*, Florence: Sansoni

Gibbs, B. (2001) 'Pleasure, pain and rhetoric in *Republic 9*', in D. Baltzly, D. Blyth, and H. Tarrant (eds.), *Power and Pleasure, Virtues and Vices* (*Prudentia* supplementary volume), Auckland: 7–34

Gioé, A. (2002) *Filosofi medioplatonici del II secolo D. C. Testimonianze e frammenti: Gaio, Albino, Lucio, Nicostrato, Tauro, Severo, Arpocrazione*, Naples: Bibliopolis

Giovacchini, J. (2007) 'Le souvenir des plaisirs: le rôle de la mémoire dans la thérapeutique épicurienne', in L. Boulègue and C. Lévy (eds.), *Hédonismes: penser et dire le plaisir dans l'Antiquité et à la Renaissance*, Lille: Presses Universitaires Septentrion: 69–83

Gonzalez, F. (1991) 'Aristotle on pleasure and perfection', *Phronesis* 36, 141–59

Gordon, P. (2012) *The Invention and Gendering of Epicurus*, Ann Arbor: University of Michigan Press

Görler, W. (1997) 'Storing up past pleasures. The soul-vessel-metaphor in Lucretius and in his Greek models', in K. A. Algra, M. H. Koenen, and P. H. Schrijvers (eds.), *Lucretius and his Intellectual Background*, Amsterdam: Royal Netherlands Academy of Arts and Sciences: 193–207

Gosling, J. C. B. (1975) *Plato: Philebus*, Oxford University Press

Gosling, J. C. B. and Taylor, C. C. W. (1982) *The Greeks on Pleasure*, Oxford University Press

Graver, M. (2002a) *Cicero on the Emotions: Tusculan Disputations 3 and 4*, University of Chicago Press

(2002b) 'Managing mental pain: Epicurus vs. Aristippus on the pre-rehearsal of future ills', *Proceedings of the Boston Area Colloquium in Ancient Philosophy* 17: 155–77; with commentary by G. Striker: 178–84

Hackforth, R. (1945) *Plato's Examination of Pleasure*, Cambridge University Press

Hall, J. C. (1966–7) 'Quantity of pleasure', *Proceedings of the Aristotelian Society* 67: 35–52

Halliwell, S. (1992) 'Pleasure, understanding, and emotion in Aristotle's *Poetics*', in A. O. Rorty (ed.), *Essays on Aristotle's Poetics*, Princeton University Press: 241–60

(2011) *Between Ecstasy and Truth: Interpretations of Greek Poetics from Homer to Longinus*, Oxford University Press

Hamlyn, D. W. (1968) *Aristotle's De anima Books II and III (with Certain Passages from Book I)*, Oxford University Press

Harte, V. (2002) *Plato on Parts and Wholes: the Metaphysics of Structure*, Oxford University Press

(2004) 'The Philebus on pleasure: the good, the bad and the false', *Proceedings of the Aristotelian Society* 104: 111–28

(2014a) 'Desire, memory, and the authority of soul: Plato, *Philebus* 35c–d', *Oxford Studies in Ancient Philosophy* 46: 33–72

(2014b) 'The life of Protarchus' choosing: Plato *Philebus* 20b–22c', in M. K. Lee (ed.), *Strategies of Argument: Essays in Ancient Ethics, Epistemology, and Logic*, Oxford University Press: 3–20

Heath, M. (2009) 'Cognition in Aristotle's *Poetics*', *Mnemosyne* 62: 51–75

Heinaman, R. (2011) 'Pleasure as an activity in the *Nicomachean Ethics*', in M. Pakaluk and G. Pearson (eds.), *Moral Psychology and Human Action in Aristotle*, Oxford University Press: 7–45

Hershbell, J. P. (1992) 'Plutarch and Epicureanism', *Aufstieg und Niedergang der Römische Welt* 2.36.5: 3353–83

Hutchinson, D. S. and Johnson, M. R. (2005) 'Authenticating Aristotle's *Protrepticus*', *Oxford Studies in Ancient Philosophy* 29: 193–294

Indelli, G. (1978) *Polistrato: sul disprezzo irrazionale delle opinion popolari*, Naples: Bibliopolis

Indelli, G. and Tsouna-McKirahan, V. (1995) *[Philodemus] [On Choices and Avoidances]*, Naples: Bibliopolis

Irwin, T. (1991) 'Aristippus against happiness', *The Monist* 74: 55–82

Johansen, T. K. (2012) *The Powers of Aristotle's Soul*, Oxford University Press

Kechagia, E. (2011) *Plutarch Against Colotes: a Lesson in History of Philosophy*, Oxford University Press

King, R. A. H. (2009) *Aristotle and Plotinus on Memory*, Berlin: de Gruyter

Konstan, D. (2008) *A Life Worthy of the Gods: the Materialist Psychology of Epicurus*, Las Vegas: Parmenides Publishing

(2013) 'Lucretius and the Epicurean attitude towards grief', in D. LeHoux, A. D. Morrison, and A. Sharrock (eds.), *Lucretius: Poetry, Philosophy, Science*, Oxford University Press: 193–209

Körte, A. (1890) 'Metrodori Epicurei fragmenta', *Jahrbuch für classische Philologie*, Suppl. 17, Leipzig: Teubner: 529–70

LaBarge, S. (2012) 'How (and maybe why) to grieve like an ancient philosopher', in R. Kamtekar (ed.), *Virtue and Happiness: Essays in Honour of Julia Annas* (Oxford Studies in Ancient Philosophy supplementary volume), Oxford University Press: 321–42

Lakmann, M.-L. (1995) *Der Platoniker Taurus in der Darstellung des Aulus Gellius*, Leiden: E. J. Brill

Laks, A. (1993) 'Annicéris et les plaisirs psychiques: quelques préalables doxographiques', in J. Brunschwig and M. Nussbaum (eds.), *Passions and Perceptions*, Cambridge University Press: 18–50

Lane, M. (2007) 'Virtue as the love of knowledge in Plato's *Symposium* and *Republic*', in D. Scott (ed.), *Maieusis: Essays on Ancient Philosophy in Honour of Myles Burnyeat*, Oxford University Press: 44–67

Lang, P. (2010) 'The ranking of the goods at *Philebus* 66a–67b', *Phronesis* 55: 153–69

Lear, J. (1988) *Aristotle: the Desire to Understand*, Cambridge University Press

Leone, G. (1984) 'Epicuro *Della natura* libro XIV', *Cronache Ercolanesi* 14: 17–107

Lloyd, G. E. R. (1983) *Science, Folklore and Ideology: Studies in the Life Sciences in Ancient Greece*, Cambridge University Press

Long, A. A. (1999) 'The Socratic legacy', in K. Algra, J. Barnes, J. Mansfeld, and M. Schofield (eds.), *The Cambridge History of Hellenistic Philosophy*, Cambridge University Press: 617–41

   (2005) 'Platonic souls as persons', in R. Salles (ed.), *Metaphysics, Soul, and Ethics in Ancient Thought: Themes from the Work of Richard Sorabji*, Oxford University Press: 173–91

   (2011) 'Aristotle on *eudaimonia, nous,* and divinity', in J. Milled (ed.), *Aristotle's Nicomachean Ethics. A Critical Guide*, Cambridge University Press: 92–113

Lorenz, H. (2006a) *The Brute Within: Appetitive Desire in Plato and Aristotle*, Oxford University Press

   (2006b) 'The analysis of the soul in Plato's *Republic*', in G. Santas (ed.), *The Blackwell Companion to Plato's Republic*, Oxford: Blackwell: 146–65

   (2007) 'Aristotle's assimilation of sense to sense-object', *Oxford Studies in Ancient Philosophy* 33: 179–220

Lovibond, S. (1989–90) 'True and false pleasures', *Proceedings of the Aristotelian Society* 90: 213–30

Madvig, N. (1879) *M. Tulli Ciceronis De finibus bonorun et malorum libri V* (3rd edition), Copenhagen: Impensis Librariae Gyldendelianae

Mannebach, E. (1961) *Aristippi et Cyrenaicorum fragmenta*, Leiden: E. J. Brill

Margalit, A. (2002) *The Ethics of Memory*, Harvard University Press

Matson, W. I. (1998) 'Hegesias the Death-Persuader; or, the gloominess of hedonism', *Philosophy* 73: 553–7

McCabe, M. M. (2000) *Plato and his Predecessors: the Dramatisation of Reason*, Cambridge University Press

   (2006) 'Is dialectic as dialectic does? The virtue of philosophical conversation', in B. Reis (ed.), *The Virtuous Life in Greek Ethics*, Cambridge University Press: 70–98

Mellor, D. (1981) 'Thank goodness that's over', *Ratio* 23: 20–30

Meyer, S. Sauvé (2012) 'Pleasure, pain, and "anticipation" in Plato's *Laws*, Book 1', in L. Patterson, V. Karasmanis, and A Hermann (eds.), *Presocratics and Plato: Festschrift at Delphi in Honor of Charles Kahn*, Las Vegas: Parmenides Publishing: 311–28

Mitsis, P. (1988) *Epicurus' Ethical Theory: the Pleasures of Invulnerability*, Ithaca: Cornell University Press

Mooradian, M. (1996) 'Converting Protarchus: relativism and false pleasures of anticipation in Plato's *Philebus*', *Ancient Philosophy* 16: 93–112

Moore, G. E. (1903) *Principia Ethica*, Cambridge University Press

Moss, J. (2006) 'Pleasure and illusion in Plato', *Philosophy and Phenomenological Research* 72: 503–35

  (2009) 'Akrasia and perceptual illusion', *Archiv für Geschichte der Philosophie* 91: 119–56

  (2012a) *Aristotle on the Apparent Good: Perception, Phantasia, Thought, and Desire*, Oxford University Press

  (2012b) 'Pictures and passions in the *Timaeus* and *Philebus*', in R. Barney, T. Brennan, and C. Brittain (eds.), *Plato and the Divided Self*, Cambridge University Press: 259–80

Nagel, T. (1970) *The Possibility of Altruism*, Oxford University Press

Nightingale, A. (2004) *Spectacles of Truth in Classical Greek Philosophy*, Cambridge University Press

Nussbaum, M. C. (1978) *Aristotle's De motu animalium*, Princeton University Press

  (1986) *The Fragility of Goodness: Luck and Ethics in Greek Tragedy and Philosophy*, Cambridge University Press

  (1995) 'Aristotle on human nature and the foundations of ethics', in J. E. J. Altham and R. Harrison (eds.), *World, Mind, and Ethics: Essays on the Ethical Philosophy of Bernard Williams*, Cambridge University Press: 86–131

Oaklander, L. N. and Smith, Q. (eds.) (1994) *The New Theory of Time*, New Haven: Yale University Press

Ogihara, S. (2012) 'False pleasures: *Philebus* 36c–40e', in L. Patterson, V. Karasmanis, and A Hermann (eds.), *Presocratics and Plato: Festschrift at Delphi in Honor of Charles Kahn*, Las Vegas: Parmenides Publishing: 291–309

O'Keefe, T. (2002) 'The Cyrenaics on pleasure, happiness, and future-concern', *Phronesis* 47: 395–416

Opsomer, J. (2005) 'Plutarch's Platonism revisited', in M. Bonazzi and V. Celluprica (eds.), *L'eredità platonica: studi sul Platonismo da Arcesilao a Proclo*, Naples: Bibliopolis: 161–200

  (2012) 'Plutarch on the division of the soul', in R. Barney, T. Brennan, and C. Brittain (eds.), *Plato and the Divided Self*, Cambridge University Press: 311–330

Osborne, C. (2007) *Dumb Beasts and Dead Philosophers. Humanity and the Humane in Ancient Philosophy and Literature*, Oxford University Press

Pakaluk, M. (1998) *Aristotle: Nicomachean Ethics Books VIII and IX*, Oxford University Press

Pangle, L. (2003) *Aristotle and the Philosophy of Friendship*, Cambridge University Press

Pappas, N. (1995) *Routledge Philosophy Guidebook to Plato and the Republic*, London: Routledge

Parfit, D. (1984) *Reasons and Persons*, Oxford University Press

Pearson, G. (2012) *Aristotle on Desire*, Cambridge University Press

Penner, T. (1970) 'False anticipatory pleasures: *Philebus* 36a3–41a6', *Phronesis* 15: 166–78

Pepe, L. (2002) 'Le livre d'Anaxagore lu par Platon', in M. Dixsaut and A. Brancacci (eds.), *Platon, Source des Présocratiques*, Paris: J. Vrin: 107–28

Persson, I. (2005) *The Retreat of Reason*, Oxford University Press

Price, A. (2009) 'Emotions in Plato and Aristotle', in P. Goldie (ed.), *The Oxford Handbook of Philosophy of Emotion*, Oxford University Press: 121–42

Prior, A. N. (1959) 'Thank goodness that's over', *Philosophy* 34: 12–17

Puglia, E. (1988) *Demetrio Lacone: aporie testuali ed esegetiche in Epicuro (PHerc 1012)*, Naples: Bibliopolis

Purinton, J. (1993) 'Epicurus on the telos', *Phronesis* 38: 281–320

Quoidbach, J., Gilbert, D. T., and Wilson, T. D. (2013) 'The end of history illusion', *Science* 339 no. 6115: 96–8

Rapp, C. (2009) '*NE* VII.12–14: pleasure and *eudaimonia*', in C. Natali (ed.), *Aristotle: Nicomachean Ethics VII*. Oxford University Press: 209–236

Rawls, J. (1971) *A Theory of Justice*, Cambridge Mass.: Belknap Press

Richardson, H. S. (1990) 'Measurement, pleasure, and practical science in Plato's *Protagoras*', *Journal of the History of Philosophy* 28: 7–32

Richardson Lear, G. (2006) 'Aristotle on moral virtue and the fine', in R. Kraut (ed.), *The Blackwell Companion to Aristotle's Nicomachean Ethics*, Oxford: Blackwell: 116–36

Roberts, R. C. and Wood, W. J. (2007) *Intellectual Virtues: an Essay in Regulative Epistemology*, Oxford University Press

Rosen, S. (2005) *Plato's Republic: a Study*, New Haven: Yale University Press

Roskam, G. (2005) 'The displeasing secrets of the Epicurean life. Plutarch's polemic against Epicurus' political philosophy', in A. Casanova (ed.), *Plutarco e l'età ellenistica. Atti del convengo internazionale di studi. Firenze, 23–24 settembre 2004*, Florence: Università degli studi di Firenze, Dipartimento di scienze dell'antichità 'Giorgio Pasquali': 351–68

(2007) *A Commentary on Plutarch's De latenter vivendo*, Leuven University Press

Rowett, C. (2013) 'Relativism in Plato's *Protagoras*', in V. Harte and M. Lane (eds.), *Politeia in Greek and Roman Philosophy*, Cambridge University Press: 191–211

Rudebusch, G. (1999) *Socrates, Pleasure, and Value*, Oxford University Press

Russell, D. (2000) 'Protagoras and Socrates on courage and pleasure: *Protagoras* 349d *ad finem*', *Ancient Philosophy* 20: 311–38

(2005) *Plato on Pleasure and the Good Life*, Oxford University Press

Scheiter, K. M. (2012) 'Images, appearances, and *phantasia* in Aristotle', *Phronesis* 57: 251–78

Schofield, M. (1978) 'Aristotle on the imagination' in G. E. R. Lloyd and G. E. L. Owen (eds.), *Aristotle on Mind and the Senses*, Cambridge University Press: 99–140

(1996) '*Epilogismos*: an appraisal' in M. Frede and G. Striker (eds.), *Rationality in Greek Thought*, Oxford University Press: 221–37

(2007) 'Metaspeleology', in D. Scott (ed.), *Maieusis: Essays in Ancient Philosophy in Honour of Myles Burnyeat*, Oxford University Press: 216–31

(2011) 'Phantasia in the De Motu Animalium' in M. Pakaluk and G. Pearson (eds.), Moral Psychology and Human Action in Aristotle, Oxford University Press: 119–34

Scott, D. (2000) 'Plato's critique of the democratic character', Phronesis 45 : 19–37
(2006) Plato's Meno, Cambridge University Press

Sedley, D. N. (1973) 'Epicurus, On Nature book XXVIII', Cronache Ercolanesi 3: 5–83
(1976) 'Epicurus and his professional rivals', in J. Bollack and A. Laks (eds.), Études sur l'Epicurisme antique (Cahiers de philologie 1), Publications de l'Université de Lille III: 121–59
(1996) 'The inferential foundations of Epicurean ethics', in M. Gigante and G. Giannantoni (eds.), Epicureismo greco e romano, Naples: Bibliopolis: 313–39
(2002) 'Diogenes of Oenoanda on Cyrenaic hedonism', Proceedings of the Cambridge Philological Society 48: 159–74

Shields, C. (2011) 'Perfecting pleasures: the metaphysics of pleasure in Nicomachean Ethics X', in J. Miller (ed.), Aristotle's Nicomachean Ethics: a Critical Guide, Cambridge University Press: 191–210

Sidgwick, H. (1907) The Methods of Ethics (7th edition), London: Macmillan

Sihvola, J. (1996) 'Emotional animals: do Aristotelian emotions require beliefs?', Apeiron 29: 105–44

Slote, M. (1983) Goods and Virtues, Oxford University Press

Small, J. P. (1997) Wax Tablets of the Mind: Cognitive Studies of Memory and Literacy in Classical Antiquity, London: Routledge

Smith, M. F. (1993) Diogenes of Oinoanda: the Epicurean Inscription, Naples: Bibliopolis

Sorabji, R. R. K. (1993) Animal Minds and Human Morals: the Origins of the Western Debate, London: Duckworth
(2000) Emotion and Peace of Mind: From Stoic Agitation to Christian Temptation, Oxford University Press
(2004) Aristotle on Memory (2nd edition), London: Duckworth

Striker, G. (1988) 'Commentary on Mitsis', Proceedings of the Boston Area Colloquium in Ancient Philosophy 4: 323–8
(1993) 'Epicurean hedonism', in J. Brunschwig and M. Nussbaum (eds.), Passions and Perceptions, Cambridge University Press: 3–17
(1996a) 'Emotions in context: Aristotle's treatment of the passions in the Rhetoric and his moral psychology', in A. O. Rorty (ed.), Essays on Aristotle's Rhetoric, Berkeley: University of California Press: 286–302
(1996b) 'Κριτήριον τῆς ἀληθείας', in her Essays on Hellenistic Epistemology and Ethics, Cambridge University Press: 22–76 (originally published in German in Nachrichten der Akademie der Wissenschaften zu Göttingen 1. Phil.-hist. Klasse 2 (1974), 48–110)

Strohl, M. S. (2011) 'Pleasure as perfection: Nicomachean Ethics 10.4–5', Oxford Studies in Ancient Philosophy 41: 257–87

Tarrant, H. (1996) 'Platonic interpretation in Aulus Gellius', Greek, Roman, and Byzantine Studies 37: 173–93

(2007) 'Platonist educators in a growing market: Gaius; Albinus; Taurus; Alcinous', in R. R. R. Sorabji and R. W. Sharples (eds.), *Greek and Roman Philosophy 100 BC–200 AD* (*BICS* Supplementary volume 94): London Institute of Classical Studies: 449–65

Taylor, C. C. W. (1991) *Plato: Protagoras* (revised edition), Oxford University Press
(1998) 'Platonic ethics', in S. Everson (ed.), *Ethics* (Companions to Ancient Thought 4), Cambridge University Press: 49–76
(2003) 'Pleasure: Aristotle's response to Plato', in R. Heinaman (ed.), *Plato and Aristotle's Ethics*, Aldershot: Ashgate: 1–20 (with response by S. Broadie, 21–7)
(2008) 'Plato and Aristotle on the criterion of real pleasures', in his *Pleasure, Mind and Soul: Selected Papers in Ancient Philosophy*, Oxford University Press: 91–106

Teiserrenc, F. (1999) 'L'empire du faux ou le plaisir de l'image (37a–41a)', in M. Dixsaut (ed.), *La fêlure du plaisir: études sur le Philèbe de Platon*, vol. 1: *Commentaires*, Paris: J. Vrin: 267–98

Tepedino Guerra, A. (1987) '*PHerc* 1232 fr. 6 : una testimonanza del libro "Sul fine" di Epicuro?', *Cronache Ercolanesi* 17: 85–8
(1994) 'L'opera filodemea *Su Epicuro* (*PHerc* 1232 1289β)', *Cronache Ercolanesi* 24: 5–54

Thein, K. (2012) 'Imagination, self-awareness, and thought in the Philebus', *Oxford Studies in Ancient Philosophy* 42: 109–49

Trebilcot, J. (1974) 'Aprudentialism', *American Journal of Philosophy* 11: 203–10

Tsouna, V. (1998) *The Epistemology of the Cyrenaic School*, Cambridge University Press
(2002) 'Is there an exception to Greek eudaimonism?', in M. Canto and P. Pellegrin (eds.), *Le style de la pensée: recueil de textes en hommage à Jacques Brunschwig*, Paris: Les Belles Lettres: 464–89

Tsouna-McKirahan, V. (1994) 'The Socratic origins of the Cynics and Cyrenaics', in P. A. Vander Waerdt (ed.), *The Socratic Movement*, Ithaca: Cornell University Press: 367–91

Usener, H. (1887) *Epicurea*, Leipzig: Teubner

Van Riel, G. (2000) *Pleasure and the Good Life: Plato, Aristotle, and the Neoplatonists*, Leiden: E. J. Brill
(2012) 'Damascius on the contemplative life', in T. Bénatouïl and M. Bonazzi (eds.), *Theoria, Praxis and the Contemplative Life after Plato and Aristotle*, Leiden: E. J. Brill: 199–212

Velleman, J. D. (1991) 'Well-being and time', *Pacific Philosophical Quarterly* 72: 48–77

Vogt, K. (2012) *Belief and Truth: a Skeptic Reading of Plato*, Oxford University Press

Vorobej, M. (1987) 'Rationality and time preference', *Southern Journal of Philosophy* 25: 407–23

Waanders, F. M. J. (1983) *The History of* ΤΕΛΟΣ *and* ΤΕΛΕΩ *in Ancient Greek*, Amsterdam: B. R. Grüner

Wardy, R. B. B. (1990) *The Chain of Change*, Cambridge University Press

Warnock, M. (1987) *Memory*, London: Faber and Faber

Warren, J. (2000) 'Epicurean immortality', *Oxford Studies in Ancient Philosophy* 18: 231–61

(2001a) 'Epicurus and the pleasures of the future', *Oxford Studies in Ancient Philosophy* 21: 135–79

(2001b) 'Epicurus' dying wishes', *Proceeding of the Cambridge Philological Society* 47: 23–46

(2001c) 'Lucretian palingenesis recycled', *Classical Quarterly* 51: 499–508

(2001d) 'Lucretius, symmetry arguments and fearing death', *Phronesis* 46: 466–91

(2002a) *Epicurus and Democritean Ethics: an Archaeology of Ataraxia*, Cambridge University Press

(2002b) 'Democritus, the Epicureans, death, and dying', *Classical Quarterly* 52: 193–206

(2004) *Facing Death: Epicurus and his Critics*, Oxford University Press

(2006) 'Psychic disharmony: Philoponus and Epicurus on Plato's Phaedo', *Oxford Studies in Ancient Philosophy* 30: 235–59

(2007) 'Lucretius and Greek philosophy', in S. Gillespie and P. Hardie (eds.), *The Cambridge Companion to Lucretius*, Cambridge University Press: 19–32

(2009) 'Aristotle on Speusippus on Eudoxus on pleasure', *Oxford Studies in Ancient Philosophy* 36: 249–81

(2010) 'Plato on the pleasures and pains of knowing', *Oxford Studies in Ancient Philosophy* 39: 1–32

(2011a) 'Pleasure, Plutarch's *Non Posse*, and Plato's *Republic*', *Classical Quarterly* 61: 278–93

(2011b) 'Socrates and the patients: *Republic* IX 583c–585a', *Phronesis* 56: 113–37

(2013a) 'Comparing lives in Plato *Laws* V', *Phronesis* 58: 319–46

(2013b) 'Epicureans and Cyrenaics on pleasure as a *pathos*' in S. Marchand and F. Verde (eds.), *Épicurisme et Scepticisme*, Rome: Sapienza Università Editrice: 127–44

(2014) 'The Cyrenaics', in F. Sheffield and J. Warren (eds.), *The Routledge Companion to Ancient Philosophy*, London: Routledge: 409–22

(forthcoming a) 'Epicurean pleasure in Cicero's *De Finibus*', in J. Annas and G. Betegh (eds.), *Cicero: Ethics and Final Ends (Proceedings of the XII Symposium Hellenisticum)*, Cambridge University Press

(forthcoming b) 'Memory, anticipation, pleasure', in F. Leigh (ed.), *Moral Psychology in Ancient Thought. Proceedings of the 2011 Keeling Colloquium*

Webster, T. B. L. (1967) *The Tragedies of Euripides*, London: Methuen

Wedin, M. V. (1988) *Mind and Imagination in Aristotle*, New Haven: Yale University Press

Westerink. L. G. (1959) *Damascius: Lectures on the Philebus*, Amsterdam: North Holland Publishing Company

Westman, R. (1955) *Plutarch gegen Kolotes. Seine Schrift 'Adversus Colotem' als philosophiegeschichtliche Quelle* (Acta Philosophica Fennica 7), Helsinki: Filosofinen Yhdistys

Wiggins, D. (1987) 'Deliberation and practical reasoning', in his *Needs, Values, Truth*, Oxford University Press: 215–37

Williams, B. (1959) 'Pleasure and belief', *Proceedings of the Aristotelian Society Supplementary Volume* 33: 57–72, reprinted in his 2006 *Philosophy as a Humanistic Discipline* (ed. A. W. Moore), Princeton University Press: 34–46

(1976) 'Persons, character and morality', in A. O. Rorty (ed.), *The Identities of Persons*, Berkeley: University of California Press: 197–215

Wolfsdorf, D. (2009) 'Epicurus on Εὐφροσύνη and Ἐνεργεία', *Apeiron* 42: 221–57

(2011) 'Prodicus on the correctness of names: the case of *terpsis*, *chara*, and *euphrosyne*', *Journal of Hellenic Studies* 131: 131–45

(2013a) *Pleasure in Ancient Greek Philosophy*, Cambridge University Press

(2013b) 'Pleasure and truth in *Republic* 9', *Classical Quarterly* 63: 110–38

Woolf, R. (2004) 'What kind of hedonist was Epicurus?' *Phronesis* 49: 303–22

Wright, M. (2005) *Euripides' Escape Tragedies: a Study of Helen, Andromeda and Iphigenia among the Taurians*, Oxford University Press

Zacher, K.-D. (1982) *Plutarchs Kritik an der Lustlehre Epikurs. Ein Kommentar zu Non posse suaviter vivi secundum Epicurum: Kap. 1–8*, Königstein/Ts.: Hain

Zilioli, U. (2012) *The Cyrenaics*, Durham: Acumen

Index locorum

Subject index